Flash 5
Interactivity and Scripting

Flash 5
Interactivity *and* Scripting

Nigel Chapman

with Flash animations and graphics by
Jenny Chapman

John Wiley & Sons, Ltd
Chichester · New York · Weinheim · Brisbane · Singapore · Toronto

Copyright © 2001 by   John Wiley & Sons, Ltd
                     Baffins Lane, Chichester,
                     West Sussex, PO19 1UD, England
                     National   01243 779777
                     International   (+44) 1243 779777

e-mail (for orders and customer service enquiries): cs-books@wiley.co.uk
Visit our Home Page on http://www.wiley.co.uk

Nigel Chapman has asserted his right under the Copyright, Designs and Patents Act 1988, to be identified as the author of this work.

All Rights Reserved. No part of this publication may be reproduced, stored in a retrieval system, or transmitted, in any form or by any means, electronic, mechanical, photocopying, recording, scanning or otherwise, except under the terms of the Copyright, Designs and Patents Act 1988 or under the terms of a licence issued by the Copyright Licensing Agency, 90 Tottenham Court Road, London W1P 9HE, UK, without the permission in writing of the Publisher, with the exception of any material supplied specifically for the purpose of being entered and executed on a computer system for exclusive use by the purchaser of the publication.

Neither the author nor John Wiley & Sons, Ltd accept any responsibility or liability for loss or damage occasioned to any person or property through using the material, instructions, methods or ideas contained herein, or acting or refraining from acting as a result of such use. The author and Publisher expressly disclaim all implied warranties, including merchantability or fitness for any particular purpose. There will be no duty on the author or Publisher to correct any errors or defects in the software.

Designations used by companies to distinguish their products are often claimed as trademarks. In all instances where John Wiley & Sons, Ltd is aware of a claim, the product names appear in initial capital or all capital letters. Readers, however, should contact the appropriate companies for more complete information regarding trademarks and registration.

Other Wiley Editorial Offices

John Wiley & Sons, Inc., 605 Third Avenue,
New York, NY 10158-0012, USA

Weinheim • Brisbane • Singapore • Toronto

British Library Cataloguing in Publication Data

A catalogue record for this book is available from the British Library

ISBN 0-471-49781-9

Produced from PDF files supplied by the author
Printed and bound in Great Britain by Biddles Ltd, Guildford and King's Lynn
This book is printed on acid-free paper responsibly manufactured from sustainable forestry in which at least two trees are planted for each one used for paper production.

contents

	preface	ix
1	introduction	1
	The World Wide Web and Its Technologies	1
	Vector Graphics	4
	Flash	7
2	basic concepts	11
	The Timeline	11
	Creating Animation	14
	Symbols and Instances	19
	Sound	22
	Events	23
	Button Symbols	26
	Attaching Actions to Frames and Instances	28
	Targets	34
	Loading Movies	39
3	introducing actionscript	43
	JavaScript, ECMAScript and ActionScript	43
	Expressions and Variables	44

	Simple Scripting	52
	Movie Clip Properties	64
	Arrays	67
4	**user interface elements**	**75**
	Input Elements and Forms	75
	Editable Text Fields	76
	Checkboxes and Radio Buttons	81
	Pop-up Menus	85
	Scrolling Lists	90
	Using Draggable Movie Clips	93
	Keys	100
5	**abstraction**	**107**
	Reusing Scripts	107
	Objects	118
	Inheritance	129
	Libraries	138
6	**movie clips**	**143**
	Using MovieClip Objects	143
	Smart Clips	155
7	**client–server interaction**	**171**
	HTTP and CGI	171
	Sending HTTP Requests from Flash	176

		Using Generator	191
8	**flash and other technologies**		**201**
		HTML	201
		JavaScript	209
		XML	215
		Other Media Formats	232
		Printing	236
	further reading		**239**
	index		**243**

preface

Macromedia Flash started life as a tool for creating vector-based animations for use on the World Wide Web, with some primitive facilities for adding interactivity. With each release of the software, those facilities have been enhanced. Flash 4 saw the introduction of a recognizable, but simple, scripting language, which made it possible to add non-trivial computation to Flash movies. Flash 5 has taken a further step forward, by replacing the primitive collection of actions available in Flash 4 with a fully-fledged scripting language, ActionScript, sharing common roots with JavaScript. The added power that this provides comes at a price: using such a language effectively requires programming skills that are not necessarily found in conjunction with the design and animation skills needed to create the visual and time-based elements of Flash movies. The release of Flash 5 prompted one reviewer to lament that 'the golden time when one person could understand and utilize all aspects of [Flash] may well be over.' Similarly, the time when one book could provide an adequate account of all aspects of Flash may well be over too, so this book does not attempt to tell you everything there is to know about Flash. Instead, it concentrates almost exclusively on scripting and interactivity.

Even if Flash scripting is to become a specialized occupation, there will still be a diverse range of people using ActionScript, from hardcore Java and C++ programmers, called in because Flash scripting now demands higher levels of programming sophistication, through Web professionals, already familiar with JavaScript, to designers experienced with the less elaborate scripting facilities of Flash 4. This diversity among scripters means that this book is likely to have a diverse readership. In order to cater for as many of these potential readers as possible, I have included some elementary material on programming and simple language constructs, such as conditional statements and loops, before going on to look at objects and other advanced features of ActionScript. Even for experienced programmers, writing scripts for Flash movies has a new dimension — that of time — because of the way scripts are linked to the progress of a movie through time, and I have tried to show how Flash deals with this extra dimension.

However, my main concern is not with describing the mechanical details of Flash scripting and ActionScript. The philosopher Ludwig Wittgenstein is usually credited with the observation that knowing the rules of chess does not imply knowing how to play chess. Similarly, knowing the syntax and semantics of a programming language does not imply knowing how to program in it. This book does not even tell you all the rules of Flash scripting. Those are available to you already in the form of the *ActionScript Reference Guide* included with Flash 5, and there is little point duplicating the available reference material. My main purpose is to try and help you learn to play the game of Flash scripting, that is, to use the facilities to create interesting and useful systems. This necessarily involves extensive description of most of those facilites, but this does not take the form of a reference manual.

The emphasis is on doing. I assume you have access to Flash and I strongly recommend that you work with it as you read. It may often be helpful to have the Flash interface in front of you while reading the description of how to perform some task within it. I have included a section entitled *Exercises and Experiments* at the end of every chapter except the introduction, and until you have attempted these you have not really read the book. There is no hard distinction between exercises and experiments. In fact, I encourage you to think of all of them as experiments — see whether you can think of more than one solution, criticize your solutions, and in cases where you are asked to build something, try it out on the sort of people you might expect to use it and see how they react. (Encourage them to try and break it.) You should also look on every example in the book as a challenge to find better ways of doing the same thing.

Many of the examples described in the book have a vaguely ecommerce slant to them. Flash 5 is well suited to this area of application, and it is one whose requirements are pretty well understood, and which will be familiar to most readers. It should be understood, though, that the examples in this book have been developed as a vehicle for describing how to use Flash, not as industrial strength applications. While you are welcome to adapt them to real systems, you should realize that more careful work is needed before these scripts can be trusted in a serious environment.

Despite my emphasis on ecommerce, Flash is also being applied in quite different areas, including novel forms of online entertainment. My main reason for neglecting these areas is that these forms are still emerging, and it is by no means clear what the requirements will be in the longer term. If you are working on the edge of new media you should find that the principles of scripting I describe in the context of ecommerce can be profitably applied in less well-defined areas, such as interactive story telling, where computation must be combined with animation.

The dynamic nature of Flash movies means that any account in the static medium of print is necessarily incomplete. For that reason, a Web site is available to accompany the book, at http://www.wiley.co.uk/flash/. Here you will find working versions of all the non-trivial examples in the book, with the Flash source for you to download. (Some of the exercises and experiments rely on you downloading the files to modify them.)

The animations that you will see on that site and which are illustrated by stills in this book have been created in a distinctive black and white style based on simple bold calligraphic strokes, in order to transfer clearly to print, and to create a unified identity. This book is not about Flash animation but, just as you are encouraged to experiment with your Flash scripts, you (or the animators you work with) should also experiment with the visual elements of Flash movies, and the way in which the two aspects can work together.

Acknowledgements

I am grateful to Macromedia, Inc. for assistance with this project; to the many people inside and outside Macromedia who have provided information about Flash in email, on the Web and in print; and to Matt Wobensmith for looking over the manuscript. Thanks also to everybody at John Wiley & Sons who helped with the project, especially Gaynor Redvers-Mutton for taking it on, Simon Plumtree for seeing it through, Juliet Booker for taking care of production, and Gemma Quilter for taking care of just about everything else.

introduction

The World Wide Web and Its Technologies

The Internet is a global network of computer networks that communicate using a standard set of protocols loosely referred to collectively as TCP/IP. The World Wide Web (WWW) is a distributed interactive hypermedia system that runs over the Internet. Like most Internet applications, it is based on the client/server model of distributed computation. Programs called Web *servers* behave rather like somebody serving behind the counter in a cafeteria: they listen for requests from *clients* — in the context of the Internet, other programs, usually running on a different *host*, as the machines connected by the network are known — to which they respond by handing over whatever the client has requested, as if it were a bowl of soup, though Web servers more often hand over a Web page.

The three technologies that originally made the WWW possible were the Hypertext Markup Language (HTML), Uniform Resource Locators (URLs) and the Hypertext Transfer Protocol (HTTP). HTML provided a simple means of marking up the logical structure of documents. URLs provided a way of identifying the location of a document (or some other resource) anywhere on the Internet. In conjunction with HTML's anchor tags, URLs made it possible to include hypertext links in documents. Finally HTTP provided a simple and efficient method of transferring documents over TCP/IP networks — in particular, the Internet — so that pages could be retrieved and links could be followed using a suitable piece of client software, a Web browser.

The success of those three technologies in building a distributed hyper*text* system, coinciding with increased access to and commercialization of the Internet, encouraged the development of the WWW into the interactive hyper*media* system it has become. New HTML tags and enhanced browsers permitted the incorporation of additional media types — bitmapped images in the form of GIF, JPEG and latterly PNG files; QuickTime movies; and audio in a variety of formats. The plug-in architecture adopted by browsers made it possible to add support for other media and file types dynamically.

The demand from designers for better control over layout led to the adoption of Cascading Stylesheets (CSS) to provide visual layout for the structural elements identified by HTML tags. Most recently, the introduction of the Extensible Markup Language (XML) has greatly extended the range of documents that can make up the Web.

As well as enriching the content of the Web, developments that have taken place since its original deployment have added the possibility of extra computation to the basic process of retrieving and displaying Web pages. The Common Gateway Interface (CGI) is a way of passing data between a Web browser and some other program running on a remote host, via a Web server. CGI (and other proprietary and browser-specific technologies, such as PHP, ASP and WebObjects) allows Web pages to be constructed dynamically, on the basis of computation carried out on the server side, in particular using the results of database queries. Other enhancements allow computation to be carried out on the client side (in the browser). JavaScript can be used to add interactivity to Web pages, allowing them to respond to user input in more elaborate ways than the simple following of links provided by HTML. Image rollovers, menus and simple motion graphics are familiar examples of the type of effects that are commonly achieved in this way. The ability to download more or less arbitrary executable content in the form of Java applets — subject to security restrictions — has further extended the computational possibilities of the Web.

The most visible product of the enhanced Web technologies, and one of the main driving forces behind their development, is what has become known as *ecommerce*: the buying and selling of goods and services over the Internet. A great many words have been written on the subject of the Internet's potential as a 'global marketplace', and there is little point in repeating them here. Suffice to say that, where companies are using a Web site to advertise their goods, people have come to expect to be able to purchase them directly from that Web site. Whereas once it may have been sufficient to provide an email link for submitting orders, now it is expected that the site will provide a shopping facility, complete with shopping basket or trolley, credit card processing, order confirmation and tracking.

In order for commerce over the Internet to be successful, the technology must provide a means, firstly, of presenting the goods to potential buyers (preferably in an attractive form, but certainly with enough accurate detail to compensate for not being able to examine a real example), and secondly, of enabling the transaction to be carried out. Ideally, the processing of the transaction should be integrated into the vendor's normal stock control, invoicing and dispatch systems, which requires computation on the server side and a way of transferring data between the Web site and the financial systems. In addition to these two requirements, it is highly desirable that an ecommerce site presents its visitors with an interface that makes purchasing simple and, as far as possible, pleasant. This may entail the use of graphics or animation, and client-side computation to control the interface elements and to handle user input.

The development of the WWW just sketched out has not always taken place in a disciplined way. The organization responsible for overseeing this development, the World Wide Web Consortium (W^3C), has produced a plethora of standards (or Recommendations as they are officially known, reflecting the W^3C's lack of statutory powers) covering enhancements to the original Web technologies. HTML has been revised several times, up to HTML 4.0, before being superseded by XHTML, a redefinition of HTML in XML. XML is itself defined by a W^3C Recommendation, which has been extended by several others covering namespaces and enhanced linking. Two CSS standards have been produced, with a third under construction at the time of writing. The Document Object Model (DOM), which defines how elements of HTML documents and stylesheets can be manipulated by scripts and applets, is the subject of two standards, while the syntax of the scripting language generally known as JavaScript is actually defined by an international standard produced by the European Computer Manufacturers' Association (ECMA), in which it is called ECMAScript. Even HTTP has been revised. In short, the Web standards picture has become complicated.

At the same time, Web browser manufacturers have not always felt obliged to conform to the standards. Both Microsoft and Netscape, who between them account for the vast majority of the browsers in use, have on occasion implemented their own extensions, while at the same time not implementing the standards completely or correctly. The situation as regards client-side scripting is particularly unsatisfactory: both browser manufacturers implemented their own document model independently. Although the two have now been unified in the W^3C DOM, the implementations in fourth generation browsers — which are still widely used — are incompatible, and many client-side scripts include extensive amounts of code that are there only to ensure that they work on all browsers and platforms. It is to be expected that the situation will improve and that Web browsers conforming to the standards will become ubiquitous, but at the moment, constructing elaborate Web sites that use the multimedia and interactive capabilities of the mature WWW and work as expected on the most widely used browsers and platforms has become an arcane art, only partially helped by Web authoring software, which itself does not always produce code that conforms to the relevant standards.

As we shall see, Flash provides an alternative way of producing interactive Web pages in the form of Shockwave Flash (SWF) files. Since SWF files are interpreted by a browser plug-in, freely provided by Macromedia, an *ad hoc* standard exists to which browsers automatically conform. (This isn't how standards are supposed to work, but the WWW has a life and logic of its own in these matters.) Furthermore, Flash provides a vehicle for a media type that is not otherwise implemented by browsers, vector graphics.

Vector Graphics

The images that have been used in Web pages almost since the first days of the WWW — GIFs and JPEGs — are *bitmapped* images. That is, an image is represented as an array of values, one for each pixel in the image, that specify the colour of the corresponding pixel. Since, even at screen resolution, such an array may occupy hundreds of kilobytes for a single image, bitmaps are usually compressed. Compression may be lossless, as in GIFs, where data values are cleverly re-encoded so that they occupy less space, or lossy, as in JPEGs, where visually insignificant information is discarded. Generally, lossy compression is more effective, especially on photographic material or other images that include continuous tones; it can reduce the size of images by a factor of up to 20 without perceptible loss of quality.

An alternative way of representing images digitally is as *vector graphics*. In this representation, pixel values are not stored explicitly. Instead, the image is represented as a collection of objects, made up of lines and curves that can be simply and compactly described mathematically. For example, a straight line can be specified just by the coordinates of its endpoints, a Bézier curve by the coordinates of its control points, and so on. If, in addition, attributes of lines and curves, such as their width and colour, and a specification of how shapes are to be filled with colour or gradients can be specified, complex images can be represented in this form.

For suitable material — images naturally made up of fairly simple shapes, with flat colours or gradients and little fine detail —vector graphic representations can be much more compact than bitmaps. This means that they not only occupy less disk space when stored in files, but they require less bandwidth when transmitted over a network. In other words, they can be downloaded in a short time even over a slow connection. Furthermore, unlike bitmaps, they are not stored at a specific resolution and so can be smoothly displayed on a range of devices. Similarly, they can be scaled or otherwise transformed geometrically (e.g. rotated, reflected or skewed) without loss of quality, using simple and efficient computations based on the mathematics of the representation. This makes vector graphics particularly suitable for animation, since shapes can be moved and transformed over time, without the need to store an explicit image for every frame. An animation can consist of a set of definitions of all the objects that appear in it, together with a set of instructions for each frame indicating where each object is to be placed, and any transformations that should be applied to it.

The statement that vector shapes can be smoothly displayed at any resolution needs some qualification. To display a straight line, for example, which is stored as two pairs of coordinates identifying its endpoints, it is necessary to determine which pixels lie on the line, and colour them appropriately, a process known as *rendering*. The mathematics required to do this is simple. However, the classical coordinate geometry that is used is based on the use of real coordinates, whereas pixels are finite in size and identified by integer coordinates. Hence, some rounding errors will occur, and will be visible in the form of jagged edges, an effect known as *staircasing* or *the jaggies*. A method that may be employed to mitigate this effect consists of colouring pixels adjacent to the edge in intermediate shades so as to soften the edges (see Figure 1.1). This smoothing technique is known as *anti-aliasing* (because the jaggies can be explained in terms of sampling theory as an example of a general phenomenon called aliasing). The extent of the shading and the exact shades used are not arbitrary, but are calculated to provide an approximation to the brightness distribution of an ideal line that would be produced if pixels were infinitesimally small. Flash graphics are displayed with anti-aliasing, so that they render smoothly at all resolutions.

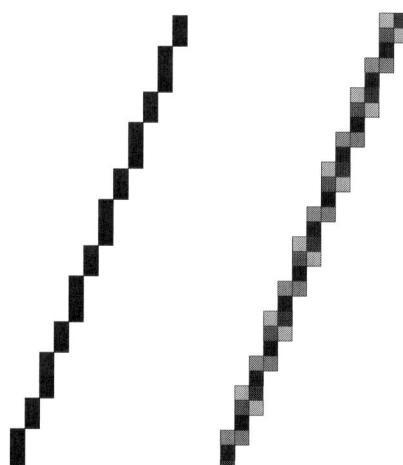

Figure 1.1 *Aliased (left) and anti-aliased (right) lines.*

It's worth emphasizing that, in a vector image, it is possible to identify individual objects and manipulate them separately, in a way that is not possible with bitmaps. It is generally possible for a person to identify objects when they look at a bitmapped image. For example, in a JPEG displayed on a Web page you may see a person and some furniture or a house plant, and so on. However, within the bitmap, the pixels making up these objects are not distinguished from the adjoining pixels; it is our brains that analyse the image and make that distinction. Consequently, moving and transforming individual objects in a bitmapped image is difficult, and requires the use of sophisticated selection tools.

It's also worth emphasizing that vector graphics are limited in the range of images they can efficiently represent. Although programs such as Illustrator and Freehand allow images to be drawn with a wide variety of textures and different qualities of line, the result always looks like some kind of drawing. Photographic material and painterly images cannot be produced using this technology (except perhaps by the absurd expedient of representing each pixel as a line of length one). Furthermore, as the degree of detail in a vector image increases — in particular, as smaller curve segments are used to produce freeform shapes, and complex gradients are used to fill them — the size of the vector representation increases, until, despite the general rule that vector graphics are much smaller than bitmaps, the reverse may actually be the case.

Despite the generally low bandwidth requirements which make them suitable for use over networks, vector graphics were not widely used on the WWW until Flash was released. This is because there was no standard vector graphic format supported by Web browsers. The dominant format used for such images in print media was, until recently, Encapsulated PostScript (EPS). PostScript is a page description language of comparable complexity to a moderately powerful programming language, and it requires correspondingly complex software in the form of a PostScript interpreter in order to display images described using it. (EPS allows the full use of PostScript's facilities, merely imposing some structural restrictions that ensure that images are self-contained and can be painlessly incorporated in larger documents.) As a result, incorporating the display of EPS graphics into Web browsers was not considered worthwhile. The W^3C's efforts to develop a standard for an alternative vector format more suitable for use on the Web have led to the definition of the Scalable Vector Graphics (SVG) language, which is based in part on PostScript, but is actually defined using XML. However, this development has taken a long time, and implementations of SVG are only beginning to appear as this is being written, in mid-2000. In the meantime, Flash's SWF files, although not endorsed as an official Recommendation, have been adopted as a *de facto* standard for Web vector graphics, both for still images and for animation.

Flash

Flash is a tool for producing interactive vector graphic animations. It is primarily used in the production of Web sites, although Flash animations can be generated in stand-alone form, made into screen savers, included in Director or QuickTime movies and incorporated in other forms of multimedia production. If Flash were no more than an animation tool, it could be used by Web designers to enliven pages with moving pictures without the bandwidth requirements of digital video, but it would probably be little more than a short-lived gimmick. However, recent versions of Flash also incorporate a scripting language, which makes it possible for animations to react to user input; facilities for adding conventional user interface elements, such as text entry fields and menus; and a means of fetching documents identified by URLs and communicating with CGI scripts. With the use of additional server technology (Generator), Flash movies can be generated dynamically, with content tailored to individual users, geographical areas or times. Despite its primary emphasis on vector graphics, Flash can also manipulate bitmapped images and other media types, including sound in a variety of formats and QuickTime movies. In fact, Flash has adequate facilities to offer an alternative to the farrago of HTML, CSS, ECMAScript and the DOM as a multimedia user interface to the WWW. With its low bandwidth requirements it is suitable for constructing interfaces for mobile computing devices, such as personal digital assistants (PDAs) and WAP phones. To add to its attractions, Flash has reasonably powerful text layout facilities, and allows fonts to be embedded in movies, thus providing a solution to the problems of typographical control that plague Web designers dependent on HTML and CSS. Finally, it provides facilities for high quality printing, which, like PDF but unlike HTML, ensures that printed output matches the appearance on the screen.

The term *Flash movie* is widely used to designate the output generated by Flash, but the usage is somewhat imprecise. It would be more accurate to say that a Flash movie is the animation that is constructed and edited within the Flash authoring environment, which is stored in a movie file, usually with extension .fla using the File>Save As command. Such a movie may be realized in several formats, using File>Export Movie. The most common format is a *Flash Player Movie*, or *Macromedia Flash file*, better (if enigmatically) known as an *SWF* file. SWF files can be played by the freely distributed Flash Player program, by its accompanying Web browser plug-in, and increasingly, now that the SWF file format has been made publicly available, by other software. SWF files are not strictly the same as Flash movies, though, since they can be generated by programs other than Flash; Adobe's LiveMotion is an example. Conversely, Flash movies can be exported in other forms, including Flash tracks in QuickTime movies, animated GIFs, or sequences of image files in many formats. (Except for SWF files and QuickTime tracks, exported movies lose their interactive capabilities.)

Where a movie is intended to be played within a Web page, suitable tags must be included in the page's HTML. The HTML 4.0 standard specifies the use of <object> for embedding multimedia content, including SWF files, but most browsers support <embed>, although it has never been endorsed by any W^{3}C Recommendation (while <object> has been abducted for the use of ActiveX controls). Fortunately, Flash will construct an HTML page with appropriate tags when the File>Publish command is used. This page can subsequently be edited to add conventional HTML content, if that is required. More details of how to embed Flash content in HTML can be found in Chapter 8.

Throughout the rest of this book, it will be assumed that Flash is a suitable tool for whatever job you have in mind, but this will not always be the case. The current tendency in computing is towards pluralism, which means that computer professionals, and Web designers and programmers in particular, must understand and use a whole collection of tools and technologies, and be able to choose the most appropriate ones for any particular task. As the remaining chapters will show, Flash is a viable alternative to conventional Web technologies for a range of tasks, but it should always be borne in mind that not every system is best served by an interactive animated front-end — simpler and plainer alternatives will sometimes be better.

A serious cause for concern, which will sometimes be relevant, is that Flash does not conform to the W^{3}C standards concerning accessibility features. Whereas the Web Accessibility Initiative has gone a long way towards ensuring that HTML and its associated technologies include features to make Web content accessible to everybody, irrespective of physical or cognitive disabilities, Flash (and other content that is played using a plug-in) cannot even take advantage of such simple facilities as HTML's alt attribute for providing a textual alternative to images for the benefit of screen readers and other software and hardware for use by people with impaired eyesight. In order to address these concerns, additional templates (see Chapter 8) are being created, which will make the text from a Flash movie available to screen reading software.

Flash has been criticized in the past for its user interface. Most criticism boiled down to the fact that it took a different approach from most tools that are widely used in multimedia. This is not an entirely frivolous complaint. By definition, the creation of multimedia may involve the use of several different programs to manipulate a range of media types. A Flash movie may use a bitmapped image prepared in Photoshop, sound recorded in SoundForge, vector graphics drawn in Illustrator, and perhaps a QuickTime movie edited in Premiere, and it may be embedded in a Web page that is part of a site created in Dreamweaver. The five applications just mentioned share many interface features, from their general look and feel based on the use of tabbed palettes, to specific details such as shared keyboard short-cuts. Previous versions of Flash had little in common with what has become a standard for user interfaces in the design industry. Flash 5 has rectified this, adopting palettes that are almost indistinguishable from their equivalents in many other widely used media applications (although in Flash they are referred to as 'panels') and incorporating other features from the interface of other Macromedia programs, such as Dreamweaver. Keyboard short cuts can be customized to match those of other applications, including Illustrator, Freehand and Photoshop. As a result, anyone with experience in mainstream graphics and Web design applications can easily master the mechanics of Flash's user interface. (There is a drawback to the new interface: like those of the other applications just mentioned, the palettes occupy a great deal of screen space. A monitor with a resolution of at least 1024 by 768 is required; many users prefer two monitors, one for the palettes and one for the artwork.)

The premise behind this book is that Flash's support for interactivity and scripting is as much a part of its strength as its animation facilities. In Flash 5, scripts are written in ActionScript, a scripting language whose syntax is taken from ECMAScript, the formally defined language framework for scripting, of which JavaScript is the best known realization. This is the most significant difference between Flash 5 and Flash 4; in 4, the scripting language was a much cruder affair, with a clumsy syntax and limited support for abstraction and data structures. Simulating arrays, structures, objects and functions required a bag of tricks that depended on dubious programming practices, such as run-time evaluation of variables' names. Although ActionScript still lacks many features considered necessary for large-scale reliable programming — notably strong typing — it is now a serious scripting language that can be used to perform elaborate computation within Flash movies.

The more conventional and mature scripting language of Flash 5 can be seen as an acknowledgement of the fact that scripts are in fact programs, and that writing them requires programmers' skills. The promise of interactivity without programming is a chimera, the pursuit of which can only lead to stereotyped and irresponsive interfaces. Furthermore, to make the most of Flash it is necessary to understand other technologies, such as HTTP, CGI, XML, HTML and JavaScript, and the ways in which Flash interacts with them. In short, mastering Flash interactivity and scripting is not the trivial task it is sometimes made out to be. It is, however, considerably less arduous than providing all the functions of an interactive Flash movie, including animation, by writing Java code yourself. With the framework that Flash provides, constructing attractive and useful interfaces is well within the capabilities of anyone who can write HTML and JavaScript code by hand.

basic concepts

The Timeline

Animation is not the prime concern of this book, but Flash's animation facilities provide its framework for interactivity and scripting, so as a preliminary, we must briefly survey this framework, beginning with the mechanics of moving pictures.

If a sequence of still images is displayed in succession at a sufficiently rapid rate, an illusion of motion is created by the phenomenon of persistence of vision. This principle underlies all methods of producing moving pictures, including film and video. *Animation* is distinguished from other types of moving pictures by the fact that each image in the sequence is created individually, by drawing or by capturing a single frame on film or video tape, for example. In contrast, *live motion* footage is usually captured to film or tape at the same rate as it is to be played back, so that the motion that is displayed is a record of some motion that occurred in the real world. Animation, though, *creates* movement.

Each image in an animation or other moving picture sequence is called a *frame*. Normally, each frame is displayed for the same length of time, so it makes sense to speak of the *frame rate* of an animation: the number of frames displayed in a certain time. Frame rates are specified in *frames per second (fps)*. Conventional film and video have long-established standards concerning frame rates, which apply to animation that is delivered in these formats. (Film is nowadays displayed at 24 fps, while video uses a frame rate of 25 fps in countries that use the PAL standard for television, or 29.97 fps — often treated as 30 — in those that use NTSC.) These frame rates are determined by the characteristics of television sets and film projectors, and by the physiological factors that operate to produce persistence of vision. Computer monitors operate somewhat differently from televisions, and are not constrained by the need to conform to standards, so a wider variety of frame rates is employed in animations to be displayed on computers, within Web pages or as part of some other type of multimedia production. In order to produce the illusion of motion, a frame rate of around 12 fps is required. Below this rate, movement appears jerky, although certain sorts of animation which deliberately make use of this effect can use frame rates of 8 fps or even lower. Higher rates will produce smoother movement.

A Flash movie can only have a single frame rate, at which all its frames are displayed. Hence, another way of looking at frames is as a way of breaking time into pieces of equal length. This leads to a natural representation of the structure of an animation in the form of a *timeline*. A timeline is a spatial representation of an animation, where the temporal sequence of frames is represented in space by a linear sequence of images, each corresponding to a frame. Figure 2.1 shows the timeline of a simple animation. Time runs from left to right, so the timeline can be read in sequence in that direction, essentially like a comic strip (in countries where text is normally written from left to right, that is.) Since each second of animation usually requires 12 or more frames, a timeline composed of thumbnails of each frame's content like this one will occupy a lot of space, so a more condensed representation using icons is often employed when the timeline is used to show the overall structure of an animation rather than to provide a view of its content.

Figure 2.1 *A simple timeline.*

The relationship between a timeline and an animation is much like the relationship between the images on a reel of film and the film we see when it is projected. You can imagine a *playhead*, which somehow causes the frame underneath it to be displayed, just as each frame of a film is projected on to the screen as it passes between the lamp and lens of a projector. Since Flash animations are made up of bytes in a computer, they are not subject to the same physical constraints as film and video tape, which can only easily be displayed in a linear sequence. There is no reason why the frames of a Flash animation should not be displayed in an arbitrary order, so it makes more sense to consider the playhead as moving arbitrarily among frames instead of the frames passing under the playhead, and we will see in later chapters how the movement of the playhead can be controlled by scripts to produce animations with a variety of non-linear structures.

Because the timeline is a sequence, it is possible to identify any frame by a number: the first frame is frame 1, the second frame 2, and so on. We will see in later chapters that in scripts it is often necessary to identify a particular frame — for example, when we wish to move the playhead to it — and it is inconvenient and potentially error-prone to use frame numbers for this purpose. In particular, when an animation is edited by inserting or deleting frames, the number of a frame will change, requiring any scripts that refer to it to be updated. To remove this necessity, frames may be given a *label*, that is a textual name by which they can be identified. Labels always refer to the same frame, even if it moves along the timeline because of editing operations. Labels are added by typing their name in the Label field on the Frame panel when the frame to be labelled is selected.

In Flash, as well as holding visible objects a frame can have *actions* attached to it, which cause something to happen when the playhead is over that frame. These actions may be as simple as stopping the movie, or causing it to continue playing from a specified frame, or they may be complex scripts that carry out calculations, control sub-elements of the movie or communicate with a server.

Long movies may be divided into *scenes*. Much like scenes in a play, these organize the movie into separate pieces, each in some sense a unified part of the whole. Scenes can be added, deleted, renamed and reordered using the Scene panel. Programmers can use scenes rather like modules, to separate distinct parts of the computation carried out by actions in a movie.

Timelines are employed by many different programs that work with time-based media such as animation (including JavaScript animation for Web pages) and digital video, and also in multimedia authoring environments that are based on the temporal organization and synchronization of media elements. Examples include Premiere, Dreamweaver, GoLive, After Effects and Director, as well as Flash itself.

As well as dividing an animation into frames in the temporal direction, Flash divides it into *layers*. Layers are often likened to sheets of acetate, like overhead projector transparencies, on which an image may be drawn. Where there is no image, the layer is transparent, so layers provide a means of overlaying different images. The opacity of the image can be varied, so that layers can be merged. Distinct elements of the animation can be maintained on separate layers, which makes it easier to organize a complex composition. Where layers are used, Flash's timeline window has a two-dimensional structure. As we will see, layers make it simple to animate separate objects independently, and can also be used to organize interactivity.

Creating Animation

The first step in making a Flash animation is to create a movie and set some of its properties. By default, Flash creates a new movie when it is started up, but the File>New command can be used at any time, as is usual with most applications. Next, the Modify>Movie command is used to set the movie's properties via a simple dialogue. In particular, the frame rate for the movie and its dimensions can be entered if the default values are not suitable. Once this has been done and the file has been named and saved, frames can be created.

Keyframes and Tweening

As a labour-saving device for animation, Flash implements interpolation, or *tweening*, as it is called. Some frames are distinguished as *keyframes*,[1] whose contents are created explicitly, by drawing with the tools provided in Flash or by importing them from some other application. Frames lying in between these keyframes are interpolated in several ways, for example, by interpolating the position of the objects in the frame, either linearly or following a path; interpolating other properties such as brightness, transparency, size or rotation; or by interpolating their shapes (a process known as *morphing*). The distinction between keyframes and tweened frames is an important one for scripting and interactivity since actions can be attached to keyframes but not to tweened frames.

It is often the case that objects will move predictably over a sequence of frames. For example, in classic Warner Brothers cartoons, objects and characters frequently fall vertically from a great height; their position in successive frames will follow a straight line downwards, while their size increases or diminishes with perspective, depending on the viewpoint. In large studios, it is customary for chief animators just to draw the frames at the extremes of such movements, while the in-between frames are done by less skilled animators, known as `in-betweeners'. Tweening in Flash is a computerized equivalent of this practice, with Flash behaving as an in-betweener.

When a new Flash movie is created, it consists of a single empty keyframe, with a single layer. Additional keyframes can be added by selecting a frame or a consecutive range of frames in the timeline, and then either using a command key (F6) or selecting Insert Keyframe from either the Insert menu or the Frames pop-up menu. Keyframes can be added independently to separate layers, which permits objects on different layers to be

---

1. There is no general agreement about whether 'keyframe' is one word or two. In this book, I follow the Flash documentation and write it as one, Similarly, 'timeline' is sometimes written as two words, but the Flash world prefers one.

tweened independently, and allows actions to be placed in arbitrary frames, by creating a separate layer purely for the placement of keyframes where actions are needed.

Selecting a frame or a range of frames is a common operation in Flash. It is done in a similar way to selection in most applications, that is, you select a frame by clicking once in the timeline. Additional frames can be added to the selection by shift-clicking or [cmd/ctl] dragging.[1] Selecting in this way will only select the particular layer in which you click. To select multiple layers, dragging or shift-clicking vertically is employed. Beware of clicking in the ruler at the top of the timeline, above all the layers. This does not select a frame, it just moves the playhead to that frame, so that it is displayed on the stage. Keyframes can be moved by selecting them and dragging them to their new position. Holding the [opt/alt] key when the frame is dropped causes a duplicate to be created; dragging a keyframe at the end of a movie with [opt/alt] depressed extends its duration by inserting additional frames.

The content of a keyframe is created on Flash's *stage*, a window in which images can be composed. Flash provides a set of drawing tools, resembling those found in vector drawing programs such as Illustrator and Freehand, which enable you to create shapes and fill them with colours and gradients. Other tools allow individual objects to be selected, moved and geometrically transformed — scaled, rotated, reflected and skewed. Objects can also be aligned and grouped into composite objects, which can then be transformed as a unit.

Although Flash's tool box contains some fairly powerful drawing tools, it cannot match the power and sophistication of dedicated drawing programs. An alternative way of constructing frames is to use such a program. Flash can import several file formats, including AutoCAD DXF and Illustrator files, but, more usefully, recent versions of Freehand and Illustrator can export artwork in Flash's SWF format. In Illustrator 9, for example, a multi-layered drawing can be exported with each layer being converted to a separate frame in an SWF file, and each object being converted to a Flash symbol (see below). This allows keyframes to be constructed in Illustrator, using its superior tools — which are more familiar to many designers — and then imported into Flash for tweening or to have interactivity and scripts added.

Flash can also import bitmapped images in various formats, including GIF, JPEG, PICT and PNG. Once imported, bitmaps are treated as indivisible objects; they can be moved and transformed, but, unlike vectors, they may suffer a loss of quality in the process.

---

1. This behaviour can be changed by setting a preference, see *Using Flash 5*.

Furthermore, bitmaps are (usually) comparatively bulky, and their extensive use can lead to large and inefficient animations. Consequently, in Flash, they are generally used as backgrounds or other static elements. Alternatively, bitmaps can be transformed into vector graphics, using the Modify>Trace Bitmap command. Various parameters can be set to control the accuracy with which tracing is performed. The resulting image is often only an approximation to the original bitmap, with tonal detail usually being lost. Tracing can be successful, though, with certain sorts of image — pen and ink caricatures, for example — that have been made in traditional media and then scanned in to the computer.

As well as drawn shapes, a Flash animation can include type (that is, displayed text), to which a full range of typographic effects and basic HTML layout can be applied. Type can also be transformed in the same way as other objects, and it can be broken apart into its constituent outlines, which then become objects that can be transformed independently, so that the type can be distorted. Because type is treated the same way as other objects, it can be animated. As well as being used as a graphic element, though, text can also be used to create forms and other interface elements, as we will see in Chapter 4.

When an animation is created in the traditional manner, one frame at a time (i.e., every frame is a keyframe), it is often the case that each frame is created by altering just a few elements of the preceding frame. That is, the same objects are used repeatedly, at different positions, perhaps with different transformations applied. Such a pattern of usage maps on to the implementation of a vector-based animation as a set of definitions of objects and a collection of instructions specifying how objects should be placed in each frame, which was described in Chapter 1. Broadly speaking, the SWF files generated by Flash take just such a form. However, in Flash, objects can only be reused in this way if they are explicitly designated as *symbols*. Every Flash movie has an associated library in which such symbols are kept. Symbols may be dragged from the library onto the stage, creating an *instance* of the symbol. Each instance has its own properties, such as position and transparency, but it remains linked to its symbol, so that changes to the symbol — redrawing it, for example — are reflected in every instance. An instance's properties are changed in the Instance panel. (Director experts will see a parallel between symbols and instances in Flash and cast members and sprites, respectively, in Director. Object-oriented programmers will see a resemblance to objects and classes, but the analogy is not perfect.)

The same instance of a symbol can appear in more than one frame. In particular, if tweening is applied, an instance will appear in different positions in successive frames;

creating animation

a new instance is not created in each frame. An instance is said to be *active* from the first keyframe it appears in to the last.

Since tweened animation necessarily involves reusing objects in a sequence of frames, only instances of symbols can be tweened. (The exception to this rule is morphing: since shapes are changing, it is not possible to identify the object at the start of the tween with the one at the end. For this sort of interpolation, anything but instances of symbols can be tweened.) If a keyframe in a layer is followed by a sequence of frames but no tweening is applied, the image on that layer is held until a subsequent keyframe occurs (or until the last frame on the layer, if there is none). Background images are typically treated in this way, as are controls such as buttons which must be present, and function the same way, throughout a movie.

Only one instance (or group) can be tweened on a single layer, but several of its properties can be interpolated at once. Where multiple layers are used, objects on separate layers can be tweened independently. Because keyframes can be set independently in each layer, the objects on different layers can be tweened over different segments of the timeline. This is often necessary to avoid unwanted synchronization between the movement of separate objects.

A simple example should help consolidate this brief description of Flash's basic animation facilities.

The movie uses layers and tweening to produce the effect of a ship moving over the sea under a cloudy sky on a moonlit night, as indicated in Figure 2.2. Figure 2.3 shows the timeline. As you can see, the movie is composed as several layers. The ship is an instance of a symbol, drawn with the brush tool, on a layer of its own; its sail is on a separate layer. The motion is tweened so that over the length of the movie the ship moves into the frame from the left, then scuds over the sea with its sail billowing and off the right hand edge. Several intermediate keyframes are used to vary the pace of the movement; in each one the ship is rotated slightly to convey an impression of pitching in the waves. The moon is on a static layer. Three layers of clouds cover it. Their motion is tweened, so that the clouds appear to rush across the moon, driven by the wind. These clouds are stretched out as they move, to reinforce the impression of movement and to prevent them looking too obviously like a solid object that is being tweened. As the moon emerges through a gap in the clouds, the scene lightens. This was achieved by tweening the alpha (transparency) setting of a layer that forms the background to the whole composition and serves as the sea and sky. Another five layers on top of this one are

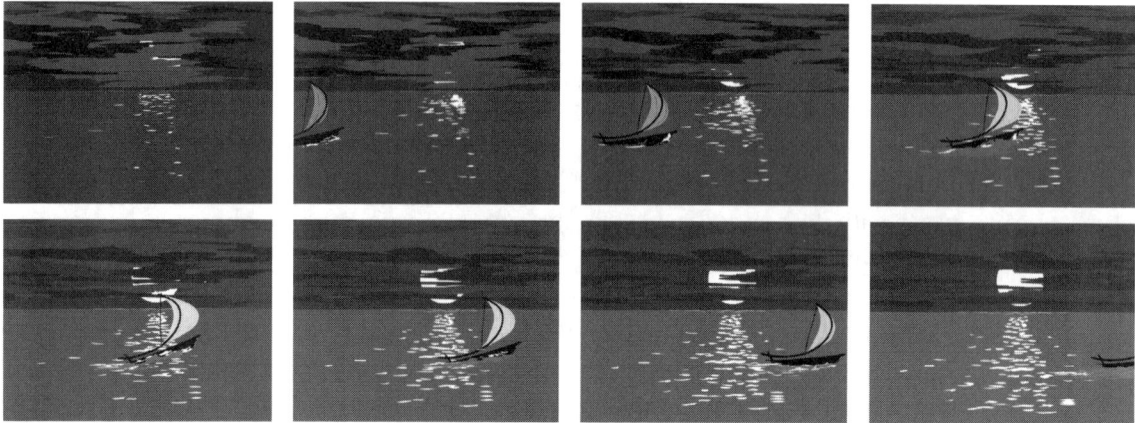

Figure 2.2   *A Flash animation.*

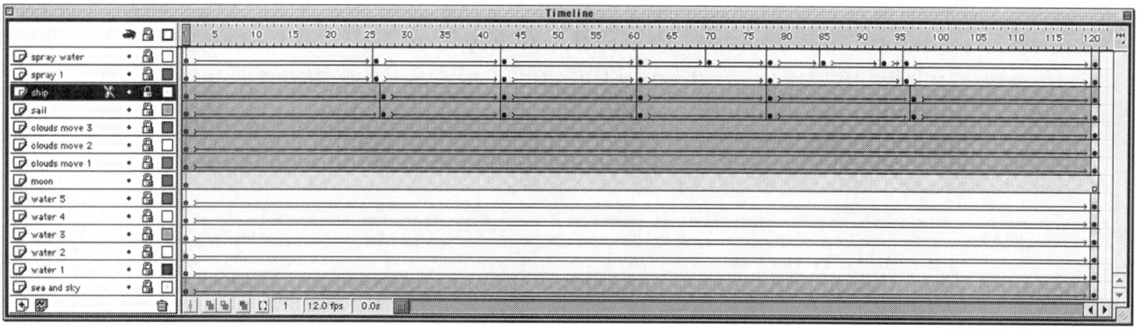

Figure 2.3   *The timeline of Figure 2.2.*

animated to provide the surface of the sea in motion. Finally, morphing is used on two different layers to provide the spray as the ship breaks the waves.

It may appear that animation in Flash is a simple matter. Certainly, the mechanics of animation are made simple by Flash, but that doesn't make the art of animation simple. Producing successful animation relies on more than mastery of the mechanics of Flash or of any other computer program or traditional equipment. It relies on an understanding of how things move, and how movement can convey information or expression. These are not things that can be obtained by reading a manual, they require years of careful study, observation and practice. If you are an experienced animator, transferring your skills to Flash should not present many problems — but they won't help you much with Flash scripting. If you are not an experienced animator — even if you are a trained graphic designer — you should think carefully before adding to the mass of poor animation that is infesting the WWW. In an ideal world, Flash projects would all be team efforts, with animators animating, designers designing and programmers programming. However, the sudden demand for Flash content does mean that people who are not trained in animation are being called on to animate; if you find yourself in this situation, at least read a serious book on the subject: *The Animation Book* by Kit Laybourne (Three Rivers Press, 1998) is highly regarded.

Symbols and Instances

Symbols are more than just reusable graphics. Flash supports three kinds of symbol, distinguished by their behaviour: *graphic symbols*, *movie clip symbols* and *button symbols*. The last of these are a specialized type, which, as their name suggests, are used to provide a simple means of accepting user input. Actions can be attached to buttons, as they can to frames, to be executed when some particular event occurs, such as the mouse being clicked while the cursor is over the button. Users can thus click on a button to make something happen, just as they can in conventional dialogue boxes and in HTML forms. Using buttons and associating actions with them will be described towards the end of this chapter. Actions can also be attached to clips, which can also respond to input in a less complex way.

Graphic symbols are usually objects that are reused or tweened, but they may also be animations, so that a movie can be included in another one. Movie clip symbols are always used as reusable pieces of animation. The difference between them and graphic symbols is that movie clips have their own timeline, which is independent of the movie in which they are included, and they can respond to certain events. This difference can be illustrated by a simple modification of the sunset movie.

Suppose I wish to have a dolphin riding the bow wave of the ship. I could do this by creating a dolphin symbol consisting of a short animation during which it leapt out of the water. (Figure 2.1 is, in fact, part of the timeline of such a symbol.). Next, I could create a new layer with keyframes at suitable points in the main animation. An instance of the dolphin symbol could be placed at just in front of the ship in these keyframes, and its motion could be tweened so that the dolphin swims in front of the ship, leaping out of the water as it goes.

So far, it makes no difference whether the dolphin is a graphic symbol or a movie clip symbol. Suppose, though, that I make the movie stop in frame 90, by using the `Stop` command in the Flash Player, for example. (We will see in the next chapter another way of stopping a movie, by attaching an action to a frame.) If the dolphin is a graphic symbol, everything will stop when the playhead reaches frame 90; the cetacean will be frozen in the water at the same instant as the ship is halted in its tracks. However, if the dolphin is a movie clip symbol, when the ship stands still the dolphin will stop moving across the frame but it will continue to jump in place. The movie clip of the leap is played independently of the main movie's timeline, though the tweened motion is part of that timeline. I could make the dolphin stop jumping when a mouse button was pressed by attaching an action to the clip to stop it playing whenever that event occurred. If the dolphin was an instance of a graphic symbol, this could not be done; such instances cannot respond to events in any way.

A symbol must be assigned one of the three types when it is created, and instances start out belonging to the same type, i.e., an instance of a graphic symbol is a graphic instance and behaves accordingly, and so on. This is probably what you expect and usually what you want, but it is possible to change the type of an instance after it is created (via the Instance panel). For example, a still image that is an instance of a graphic symbol might be turned into a movie clip or a button if you wanted it to respond to events.

There are other differences between movie clip symbols and graphic symbols. Most importantly for our purposes, interactive controls do not work in a graphic symbol but they do in a movie clip symbol. Movie clips are truly movies within movies. Where movie clip symbols are combined with interactivity it becomes possible to construct a Flash movie as a collection of movie clips which are coordinated by the use of scripts, activated in response to events. Each movie clip may include buttons and frames with associated actions, as well as having its own actions that respond to events, so that clips serve as vehicles for computation, and the organization of the movie is also the structure of the computation it carries out.

Instance and Target Names

In order for scripts to be able to refer to them, movie clip instances must be identifiable. Since there may be several instances of the same symbol, it must be possible to distinguish individual instances, not just different symbols. An instance can be given a name for this purpose, via the Instance panel, which displays a text field for entering an instance name when the selected instance is a movie clip.

Since a movie clip is like a movie, and movies can contain movie clip instances, it follows that movie clips can contain movie clip instances, and these may be instances of movie clips that contain movie clip instances, and so on. Movie clip instances can be nested in this way to an arbitrary depth. Note that a symbol is built out of *instances* not

symbols and instances

symbols. This makes it impossible for every instance in a movie to be given a unique name.

For example, suppose I create movie clip symbols for a small school of dolphins, consisting of three differently scaled instances of the dolphin symbol, calling them left, right and centre. If I now place two instances of the school symbol in a movie, each has its own three dolphin instances, with the same three instance names (see Figure 2.4). To distinguish between them, Flash allows instances within instances to be identified with a composite *target name* using a dot notation. An instance named y within an instance named x is identified as $x.y$. For example, if my two school instances are called near and far, the dolphin instances they contain will be near.left, near.right and near.centre, and far.left, far.right and far.centre. This notation is extended in the obvious way for clips within clips within clips within …

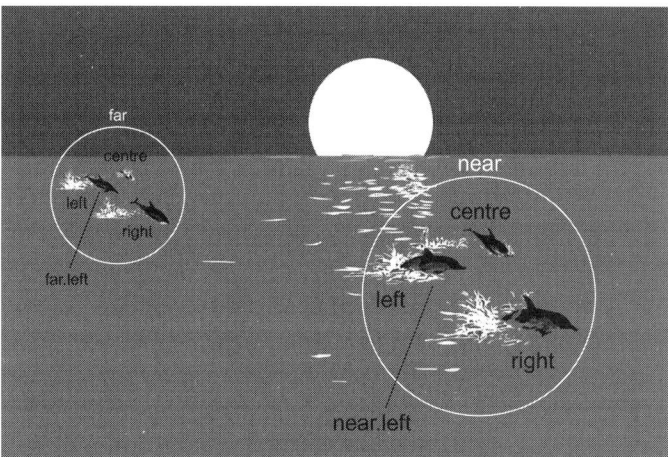

Figure 2.4   *Naming instances.*

Target names are interpreted relative to the movie clip in which they are used. For example, within far, right means far.right, but in near it means near.right. To refer to an instance within another instance, its full target name must be used. The special instance name _root is used for the main timeline of the movie, and _parent for the containing instance. Hence, inside far, the target name _parent.near.right is the same as _root.near.right. A target name beginning with _root always identifies the same instance, no matter where it is used.[1] One beginning with _parent, on the other hand, allows actions within clips to refer to clips above them in the hierarchy or in separate

1. This isn't quite true, as we will see in Chapter 3.

branches, without reference to their absolute position in a hierarchy. You will probably see an analogy here with absolute and relative URLs, with _parent playing the same role as ... The advantage of using relative targets is the same as that of using relative URLs: it makes it straightforward to move a clip to a different absolute location. In particular, it makes it easy to reuse clips in other movies.

In Flash 4, a different notation, more akin to path names in URLs, was used for target names. Components were separated by a / instead of a dot, and .. was used instead of _parent. This notation should be avoided in Flash 5, but you may see it in older scripts that have been imported from previous versions.

Sound

Sound can be used in several different ways in Flash movies, and is one of the aspects of playback that can be controlled by actions. Sounds can be imported from AIFF, WAV or MP3 files, and then stored in the movie's library. The sounds in the library appear in a pop-up menu on the Sound panel. They are added to the movie itself by creating a layer, selecting a frame where you want the sound to begin, and then choosing a sound from the pop-up. Sounds can be synchronized with the movie's playback in one of two ways. *Event sounds* start to play when the playhead enters the frame at which the sound was added, and then continue to play until they reach their end or for a specified number of repetitions, irrespective of how the playback of the animation proceeds. For example, an event sound will continue to play if the movie is stopped, like a movie clip. *Stream sounds* are synchronized to the main movie: if it stops, they stop; if frames are being displayed at less than the movie's specified frame rate (because it is being streamed over a slow network connection or played on a slow machine), frames are dropped to ensure that the relationship between sound and picture set on the timeline is maintained. Stream sounds are suitable for synchronized soundtracks, while event sounds are useful for providing ambient sound and spot effects. You use the Sync pop-up menu on the Sound panel to choose whether a sound is an event or stream sound.

Sounds can be controlled by scripts, but there is a more direct way of stopping a sound. The Sync pop-up menu includes Stop as one of its entries. If you have added a sound as described above, you can add a keyframe to its layer, select the sound again from the pop-up menu in the Sound panel and then choose Stop from the Sync pop-up. The sound will stop when the playhead reaches that keyframe.

There is one other item in the Sync pop-up: Start. This has the same effect as Event — it starts up an event sound — except that if the sound is already playing, it starts a new copy of it, allowing you to create a chorus effect, among other possibilities. If a movie contains several sounds, they are all mixed down when the movie is exported.

Simple sound editing can be performed inside Flash, though as with graphics, many users will prefer to use a dedicated application and only use Flash to assemble the final movie. A few effects, such as fading in or out and panning between stereo channels can be applied dynamically, and may be controlled by actions assigned to buttons, frames or movie clips. Sounds may also be added to buttons, to enhance user feedback (although this should be done judiciously, because sounds can be particularly annoying to many people).

Events

Graphical user interfaces are based on an *event-driven* model of program execution. That is, events such as mouse movements and clicks or key presses cause some code to be executed, which changes the state of the system in some way. Operating system interfaces, such as the Windows Explorer or the MacOS Finder follow this pattern, as do Web browsers. The same model of interactivity is used by Flash movies.

There are three classes of event that can cause scripts to be executed in a Flash movie: *frame events*, *button events* and *clip events*. The names refer to the types of object that can respond to them. Frames respond to events caused by the playhead. The only such event in Flash is the playhead entering the frame. Buttons — that is, instances of button symbols — respond to events caused by user input. Movie clips — instances of movie clip symbols — also respond to events caused by user input, although the range of events they recognize is more limited than the full set of button events. Clips also respond to events on the timeline, including the playhead entering the first frame in which the clip appears, or leaving the last such frame; they also allow scripts to be executed every time a frame is entered, in addition to any scripts attached to specific frames.

As the preceding paragraph indicates, buttons react to the widest range of events. Each button symbol defines an *active area*, within which the cursor is defined as being over the button. (The active area need not correspond to any visible boundary or object.) A button can potentially respond to the following events: a mouse button being pressed or released while the cursor is within the active area, a mouse button being released outside the active area, the cursor being moved over or out of the active area, and the cursor being dragged (i.e., being moved while a mouse button is held down) either over or out of the active area, and a specific key being pressed. Table 2.1 shows the names Flash gives to these events. There are some subtle but important details to be aware of.

Table 2.1 *Button events.*

press	rollOut
release	dragOver
releaseOutside	dragOut
rollOver	keyPress(key)

Normally, release and releaseOutside events are only received by the button that received the most recent press event. For example, if a frame contains two buttons, and the mouse button is pressed while the cursor is over the first, held down while it is moved over the second, and then released, the first button will receive a press event followed by a releaseOutside event; the second button will not receive a release event, even though the mouse button was released while the cursor was over it. Similarly, a button will only receive a dragOver event when the cursor is moved over it with the mouse button depressed if the mouse button was originally pressed while the cursor was over the button. This behaviour can be changed, by selecting Track as Menu Item from the Behaviour pop-up in the Instance panel when a button is selected. If that had been done in the first example just described, then the second button would have received the release event. In this case, the first button would not have received its releaseOutside event, even though the mouse button was released outside it. There is no way for both buttons to receive an event under such circumstances. When a button is being tracked as a menu item, it receives dragOver events any time the cursor is dragged over it. The most common use for this modified behaviour is in constructing menus — hence the terminology. This will be described in Chapter 4.

When the active areas of buttons overlap or coincide, events are only received by the frontmost button. Where buttons are on separate layers, the frontmost button will be on the frontmost layer; where overlapping buttons are on the same layer, the frontmost is determined by how the instances were placed on the stage. Normally, instances placed later are in front of ones placed earlier, but this ordering can be changed using the commands on the Modify>Arrange sub-menu.

The names of the clip events are shown in Table 2.2. The load, unload and enterFrame events are those alluded to earlier, which are dependent on the playhead. The data event occurs when input is received from a server, which will not be described until Chapter 7. The remaining events are caused by user input. Note that clips respond to this in a less refined way than buttons do. Not only do they distinguish fewer different events, they react to them less precisely: a mouseDown event is received by a clip when the mouse button is pressed no matter where the cursor is, even if it is not over the clip at the time. It follows that, if there is more than one active clip, when the mouse button is pressed, they will all receive a mouseDown event; they will still receive the event if the cursor is over a button, which will simultaneously receive a press event. Keyboard events are also treated differently by clips and buttons. Whereas for a button you can specify that a script should be triggered by the pressing of a particular key, such as k or @, a clip can only react to the pressing of any key, and the script that is invoked must then determine which key it was that was pressed. (On the other hand, clips can respond to the pressing of modifier keys, such as shift, independently of any key they are modifying, and to keys being released, which buttons cannot.) All active clips receive a keyDown event, but only the frontmost button receives a keyPress.

Table 2.2 *Clip events.*

load	mouseUp
unload	keyDown
enterFrame	keyUp
mouseMove	data
mouseDown	

Frame events are predictable: we know the circumstances under which the playhead will enter a frame. Button events, in contrast, are unpredictable, since they are caused by user input, which might happen at any time and in any order. Clip events are a mixture of the predictable and the unpredictable. Most often, frame and button events are used in combination, with scripts attached to a frame establishing a context for the user interaction provided by buttons. Clip events are used to allow clips to behave as objects, so that elaborate movies can be structured as a set of interacting clip instances.

An interactive Flash movie is created by attaching scripts to frames, buttons or movie clip instances and, for buttons and clips, specifying the events in response to which the script is to be executed. Scripts are written in ActionScript, a scripting language that closely resembles JavaScript. The main difference is that, whereas JavaScript provides objects for manipulating Web pages, ActionScript provides objects and built-in operations known as *actions*, for manipulating the elements of Flash movies.

In this chapter, we will consider basic actions that control the way in which a movie behaves. Most such actions take parameters. For example, the action gotoAndPlay takes a frame number or label as a parameter, which specifies the frame to which the playhead should move. The parameters which are permitted for each basic action depend on what it does. In later chapters we will see how the basic actions can be combined into scripts which use variables and control structures to perform relatively elaborate computation and interact with other programs.

As a preliminary to a description of basic actions, we must look in more detail at button symbols.

Button Symbols

It's best to think of button symbols as being a distinct type of symbol in Flash, because of the way they behave, but they are built as animations that have exactly four frames. These are given the special labels Up, Over, Down and Hit. The first three correspond to states of the button, relative to the cursor. Up is the normal state, when the cursor is not over the button, while Over, as you might guess, corresponds to the cursor being over the button. Thus, by putting different graphics in the Up and Over frames, a classic rollover effect can be produced: the appearance of the button changes as the cursor passes over it, providing useful feedback to the user. Typically, the two states will be similar, with different shading, for example. The Down frame is displayed when the mouse button is depressed while the cursor is over the button symbol, i.e., the user has pressed the button. Again, the intention is that the display should provide feedback, so typically the Down frame will show an image that indicates the button being operated. For example, if a three-dimensional image of an actual button was being used, the Up frame might show it slightly elevated, while the Down frame showed the same button pressed down. However, these are only conventions. The frames can show any images, or none (for invisible controls), and the same image can be used for all three, if it is felt that conventional feedback is inappropriate.

The final frame, Hit, is different from the other two, because it is not displayed. It is used to indicate the area within which the cursor is considered to be over the button — its active area. Often, this will match the image in the Up frame, but it need not do so. For example, Figure 2.5 shows the frames of a button taken from the library distributed with Flash. Here, the active area is extended beyond the button icon, to allow a text label to be placed next to the button icon within the active area, so that it seems to be part of the button although it is not. (See Figure 2.6 — clicking on the word 'Register' invokes the same action as clicking on the button icon.)

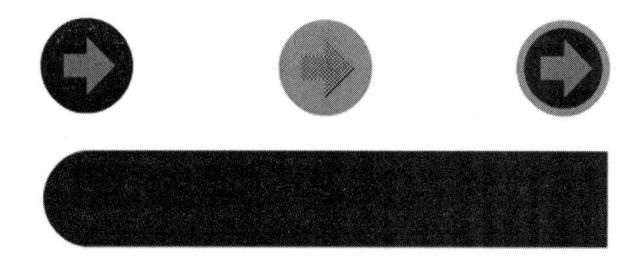

Figure 2.5   *Button states and active area.*

Figure 2.6   *A label on the button.*

The frames of a button symbol are composed on the stage like any other frame. Graphics may be imported, and symbol instances can be incorporated in the button. Movie clip instances can be used to create animated buttons. (Most of the examples I have seen of this are pretty tacky — buttons that explode when you click on them, and so on — but potentially, animated buttons offer new possibilities for providing attractive user interface elements.) Sounds can also be attached to some of a button's keyframes, by placing them on a layer as event sounds, so that the button clicks when pressed, and so on. (Again, there is plenty of scope for tackiness and irritated users here.)

As I remarked earlier, an instance of any symbol may have its type changed after it has been placed on the stage, using the Behaviour pop-up on the Instance panel. This means that graphic instances can be made to respond to events as if they were buttons. If you don't want the rollover effect, this can be a convenient way of adding responsive elements to a movie.

Normally, one tends to think of buttons as static controls, which sit on the screen waiting to be pressed. This is often the best way of using them; it conforms to users' expectations and provides a simple organization for your movie. Buttons can be placed in a keyframe that is extended over the whole movie, on their own layer. However, sometimes it may be useful to employ buttons in less conventional ways. One particularly handy technique is to create a rectangular button equal in size to the stage, place an instance of it on the frontmost layer of a movie, extending the image over as many frames as is appropriate, and setting the instance's alpha value to zero, so that it becomes transparent. The result is that the button instance will receive events anywhere on the screen. Such a button can be used to create an interface in which all a user has to do to make something happen is click somewhere. You might use this in an introductory section of a movie to allow the user who is familiar with its contents to dismiss the introduction.

A more outré variation is to animate button instances, causing them to move around or fade in and out. For example, you might wish to show an animated shopping trolley moving around a virtual supermarket, and allow the user to click on the trolley wherever it was in order to add an item to their shopping.

Attaching Actions to Frames and Instances

The procedure for attaching actions is basically the same, whether they are being attached to a button or clip instance or to a frame. First, the frame or instance is selected in the timeline or stage, respectively. Then, the script is entered in the Actions panel. This panel can be invoked in several ways: by selecting the Windows>Actions command, or by clicking on the actions icon ( ) in the mini-launcher either at the bottom of the stage or in the Instance panel. The Actions panel is context-sensitive: if a frame is selected, it is labelled Frame Actions and actions that specify events are disabled; if a clip or button is selected, the panel is labelled Object Actions and allows you to specify events. The panel is modeless, that is, you don't need to dismiss it like a dialogue box in order to do something else. You can leave it open all the time, without losing any scripts you are working on.

The Actions panel can operate in either of two modes: *normal* and *expert*, which are selected using the pop-up menu attached to the small triangle in the upper right corner of the panel. In normal mode, the panel is split into three panes, as shown in Figure 2.7. The top right pane is used to display the text of the script. The top left pane initially displays several entries corresponding to categories of ActionScript statements. Clicking on one of these categories causes it to expand into a list, as shown in the figure. Statements are added to a script by double-clicking an entry from the list. Where a statement requires some parameter values, the bottom pane of the panel is used to enter them: when an action has been selected from the list at the left, appropriate fields are displayed at the bottom to enter any associated parameters. Here, for example, a Go To action has been selected, so the bottom panel has fields to enter the destination scene and frame. (The pop-up labelled Type allows you to choose whether to enter a frame label or number, choose the next or previous frame, or use an expression to compute a destination.)

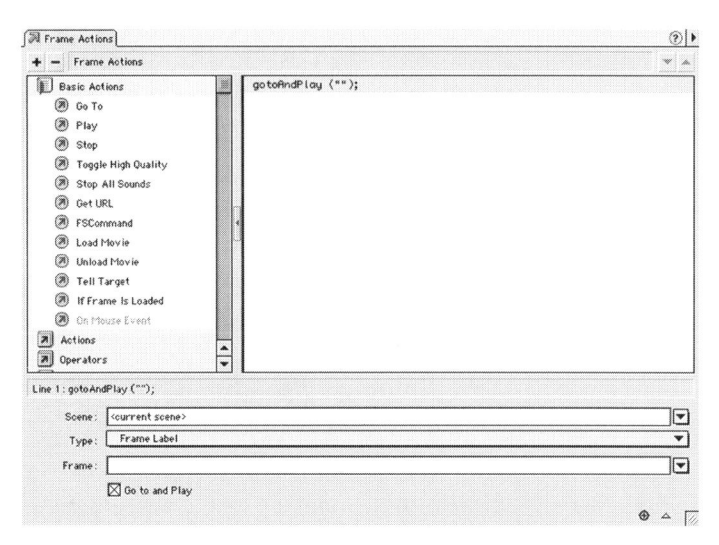

Figure 2.7 *The Actions palette in normal mode.*

In expert mode, the Actions panel behaves more like a text editor: you can type directly into the right hand pane as well as using the list on the left to select statements, and the bottom pane is not available — you have to remember which parameters are required and type them yourself. If you are an accurate typist, and used to writing scripts and programs, expert mode will probably feel more comfortable and be quicker. Otherwise, normal mode will protect you from making certain sorts of mistakes, and save you from having to remember so much detail about ActionScript syntax. You can choose the mode you work in for each script; a preference setting is used to determine which to use by default.

An alternative to using either mode of the Actions panel is to use a text editor to create scripts in files stored outside the Flash movie. Powerful extensible editors like emacs or Alpha, as well as having the advantage of being familiar tools, offer specialized editing modes for JavaScript, and in time will probably provide similar support for ActionScript. If you choose to use an external editor, you have two options for incorporating the script in the movie. Either choose Import From File... from the panel's pop-up menu, and then select the file in question, or choose include from the list of actions in the left pane to insert a #include directive, with the file's name as its parameter. The difference between the two is that importing a script from a file causes it to be textually placed in the movie, as if you had typed it in the Actions panel; using include only plants a pointer to the file, which is not incorporated until the movie is exported. This means that if you need to change the script, any changes you make in your text editor will automatically propagate to the movie, whereas if you had imported it, the imported script would have become independent of the file, and you would have to import it again to incorporate any changes. Importing does mean that you can view and edit the script inside Flash, though.

Basic Actions

The category of Basic Actions that you see in Figure 2.7 is only available in normal mode. It provides the simple functionality that was available in Flash 3, which serves as a good starting point for a description of Flash interactivity in general. (The Tell Target and If Frame Is Loaded actions which you see in Figure 2.7 are now deprecated, so they will not be described.) Because these actions are a legacy from earlier versions, they do not behave in entirely the same way as other actions. In particular, the code that is inserted into the script is not identical to that indicated on the list, but is a translation into the new ActionScript syntax. For example, you select Go To from the list, and tick the Go To And Play checkbox in the parameters pane, and a gotoAndPlay statement is added to the script. These differences are purely cosmetic, though.

Perhaps the simplest action of all is Stop, which halts the movement of the playhead at the frame it is currently over (the *current frame*, as I will call it from now on). Hence, to stop a movie at, say, its 90th frame (assuming that is a keyframe and that you are using the Actions panel in normal mode), you would select frame 90 in the timeline, display the Frame Actions panel if it is not already visible, click on Basic Actions in the left pane to expand the list, and select Stop. The single line script
stop ();
appears in the right hand pane.[1] The script is now attached to the frame and will be executed when the playhead reaches it, stopping the movie.

What, you may well ask, is the point of using an action attached to a frame to stop a movie? Or perhaps: what is the point of all the frames after the one it stops in, since the playhead can never reach them? (Frame actions are, as I remarked earlier, predictable.) A stop() statement prevents the playhead moving on to another frame, but it does not halt the Flash player. The frame's contents are still displayed and any buttons and movie clips that have been placed in the stopped frame will be able to respond to events.

---

1. The layout shown in this and the remaining examples in this chapter is that introduced by Flash when the statement is inserted using normal mode. If you use expert mode or an external editor, you can use your own layout — you might well dispense with the space before the brackets, for example. In later chapters, a more compact layout will be used.

Certainly, in the absence of any other actions, the playhead will never be able to pass a frame with a Stop action, but the presence of clips and buttons means that other actions are possible. In addition, since movie clip instances in the frame continue to play, a stopped frame can serve as a container for a set of clips that are controlled separately.

To reduce things to their simplest, suppose that in frame 90 — to which a script consisting of a stop() statement is attached — there is an instance of a button symbol, which could usefully be labelled Continue. A play() statement can be added to this button, by selecting it on the stage while frame 90 is selected in the timeline, and then proceeding as before, but choosing Play from the basic actions list. The following script will be attached to the button:

```
on (release) {
        play ();
}
```

As you can see, the play() statement is enclosed in curly brackets, and preceded by on (release). This is the syntactical boilerplate used to indicate that the action is associated with an event (in this case release) as well as with the button instance. Button actions are always associated with both an instance and an event so when you first add one the boilerplate is inserted automatically (in normal mode). If you select the first line (beginning with on), the bottom pane of the panel offers the opportunity to select a different event or add extra events, although release is the one most commonly required. (By convention, a mouse click does not occur until the button is released — this is necessary to allow dragging.) To add different actions for other events, you can explicitly select On MouseEvent from the list of basic actions (this option is disabled when you are adding actions to a frame), choose one or more button events in the parameters pane, and then use the list again to select an action to associate with them.

There is another significant difference between button scripts and frame scripts. Whereas the stop() attached to frame 90 stopped the playback of the movie in which the frame occurs, the play() attached to the button resumes playback of the main movie; it doesn't cause the button to play itself as a movie. This is probably what you would expect, but it is something of an anomaly: usually you must indicate the *target* of a button action, as we will see shortly.

If you select a movie clip instance instead of a button and then add a basic action to it, the action will be associated with the load event by default. For example, selecting Play from the list of basic actions when a clip is selected on the stage will cause the following script to be attached to the clip:

```
onClipEvent (load) {
```

play ();
}

The event can be changed by selecting the first line and choosing a different one in the parameters pane, as in the case of a mouse event. However, onClipEvent is not a basic action, so to add others you would have to use the sublist labelled Actions. The Flash 3 actions on which Flash 5's basic actions are based predate clip events, so it is more consistent not to use them for this purpose and in the remainder of this chapter I will only consider buttons and frames.

Among the list of basic actions are Toggle High Quality, which turns anti-aliasing off and on, and Stop All Sounds, which does what it says it does. These two actions cause the statements toggleHighQuality() and stopAllSounds(), respectively, to be inserted in the script.

Simple Movie Structures

Using stop() and play() in the manner outlined above enables a user to exert some control over playback, but is of limited use. The Go To basic action, which adds gotoAndPlay and gotoAndStop statements, allows more flexibility and introduces the possibility of structuring movies in ways other than as simple linear sequences, by moving the playhead to a specified frame.

One of the most useful such structures is a set of *selections*, which are chosen from a menu. Suppose, for example, that your Web site uses Flash to present a short description of half a dozen products — let's say computing books, as a definite example — which you wish to sell over the Internet. If you were using HTML, you would probably organize your site with a welcome page containing links to pages for each book. The links might be arranged as a conventional menu, or you might use images, possibly of the books' covers.

Conceptually, it should be fairly easy to see how a similar organization can be achieved with Flash. The timeline of the main part of the movie is divided into sections, one for each book. (These might be separate scenes, but this is usually only done if each section is long.) The first frame of each such section should be given a label. The first frame of the entire movie, which precedes all the individual books' sections, contains buttons for each book — as with the HTML implementation, these might be the text of each book's title, or some iconic representation or a more elaborate graphic — each of which has an action causing the playhead to go to the beginning of the section for the corresponding book. At the end of each of these sections, there is a button to take the user back to the selection menu.

Now for the details. The first frame must have a stop() statement attached to it, otherwise the playhead will carry straight on from it into the first book's section of the movie. Likewise, the last frame of each section must have a stop() statement, to prevent playback continuing into the following one. Each section's last frame can have a button which, when clicked, will take the playhead back to the first frame of the movie — we'll assume that the last frame has some text or similar content that is worth looking at for a while, otherwise a script could just be attached to the frame to return to the menu. The first frame contains one button for each book, as described above.

All of these buttons have a script attached to them by selecting the Go To action. This action takes a parameter that specifies a frame to which the playhead should be moved. You can use a frame number or a label for this purpose —the use of labels is strongly recommended for this structure, since editing any part of the movie may invalidate frame numbers. You also indicate whether the movie should play or stop at that frame, that is, whether a gotoAndPlay or a gotoAndStop action should be used; in this case, it should play. Thus, the script attached to the button in frame 1 corresponding to the book *Digital Multimedia* will look like this:

```
on (release) {
        gotoAndPlay ("dmm");
}
```

where dmm is the label on the first frame of the section of the movie describing that book. The button itself is a GIF image of the book's cover which has been converted into a button symbol so that a script can be attached to it and it can receive events. Each of the other buttons is constructed similarly and will have similar actions, with the label of the corresponding section's starting frame substituted for dmm. The buttons on the final frame of each section will have identical scripts, like this:

```
on (release) {
   gotoAndPlay ("menu");
}
```

where menu labels the first frame of the movie.

Actually, it doesn't matter whether the gotoAndPlay("menu") or gotoAndStop("menu") is used here, because the first frame has a stop() attached to it, so playback will always stop there.

A second commonly used structure comprises a sequence of stages, where each must play in its entirety before the next begins. You might use such a structure in an on-line purchasing system, for example, where you need to take several sets of details from the customer. Flash provides form elements to accept user input (see Chapter 4), which could be arranged in a sequence, so that the user first confirms their order, then provides contact details, then credit card information, and is given a chance to check everything is correct before committing themselves to the purchase. If it is possible to assert that every step in the sequence will always be carried out exactly once, in their prescribed order, stop() and play() statements will suffice to implement the sequence, but this is unlikely to be the case. In almost all cases, it will be necessary to allow the user to go back to a previous step, to correct errors or because they have changed their mind. It may also be necessary to allow certain steps to be skipped — for example, you might include a marketing questionnaire, but allow customers to decline to fill it in. For such variations, gotoAnd... statements on buttons can be used. The details are left to Exercise 6 at the end of this chapter.

Both the structures I have described share a useful property: each individual section has a single 'entry point', i.e., any statement that sends the playhead to a section sends it to its first frame. If you have much experience of programming you will appreciate why this is a desirable property, especially where a movie has much computation associated with it. It means that at any frame within the section, you can rely on any actions occurring in earlier frames to have been executed. This makes it easier to think about what is happening, and to change the movie without upsetting the logic of actions. It also makes it easier to maintain coherence among the visual elements of the movie.

Targets

The actions we have looked at so far all affect the playback of the main timeline of a movie. Where a movie contains instances of other movie clip symbols, it is often necessary to be able to control the behaviour of one clip using buttons in the main movie, or sometimes, in other clips. This is done using target names, which were described earlier in this chapter.

An easily overlooked point is that, before a clip can be controlled in this way, it must be given an instance name. This does not happen when the instance is created; you must enter it in the Name field on the Instance panel explicitly. Flash does not check whether any target name you use actually refers to anything, so if you forget to give an instance a name, but use one anyway believing you had done so, you will not be warned about the error; your action will just do nothing, silently, probably leaving you baffled. As well as having an instance name, a clip must also be in existence when it is the target of some action. A clip comes into existence in the first frame in which it is present, and ceases to exist after the last. If an action refers to it outside its time of existence, nothing happens, and once again there is no error message. (If you have written JavaScript to control elements of Web pages, you will be familiar with the necessity to ensure that document elements have been parsed by the browser before you can refer to them. The problem is similar, but is compounded by the time-based nature of Flash movies.)

As a first example of controlling movie clip instances, consider making a movie player, so that the playback of a clip can be controlled using buttons. We will only deal with the Play, Stop, Step Forward, Step Back and Rewind functions.

The first step will be to create a movie with a single frame and attach stop() to it. This frame will just be a container for the movie clip being controlled and the buttons that control it. Next, a clip symbol must be created and an instance of it placed on the stage. Any Flash movie converted to a symbol can be used for this purpose. To emphasize the point once again: the instance must be given a name. Let's suppose it is called the_clip.

At this point, you will probably realize that we are going to end up with this particular movie clip wired in to the player, rather as if your VCR came with one tape in it and no means of changing it. Well, we have to start with something... Later we will see how to turn this basic movie into something like a Flash movie jukebox that lets you select a movie to play. This will require some additional knowledge of ActionScript, so for now, let us concentrate on controlling the playback.

The next step is to add controls in the form of buttons. Among the libraries distributed with Flash is a collection of VCR buttons, and these will suffice for something that does not need a distinctive visual identity. Alternatively, if you wished to implement something like this for a real site, you might want to design buttons of your own, as we have done here. Figure 2.8 shows a possible stage layout.

The set of basic actions includes one, Tell Target, that can be used to control clips in the desired way. It is, however, a legacy from earlier versions of Flash and is now deprecated (i.e., support for it may be withdrawn in later releases of Flash). A better way is to make use of the fact that a clip is an *object*, in the technical sense that the term is used in ActionScript. First of all, therefore, we need to take a preliminary look at objects. (We will return to the subject in greater detail in Chapters 5 and 6.)

An object in ActionScript is just a collection of named data items, known as *properties*, and operations that it can perform, known as *methods*. For now, we need only be concerned with methods, which, in anthropomorphic terms, are the things an object knows how to do. When we want an object to do something, we *call* the appropriate method. If an object called an_object has a method called a_method, you call the

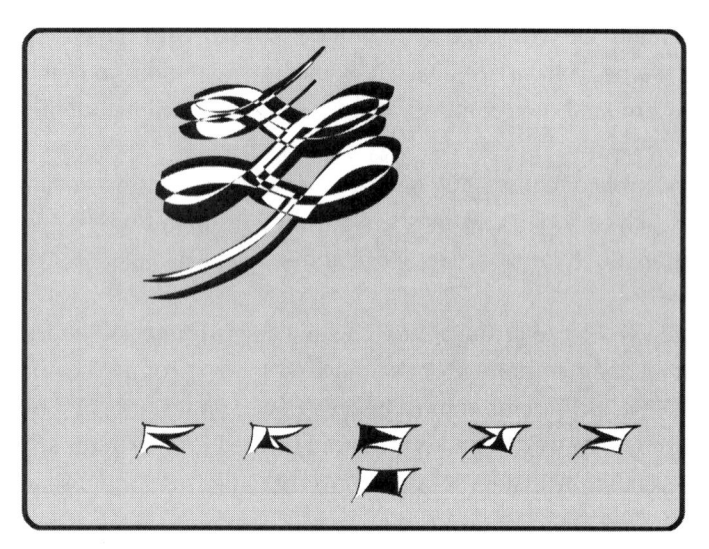

Figure 2.8 *A movie player movie.*

method with the statement an_object.a_method(), that is, the object's name is followed by a dot, and then the method's name and a pair of brackets. We sometimes say that the method is called *through* the object.

A clip is a movie within a movie, so it knows how to do all the things that a movie can do, such as stopping, playing, going to a specific frame, and so on. In fact, all the ActionScript statements that we have used so far to control a movie are actually method calls, but since they are sent to the movie itself, the object is implicit. As you may infer from this (thinking about gotoAndPlay, for instance), method calls may take arguments, which appear inside the brackets.

The point of all this is that a movie clip is an object and it can be identified by a target name, which can therefore be used to call methods. For example, the statement
```
the_clip.play ();
```
calls the play method of our clip — which causes it to play. Hence, the Play button of the movie player needs to have the following script attached to it:
```
on (release) {
        the_clip.play ();
}
```
and then when it is clicked, the clip will start to play, as required.

If you try, you will discover that you can't enter a script like this in normal mode using basic actions. In fact, you can only enter this precise script in expert mode. There is an alternative way of achieving the same effect, which can be entered in normal mode, and may be more convenient, especially if you are calling several methods belonging to the same object. The with statement is used to set up an object to which all methods that are called without an explicit object name are assumed to belong. For example,

```
with (the_clip) {
        play ();
    }
```
means the same as
the_clip.play ();

To add a with statement you must use the Actions sub-list in the left hand pane of Actions panel — it isn't a basic action. In normal mode, the parameters pane provides a text box labelled Object for you to enter the clip's target name. (Later we will see other kinds of object, too.) Rather than typing the name, and risking errors that may be hard to find later, you can click on the small target icon in the bottom right hand of the panel. This will cause a dialogue similar to the one shown in Figure 2.9 to be displayed. The top pane shows the hierarchy of clips in your movie. (In this movie, there is only one, but, as we will see later, a movie may contain many clips.) By double-clicking a particular clip, its target name will be inserted in the script. Notice the buttons at the bottom right that let you choose between absolute and relative target names. (As I explained earlier, relative target names are usually to be preferred.) Of course, if you need to refer to a clip before it has been added to the movie, you will have to type its name by hand.

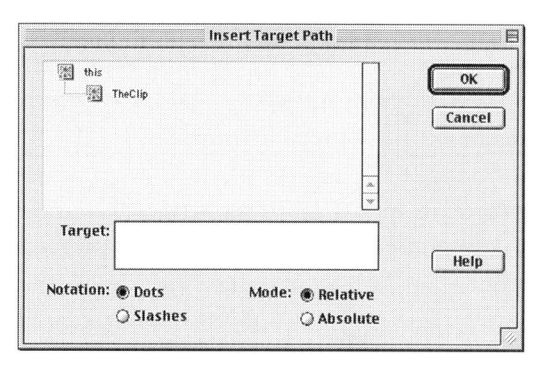

Figure 2.9 *The target dialogue.*

Using a with statement, the script for the Play button is:
```
on (release) {
        with (the_clip) {
```

```
            play ();
        }
}
```
You should be able to see from this what scripts should be attached to the Stop and Rewind buttons.

The Step Forward and Step Back buttons are similar. The action attached to the Step Forward button is:
```
on (release) {
        with (the_clip) {
                nextFrame ();
        }
}
```
The nextframe() method call can be inserted in normal mode by choosing Go To from the basic actions list and selecting Next Frame from the Type pop-up in the parameters pane. For the Step Back button, the prevFrame method is called instead of nextFrame in the obvious way.

There is one final action that is required in this movie. As it stands, the clip will start to play immediately — recall that clip instances play independently of the timeline of the main movie. We could prevent this by inserting a stop() at the first frame of the clip, but a cleaner alternative is to attach the following script to the first (only) frame of the main movie:
```
with (the_clip) {
    stop ();
}
```
As this demonstrates, method calls can be used to make clips perform actions when the playhead reaches a particular frame in the main movie.

If, for some reason, you prefer to stick with the basic actions, you can use Tell Target to achieve the same effects. Essentially, the tellTarget statement which this action inserts is a synonym for with that uses a non-standard syntax: the target name must be enclosed in quotation marks, as in
```
tellTarget ("the_clip") {
        play ();
}
```
If the target name is complex, the slash notation mentioned on page 22 is used, instead of the dot notation. Obviously, the difference is cosmetic and insignificant, but tellTarget does not fit in with the syntax of ECMAScript, on which the current version

of ActionScript is based, so it is best avoided. Despite this, you will almost certainly see tellTarget used by programmers who are used to Flash 4, and in books that have been hastily revised for the new version.

Loading Movies

Normally, the Flash Player plays a single movie, by default in a continuous loop. To play a different movie, you open it in a new window. It is possible to make the player play a new movie in the old window using the loadMovie statement. This statement can also be used to play more than one movie simultaneously (which is different from playing a movie containing more than one clip instance).

Loading provides a means of implementing movies structured as a set of selections that may be more efficient than stitching all the sections together and using gotoAndPlay in the way that was described earlier in this chapter. Each section to be selected is stored in a separate movie, and loaded in response to a button click. This way, sections that are never selected are never loaded into the Flash Player; if the movie is being viewed over the Internet, unused sections need never be transmitted over the network. Keeping the sections in separate movies also makes it easier to reuse them in different contexts.

When more than one is being played, movies are stacked, both physically, by being placed on top of each other with the top left hand corners aligned, and logically, by being assigned a *level*, which is just a number showing how many movies are below it. A movie that is opened in the Flash Player is deemed to be at level 0; the first movie it loads is then placed on top of it and would normally be assigned level 1; the next is placed on top again, and assigned level 2; and so on. The background of any movie at a level higher than 0 is made transparent, so that movies at lower levels show through. This provides a crude means of dynamically compositing movies.

The loadMovie function takes several arguments. The first is always a URL identifying the movie to be loaded. The URL may be relative or absolute; if it is absolute then, for security reasons, the movie it identifies to be loaded must be in the same subdomain as the movie doing the loading.[1] The second argument takes one of two forms: either it is a number, specifying a level to load the movie into, or it is a target name; the second option will be considered later, as will an optional third argument.

---

1. See page 178 for an explanation of subdomains.

If the level specified is already occupied, the loaded movie replaces the existing one. This is more often what you want to do than stacking up movies into new levels indefinitely. It is certainly what you would want to do if you were using loadMovie to implement a set of selections. The selection mechanism can be in level 0, and it can load each individual movie into level 1. For example, in the set of selections described on page 33 the action attached to the button for selecting the description of *Digital Multimedia* could be replaced by

```
on (release) {
    loadMovie ("DMM.swf", 1);
}
```

assuming DMM.swf was the file name of a movie describing that book. The other buttons' scripts would be altered in the same way, so that each time a book was selected its movie would be loaded, replacing the one that was previously being displayed. Provided each movie had a blank frame with a stop() attached, no script is needed to return to the menu, since it would always be there in level 0 underneath the loaded movie.

If the second argument to loadMovie is 0, the original movie that was opened in the Flash Player (i.e., the movie at level 0) is replaced. At the same time, all movies at higher levels are removed (this does not happen when a movie is loaded at any other level). Thus, loading a new movie into level 0 is like closing the one currently playing and opening a new one, except that the same window is used and the overhead of restarting the player is avoided. It should be clear how this operation can be used to string together several movies into a sequence.

When several movies are playing at once, each potentially containing clip instances, an extra layer of naming is required to provide a unique target name for every clip in every movie. Earlier I said that absolute target names begin with _root; as a footnote admitted, this is not true. Absolute target names begin with _level$n$, where n is a level number. So a clip called near in a movie playing at level 5 would have as its target name _level5.near. Inside a movie at level n, the pseudo-target _root is a synonym for _level$n$. In a movie at level 0, it stands for _level0, which is consistent with my original description.

Movies loaded into levels can be treated as movie clips. Methods can be called using their level as a target name. For example, if you had loaded a movie into level 2, you could stop it by calling _level2.stop().

Arguably, making references to clips in movies at different levels is inadvisable. It means that the movie making the reference has to know about the internal structure of the movie containing the targeted clip. It means that changing that movie can potentially have repercussions in any movie that loads it, and it means that its behaviour cannot be determined by looking at it in isolation. This may be acceptable for clip instances, but for movies that potentially can be played on their own as well as being loaded into some other movie, it is not. In software engineering terms, the coupling between the loading and loaded movies is too strong. If they are that intimately related, they ought to be combined into one movie, unless there are compelling efficiency reasons not to.

Instead of loading movies into different levels, loadMovie can be used to load a new movie into an existing clip instance. If the second argument is a target name instead of a number, the loaded movie replaces the target clip. In so doing, it takes on its identity, assuming the target name, position, rotation, scaling and transparency of the original clip. As a clip, it can receive events, and scripts in the loader can call methods using its target name. A movie loaded into a level is not a clip, so it cannot receive events and does not have any methods.

In fact, if you prefer using object-oriented notations, you can call loadMovie itself as a method in the case that the movie is to be loaded into a clip. That is, if the_clip is a clip instance, you could load the DMM.swf movie into it using either the function call
loadMovie("DMM.swf", "the_clip");
(note the quote marks around the target name) or the method call
the_clip.loadMovie ("DMM.swf");
(note their absence). The latter is more consistent with the way methods are used for performing other operations on clips. There are several other examples of methods that duplicate functions. In this book, methods will be preferred where there is a choice.

The optional final argument to loadMovie specifies a method ("POST" or "GET") for sending data to the URL from which the new movie is to be loaded. This is only a meaningful thing to do if the URL identifies a program that is going to generate the SWF file dynamically. In that case, data can be sent to it in order to affect the computation that produces the movie. We will consider this sort of communication between the Flash Player and some other program in Chapter 7.

Exercises and Experiments

1. When might you want to change the type of an instance of a movie clip symbol to graphic?

2. If you are devising movie clip symbols to be reused in different movies, it is advisable to use relative target names wherever possible. Why?
3. Suppose you had a movie that began with a 30 frame introduction. Devise two different ways of letting a user dismiss the introduction by clicking anywhere on the screen.
4. A naive way of providing a Mute button for a movie with sound is to attach Stop All Sounds to it. Why is this likely to be unsatisfactory?
5. What is the effect of the statement gotoAndStop("Home") if the frame labelled Home has a script that includes a play() statement attached to it? (Try to answer this question without experimenting first, then construct a movie to check your answer.)
6. Implement a movie as a sequence of steps. Make it possible for a user to go back to a previous step, repeat the current step instead of continuing to the next, skip any step, and abandon the interaction at any point.
7. Fill in the rest of the VCR example by adding the actions for the Stop and Rewind buttons.
8. Exactly how would you use loadMovie to string together a sequence of movies? Re-implement your solution to Exercise 6 using this technique. Can you make a sequence of movies without adding any scripts to the individual members of the sequence?

3

introducing actionscript

JavaScript, ECMAScript and ActionScript

First of all there was LiveScript, a scripting language devised by Netscape for simple Web programming tasks, especially client-side scripting jobs such as verifying input to forms and dynamically modifying aspects of pages' appearance. LiveScript changed its name to JavaScript shortly after its release, even though its actual relationship to the Java programming language is slight and the resemblance between the names has been a source of some confusion ever since. Microsoft, in its role as the other major browser manufacturer, produced its own version of JavaScript, known as JScript, which was not quite identical to Netscape's. To avoid yet another source of browser incompatibility, the European Computer Manufacturers' Association (ECMA) was called upon to produce a standard based on JavaScript and Jscript. This standard gave the name ECMAScript to the language it defined.

It was always the case that JavaScript comprised a *core language*, providing general-purpose programming facilities and some rudimentary object-oriented features, and a set of *built-in objects* that allowed JavaScript programs to interact with some other system. In the most familiar case, the other system is a Web browser, and the built-in objects correspond to elements of Web pages and browser windows. By providing a different set of built-in objects, the same language can be used to interact with other systems. Server-side JavaScript, for instance, lets scripts interact with Netscape Web servers and with files and databases.

ECMAScript is a formally defined version of the core language only. The standard explicitly concedes that ECMAScript is not 'computationally self-sufficient': it has to be combined with what it calls *host objects* that allow scripts to 'manipulate, customize and automate the facilities of an existing system'. Flash is an 'existing system' in the sense implied here, and ActionScript is almost ECMAScript combined with host objects that allow it to manipulate Flash movies. It is only almost that, because the need to maintain compatibility with Flash's previous scripting system has made some compromises with the ECMAScript standard necessary. However, ActionScript is close enough to ECMAScript and ECMAScript is close enough to JavaScript for the syntax and core semantics of ActionScript to be immediately comprehensible to anyone who already knows JavaScript.

In the previous chapter, we considered adding a single action selected from the list in the Actions panel to a frame or button instance. Generally, this inserted a single ActionScript statement into the script. Many simple Flash movies are constructed using no more than this, but to produce more elaborate effects, these primitive actions (and others that we have not considered yet) can be combined into more elaborate scripts that carry out an organized set of operations. This enables Flash movies to perform computation and to react flexibly to users' input. When we are dealing with scripts with more than one action, it makes sense to think of them as little programs written in ActionScript. We therefore need to look at ActionScript as a programming language.

Expressions and Variables

The best place to start a description of any programming language is by considering the different types of value that are available.

Values and Expressions

ActionScript recognizes three different types: number, string and Boolean. Numbers are used for arithmetic, and strings for storing and altering text, while Booleans are truth values, which can be used to control the flow of execution of a script.

Generally speaking, the way ActionScript handles numbers and arithmetic follows the way it is normally done on paper, with no arbitrary additional rules for the benefit of the computer, although some notational compromises are made with the keyboard. No distinction is drawn between integers and floating point numbers. (Internally, all operations are performed on IEEE 754 double-precision floating point quantities.) Numerical constants (or *literals*) are written using ordinary decimal notation, as, for example, 158 or 14.673, or 'scientific' notation, using e to indicate a decimal exponent, as, for example, 12e35 (for 12.10^{35}) or 1e-4 (for 0.0001). The usual operations of addition, subtraction, multiplication and division are available, using the conventional operators (conventional in programming languages, that is) +, -, * and /. Unary - can be used to negate a value, and unary + can be used to do nothing. The remainder (or modulo) operator is written as %, and differs from that provided in many languages by not being restricted to integers. That is, as well as being able to write 8%3, which gives 2, the remainder on dividing 8 by 3, you can also write 4.5%2.1, which gives 0.3, the

expressions and variables

remainder on dividing 4.5 by 2.1. Also unlike most languages, ActionScript defines what happens if the operands of % are negative: the result is negative if and only if the left operand is negative; the magnitude is the same whatever the signs.

ActionScript also deals with the tricky questions that arise from division by zero and other dubious operations. The number data type includes special values Infinity and NaN. Infinity is the result of operations whose size exceeds the range of numbers that can be represented; for example, 1/0 yields Infinity. NaN stands for 'Not a Number' and is the result of undefined operations. In particular, 0/0 produces NaN.

Because all arithmetic is done on floating point numbers, you cannot rely on the results of arithmetic operations being precise: floating point numbers are only approximations, and the way in which floating point arithmetic is carried out can introduce errors, which can accumulate if a series of operations is performed. Because the machine uses binary numbers and we use decimal, such errors often crop up in calculations that look as if they ought to be trivially precise. For example, evaluating 4.1 - 4 produces 0.0999999999999996. Numerical experts will tell you that you shouldn't really even compare floating point numbers for equality, but instead you should see whether their difference is less than some small value that gives you the precision you require. Most of the time, nobody bothers about these matters, but sometimes you will have to care. For example, when the numbers you deal with represent money, people are likely to be upset if you lose some of it in the arithmetic. If you are implementing a system that works with monetary quantities, you should consult a numerical analyst, or at least always work in pennies or cents or the smallest unit in whatever currency you are dealing with.

The precedence of the arithmetical operators holds no surprises: 8*4+3 is equal to 35, for example. Round brackets are used for grouping where it is necessary to override the usual precedence rules: 8*(4+3) is 56.

Other useful mathematical operations, including exponentiation, random number generation, trigonometric functions and logarithms are provided through the built-in Math object. You will recall from Chapter 2 that an object is a collection of properties and methods. The Math object's properties are useful mathematical constants, such as π, e and $\sqrt{2}$. Properties are referred to using the same dot notation as we used for methods previously, but since a property is a value, not an operation, it is not followed by brackets. The constants just mentioned are written as Math.PI, Math.E and Math.SQRT2. This illustrates the convention that constants are given names in upper case. The properties of Math can be used in just the same way as numerical literals. For example, the area of a circle whose radius is 18 is given by the expression Math.Pi * 18 * 18.

The Math methods are called like the methods we have seen earlier, using the dot notation and putting their arguments in brackets. For example, Math.sqrt(47) returns the positive square root of 47, sqrt being the name of the square root method. For the full list of methods and properties of the Math object, consult the ActionScript reference guide. This object acts as a container for the constants and functions that are traditionally found in mathematical libraries in other programming languages.

Strings are sequences of characters. String literals are written enclosed in either double quote marks "like this" or single quote marks 'like this'. Double quotes are more common (they were the only option in versions of Flash before Flash 5). A string can include any characters from ISO Latin1 (otherwise known as ISO 8859-1),[1] a standard 8-bit character set, which includes various accented letters and special symbols in addition to the familiar ASCII characters — upper and lower case letters, digits, punctuation and a few mathematical symbols. In this respect, ActionScript differs from the ECMAScript standard, which specifies the use of the 16-bit Unicode character set. (But few JavaScript implementations support Unicode yet, either.)

Any programming language that uses quote marks to enclose string literals presents the problem of how to include quote marks inside a string. If the delimiters are double quotes, a single quote presents no problem, and vice versa. For the problematical case of the same quote mark being used as the delimiter and within the string, ActionScript adopts what has become the classic solution to this problem: inside a string literal, special *escape sequences* can be used. An escape sequence consists of a backslash character, \ , followed by some other character or sequence of characters; the whole sequence stands for a single character that cannot otherwise be included in the string literal, either because, like the quote mark, it is used for some other purpose, or because it is difficult or impossible to enter using a conventional keyboard. In particular, a double quote mark is represented inside a string literal by the escape sequence \" and a single one by the sequence \'. Note that the escape sequence is only used to write down the string literal; it is the single character, " or ', that is stored in the string itself.

As soon as you introduce escape sequences, a new problem arises: how do you represent the \ , since that is now used as the escape? Fortunately, this problem can be solved without starting off an infinite regression. The escape sequence \\ is used to represent a

---

1. For Japanese text, the 'Shift-JIS' character set is supported.

single backslash in a string literal. Table 3.1 lists all the escape sequences provided by ActionScript. Although Unicode escapes beginning with \u are available for ECMAScript compatibility, at present the full range of Unicode characters is not supported.

Table 3.1 *Escape sequences used in string literals.*

Escape sequence	Character	ISO 8859-1 code (hex)
\b	backspace	08
\t	tab	09
\n	line feed (newline)	0A
\f	form feed	0C
\r	carriage return	0D
\"	double quote	22
\'	single quote	27
\\	backslash	5C
\$o_1 o_2 o_3$	octal byte	$o_1 o_2 o_3$ octal
\x$x_1 x_2$	hexadecimal byte	$x_1 x_2$
\u$x_1 x_2 x_3 x_4$	Unicode character	$x_3 x_4$

The only infix operator available for strings performs concatenation — sticking one string on the end of another — and is written as a + symbol. For example, "this"+"that" is equal to "thisthat".

The String object provides additional operations for analysing and manipulating strings, in the same way that the Math object provides the more advanced numerical operations. The way in which it actually works is obscure, but need not concern us; the effect is that any string appears to be an object with methods for performing useful operations on its characters, and a property, length, that holds the number of characters it contains. These methods and this property can be accessed using the dot notation, like any other methods and properties. They are most interesting when strings are stored in variables (which will be described shortly), but they can be used in conjunction with string literals. For example, "Flash".length is an obscure way of writing 5.

The methods in String include several different ways of taking strings apart: charAt takes a number and returns the character that it finds at the corresponding position in the string: "Flash".charAt(2) is "a". Note that character positions start at 0 for the first character, and that the value returned is itself a string, of length one — there is no such thing as a character type in ActionScript. (You can access character codes, using the charCodeAt method, which returns a number, but it is rarely wise to be messing about with numerical character codes.) The substr and substring methods allow you to extract parts of a string; they differ in the way you specify the part you want to extract. The simpler method is substr, which takes a starting position and length: "Flash".substr(1, 4) is "lash". If a negative starting position is specified, characters are counted from the end of the string, with -1 being the last character, so "Flash".substr(-2, 2) produces "sh". The substring method allows you to specify a substring by its first and last characters, if that is more convenient. To be precise, it takes two arguments, the first is the offset of the first character in the substring, the second is one greater than the offset of the last: "Flash".substring(1, 4) is "las". (Although an invitation to confusion, this is not entirely capricious: the length of the substring is always equal to the difference between the arguments.) If the offsets passed to any of these methods lie outside the string, an empty string is returned.

Other methods of String provide simple facilities for searching in strings. Among them, indexOf (in its simplest form) takes a substring and returns the position of the first character of an occurrence of the substring in the string, or -1 if it does not occur. So, "Flash".indexOf("sh") is 3. Other methods allow you to search from the end instead of the beginning (lastIndexOf), and convert all the letters in a string to upper case (toUpperCase) or lower case (toLowerCase). For full details, see the *ActionScript Reference Guide*.

In most contexts, if a string that looks like a number, such as "512", is used as the operand of an arithmetical operator, it is converted to the number it looks like and the operation is performed. (If it doesn't look like a number, it is converted to the special value NaN.) For example, "512" * "20" produces the number 10240. The exception to this behaviour is the + operator, because this can take strings as its operands anyway: "512" + "20" is the string "51220". In the event of + being applied to operands of a mixture of types, the string interpretation takes precedence, with numbers being converted to the corresponding strings of digits: 512 + "20" and "512" + 20 both give "51220". Thus, appending an empty string to a number, as in 512 + "", forces it to be converted to a string, while adding zero to a string, as in "512" + 0, converts it to a number. This can be useful, but a more perspicuous way of carrying out such conversions is by using String and Number explicitly, as in String(512), which gives "512", or Number("Flash"), which gives NaN.

Comparisons between values are performed using the variations on conventional operators introduced by C and copied by many subsequent programming and scripting languages: > and < have their usual arithmetical meaning; >= and <= are used for ≤ and ≥, while == and != are used for equality and inequality respectively. The result of a comparison is a Boolean value, true or false, depending on whether the comparison succeeds or fails.

The unary operator ! (logical NOT) is used to invert the result of a comparison, or any other expression producing a Boolean value: if *E* is an expression, !*E* is true if *E* is false, and false if *E* is true. The infix operator && (logical AND) produces true if both its operands are true; || (logical OR) produces true if one or other of its operands, or both, is true. These Boolean operators have a low priority, so that an expression such as 2 > 10 && "2" != 2 has its apparent meaning. It never does any harm to insert brackets if you are in doubt about the binding of operators, and it often makes your meaning clearer. As the example just shown suggests, strings of digits are converted to numbers when they are compared with actual numbers in the same way as they are when used with arithmetic operators. If, however, strings of digits are compared with each other, they are not converted and a lexical comparison is used: "2" > "10" is true.

If a number is used where a Boolean value is required, 0 is converted to false, and all other numbers are converted to true. If a string is used, it is first converted to a number, and then the rule for numbers is applied. This is not what the ECMAScript standard specifies, but it maintains compatibility with Flash 4.

The logical NOT, AND and OR operations should not be confused with bitwise operations, which combine the individual bits of a number using Boolean algebra on the 1s and 0s. These will rarely be useful in Flash scripts (their only real use is in manipulating bit masks), but you should be aware of their existence, because it is easy to use them by mistake. Bitwise AND and OR are written as & and |; that is, they use the same character as their logical counterparts, but only a single one instead of a pair, as in &&. If you experiment or read the reference manual, you will discover that true and false are converted to 1 and 0 if you use them as numbers, so you can meaningfully apply & and | to Boolean values and get the right answers. The important difference between the two is that the logical operators use *short-circuit evaluation*, which means that they only evaluate as many of their operands as they need to in order to find the result. Thus, in the expression 2 > 10 && 10 < 11, it is only necessary to evaluate the first comparison, since, as this is false, the whole expression cannot possibly be true. If expressions have side-effects, it may be that using the bitwise operators instead of the logical ones produces a different answer. As a general rule, use the logical operators for logical operations.

Variables and Assignment

Expressions that only consist of constants and operators are of no interest — you always know their value already. It is only when variables are introduced that any useful computation can be done.

In programming, variables are containers — or *locations*, in the jargon of programming languages — that have a name and can hold a value. It is common to consider the variable's name and the location it names as the same thing, and where no ambiguity results I will do so. Sometimes, though, to distinguish, the name will be called an *identifier*. The value stored in a location can be changed by the operation of *assignment*. It has been argued that assignment is the essence of programming; it is certainly what distinguishes it from mathematics (where variables don't have values that can be changed), and it is central to the way in which computation is organized as a sequence of steps, since assignment allows you to remember values computed in previous steps.

In ActionScript, a variable can be created just by being used. There is no need to introduce it into your script beforehand with a separate declaration. Usually, the first thing you do with a variable is assign a value to it — before it has explicitly been given a value a variable holds the special pseudo-value undefined. Using an undefined variable is almost always an error, and always unwise. If you use it as a string it is converted into the empty string; if you use it as a number, it is converted to zero. This behaviour differs from that specified from ECMAScript, and should not be relied on.

In ActionScript, = is used as the assignment operator (which is why equality is written ==). A value is assigned to a variable using an assignment of the form
identifier = expression
For example, to initialize a counter to zero, you would use the assignment
the_count = 0;
where the_count was the name of your counter variable. An assignment is actually an expression itself, whose value is the value assigned. This means that you can use assignments as sub-expressions within other expressions. In particular, you can use assignments on the right hand side of assignments, as in
i = j = 0;
Although this provides a neat shorthand for assigning the same value to several variables at once, using it in any more complicated way tends to produce obscure programs and sometimes unexpected results, so it is best avoided.

ActionScript is slightly more liberal than most programming languages in the characters that can be used as part of an identifier: upper and lower case letters, digits, underlines and dollar signs are all permitted, subject only to the restriction that the first character cannot be a digit. By convention, identifiers beginning with underlines or dollar signs are used for properties of built-in objects and other predefined values. In theory, an identifier can be as long as you like, though the finite size of computers means that ultimately there will be a limit.

expressions and variables

Some legally formed identifiers can't be used as variable names because they are *reserved words*, which have a special meaning in ActionScript. Examples include on and with, which we met in Chapter 2. Other reserved words will be pointed out as we meet them.

Although you don't have to introduce variables with a declaration before you use them, you can if you like. (Personally, I do like, and will in my examples.) The reserved word var introduces a declaration. It can be followed by a list of identifiers, or, more usefully, by a list of assignments, as in:
var program = "Flash", version = 5.0;
The individual assignments are separated by commas. Using this form of declaration ensures that you always give a variable an initial value before you use it. In Chapter 5, we will see that sometimes using an explicit declaration may be necessary to produce certain sorts of behaviour.

Once a variable has been given a value, the value can be used in expressions just by writing the variable's name. Hence, if the_count had been initialized as above, the expression the_count + 1 would have the value 1, and the following statement could be used to add one to the counter:
the_count = the_count + 1;

Assignments such as the one just shown, that compute a new value for a variable by applying a simple operation to its old value are common, and ActionScript follows Algol68 and many subsequent languages (most influentially, C) by providing shorthand compound assignment operators that combine the operation and assignment. For example, += is an operator that adds its right operand to its left and assigns the result back to the left, so the assignment above could be written as
the_count += 1;
Such compound *assignment operators* are available for all the binary operators in ActionScript.

The case of adding one to a variable is so common that an even more compact notation is provided, in the form of the ++ operator. The precise effect of this operator depends on whether it is written before or after its operand. If written before, as in ++the_count, it increments the value, and the result of the expression is the new value; if written after, as in the_count++, it performs the same increment, but the value of the expression is the original value of the_count. The difference only matters if the increment is used as a part of a more complex expression (for example, new_count = ++the_count), or in a condition (for example ++the_count > 10). The most common way of using ++, though, is in a statement on its own, when, unless you are doing something very obscure, the difference between the prefix and postfix versions is a matter of taste.

When you are entering scripts in the Actions panel, you can find a list of all the available operators by expanding the Operators sub-list in the left panel.

Simple Scripting

Once you have understood the use of variables, it is possible to write scripts using basic *control structures* to perform some simple computation.

Control Structures

The 'structured programming' movement in the late 1970s identified three basic control structures: *sequencing, selection* and *iteration*, as being necessary and sufficient for implementing any algorithm. In a sense, therefore, the corresponding ActionScript statements are enough to allow you to write scripts to perform any computation you want. However, for most non-trivial tasks, higher level features, such as functions and objects, are needed to make scripts comprehensible and easy to maintain. ActionScript provides these features, too, but in a less fully developed form than they are found in mainstream programming languages, such as Java and C++. Some of the help that objects, in particular, provide for large scale program construction in these languages is not available in ActionScript because it lacks static type checking. Where ambitious computation is needed, it is often better to pass it on to some other system written in a conventional programming language, in ways we will consider in later chapters.

The semantics of the three structured control forms is probably familiar, and the syntax used in ActionScript for each is similar to that used in many other programming languages. The statements in a sequence are written in order, with each one terminated by a semicolon, as $S_1;S_2;...$, and are executed one after the other. A selection is written if (E) S_1 else S_2. The expression E is evaluated and if it is true the first statement S_1 is executed, otherwise the second S_2. An iterated statement, written while (E) S, is repeated as long as the expression in brackets after the reserved word while continues to hold true. In all these forms, the names S, S_1 and S_2 denote either a single statement (including conditional and iteration) or a *block*, which is a sequence of statements written between curly brackets. E denotes an expression, usually some sort of comparison.

Note that loops can be nested inside other loops and a selection can have more than two alternatives —since either or both can themselves be selections. (In fact, one of them can be empty, in which case else is omitted, giving the single-branched conditional if (E) S.) Since a block is really just a sequence, with curly brackets round it to show where it begins and ends, loops can also contain sequences and selections, sequences can include loops and selections, and so on.

Although it is not necessary to put curly brackets round a single statement when you use it as the body of a loop or an alternative in a conditional, it does no harm to put them, and a lot of people — especially Perl programmers — prefer to do so.[1] If you use normal mode to enter these statements in the Actions panel, the brackets are automatically inserted. (The same applies to the with statement introduced in Chapter 2.) I prefer to omit them unless they are needed, but there is no virtue in this. If you choose to follow my example, note that the curly brackets in on and onClipEvent statements *are* required.

Simple Use of Control Structures

The use of sequences is straightforward: you use them when you need to perform several actions one after the other. For example, you might need to add an action to a button that started several movie clips playing. You would do this with a sequence of calls to the play() methods of each clip. Non-trivial scripts invariably use selections and iterations, often in sequence or containing sequences.

The following examples will necessarily have a somewhat artificial air, since many of the features necessary to build meaningful systems that communicate with users and other programs in Flash have not yet been described. They should, however, suffice to demonstrate how the basic programming features of ActionScript are used. Later we will see plenty of examples where the programming interacts with Flash's interface, communication and animation features.

As a first example, suppose to begin with that you wish to compute a payment, perhaps a commission. Say the payment is 10% of some total amount, except that amounts less than 10 (Euros, dollars, zlotys, or whatever) are not paid. Assume that the total is held in a variable called total, defined elsewhere, and we want to compute the payment and store it in a variable called payment, also defined elsewhere. This can be achieved in the following way:

```
var commission = amount * 0.1; // 10% = 0.1
if (commission < 10)
    payment = 0;
```

---

[1]. The *ActionScript Reference Guide* insists that they are required, but this is not true.

else
    payment = commission;

The characters from // to the end of the first line are a *comment* — text that is ignored by Flash, and serves as an annotation for the benefit of people reading the script. You will see few of them in this book, because the accompanying text does the job of explanation. However, large or subtle scripts benefit from the use of meaningful comments, and you should develop the habit of adding them, if only to help you remember what you have done when you come back to it after an interruption. Note here (and in the examples in previous chapters) that all the single statements are terminated with semicolons. You can, in fact, leave these out when they occur at the end of a line, but most people either find it easier to put them in than to remember the few special cases where they can't be omitted, or are so used to writing in other programming languages that they insert semicolons from habit. Accordingly, I will always use them in examples.

The correctness of this code should be evident. If you were unsure about this, Flash provides a basic facility for tracing the execution of your scripts that would allow you to look at the value computed for payment. The trace function takes a string as its argument and displays it to a special output window. The string can be constructed as an expression including variables, so it is possible to get trace to display helpful messages. For example,
trace(payment + " on total of " + amount);
produces messages like
0 on total of 10
This tracing facility is generally useful for finding out what is going on inside your scripts, especially when they are going wrong. Don't forget to remove or disable the tracing code before distributing your finished movie, though. If you need more sophisticated help with tracking down problems in your scripts, you can use the debugger, which is documented in Chapter 6 of the *ActionScript Reference Guide*.

Tracing and the debugger help catch the logical errors in scripts. Syntactical errors, such as missing brackets or forgotten quote symbols, will always be caught by Flash when you test your movie. Alternatively, you can explicitly perform a syntax check by selecting Check Syntax from the pop-up menu under the triangle in the top right hand corner of the Actions panel. In either case, any errors will be reported in the Output window, with messages that should enable you to find the source of the error and correct it. Do not necessarily believe the message that tells you This script contains no errors, which is produced after an explicit syntax check has found no problems. It only means that the syntax is correct, which is no guarantee that the script does what it is supposed to.

simple scripting

Conditional statements that assign one of two values to a variable depending on some condition are common, and an alternative notation, that you may find more attractive, can be used to achieve the same effect. A conditional *expression* has the form
E ? E₁ : E₂
where all the *E*s are expressions. Its value is either E₁ or E₂, depending on whether E is true or false. In this example, I would normally have written
payment = commission < 10 ? 0: commission;

A word of warning is in order for hardened Perl or JavaScript programmers. You might be tempted to use the logical operators as an even more compact way of performing some conditional assignments, on the basis that $E_1||E_2$ is actually evaluated as $E_1?E_1:E_2$ and $E_1\&\&E_2$ as $E_1?E_2:E_1$. If the expressions are Boolean, this is just a description of short-circuit evaluation, but if they are not, it tells you that the result need not be Boolean. This leads people to write code like this:
var x = a || default;
which assigns a to x if it is defined, and assigns default otherwise. This doesn't always work in ActionScript, which differs from ECMAScript in the way it converts strings to Booleans. Any string that would give zero if it was converted to a number is converted to false, so not only empty or undefined strings will be replaced by the default. It is best to avoid the idiom entirely in ActionScript, since it only sometimes behaves as expected.

Before leaving the payment example, consider one more variation. You may have realized that the variable commission is redundant. I could have assigned the commission provisionally to payment and then reset it if it was too small. This would use a single-branched conditional, like this:
payment = amount * 0.1;
if (payment < 10) payment = 0;

You use a conditional statement when you need to make a choice, as in the example just given. Loops are used when you need to repeat an operation. As a simple example, suppose you wished to replicate a string a certain number of times, and that variables s and repetitions held the string and the replication count, respectively. So, if the value of s was "Flash" and that of repetitions was 4, you would want to produce "FlashFlashFlashFlash". The following code will accomplish the task.
var ss = "", i = 0;
while (i < repetitions) {
    ss += s;
    ++i;
}

The strategy, which will become familiar to you if it is not so already, is to use a variable, in this case i to serve as a *loop counter* that keeps track of the number of times we have gone round a loop. It is initialized to zero before the loop starts. (We haven't gone round any times yet.) Another variable ss, which is going to store the result must be initialized to the empty string. It will always be the case that ss holds i copies of s; presently it holds none, since i is zero. The number of times that the loop must be executed is equal to the value stored in repetitions, so, provided we add one to i every time round the loop and do not change the value of repetitions, we know we have to go on executing the loop body as long as the value of i is less than that of repetitions, which is what the condition at the head of the loop in this script asserts. Inside the loop we first do the actual work of constructing the result ss by appending a copy of s to the end of it (I have used an assigning operator), and then increment the loop counter, thus maintaining the truth of the claim that ss holds i copies of s. It follows that when the test at the head of the loop fails, and we exit from the loop, ss holds the required string.

Loops like this one, which are controlled by a counter that is incremented on every iteration are very common. In many programming languages, some special syntax is provided for them. The *for loop* provided in C is probably the most elaborate example, and it has been adopted with minor modifications in many later languages, including ActionScript. The for loop has the following syntax:

for (*initialization* ; *condition* ; *increment*) *statement*

and it is equivalent to the following loop:

initialization;
while (*condition*) {
    statement
    increment
}

That is, the *initialization* is performed before the loop begins; the *condition* is tested to see whether the loop body should be executed; the *statement* is repeatedly executed, followed by the *increment*. The previous loop could be rewritten as:

for (var ss = "", i = 0; i < repetitions; ++i)
   ss += s;

As you see, the initialization can include var declarations, though the equivalent while loop tells you that the variables are not confined to the loop (as in C++).

In a for loop, all the book-keeping concerned with iteration is kept together at the top of the loop, separate from the loop body in which the iterated computation is specified. Such special loops are convenient: most programmers have at some time in their career written a while loop and forgotten to add the code to increment the loop counter or whatever it is that is needed to move the loop on for the next iteration. It is strangely easy to do; the result is a loop that goes round forever. It is provably the case, though, that any looping computation can always be written using no more than the while loop and sometimes this will be more suitable than a for loop. In the end, the difference comes down to style and choice.

Loops controlled by a counter can be used, in conjunction with the charAt method, to inspect each character of a string in turn. The next example searches a string, held in the variable source, for a character held in target, and counts how many it finds. As in the previous example, either a while or a for loop could be used. This time, I'll use while. Before starting the loop it is necessary to set up the loop counter and a variable to hold the result.

var occurrences = 0;
var i = 0;

This time, the required number of iterations of the loop is equal to the number of characters in the source string, which is stored in its length property, so the loop begins like this:

while (i < source.length)

We only want to count occurrences of the target, so within the loop a conditional statement is needed. The charAt method is used to extract a single character from source to compare with target; only if they match is the variable occurrences incremented. Then finally, the all-important increment of the loop counter completes the loop.

```
{
    if (source.charAt(i) == target)
        ++occurrences;
    ++i;
}
```

(There is, of course, no need for every loop counter to be called i, but it's as good a name as any.)

Purists frown on the practice, but sometimes it is convenient to jump out of a loop before its termination condition becomes true. The break statement is provided for this purpose. The most common pattern of use is illustrated by the following script, a variation on the preceding one, which just searches for an occurrence of the target, and sets found to true if there is one. (The example is for expository purposes only — if you really wanted to do this you would use String.indexOf.)

var found = false;
var i = 0;
while (i < source.length) {

```
        if (source.charAt(i) == target) {
            found = true;
            break;
        }
        ++i;
}
```

A closely related statement, continue, causes the next iteration of a loop to be started immediately, without finishing the current execution of the body. This is only rarely useful.

A final loop variant has the form
do *statement* while (*condition*)
It has the same semantics as the while loop, except that the condition is tested after the loop body, which means that the loop is always executed at least once. In my experience, this always turns out to be wrong. I cannot explain why, I merely state that this is so, and will therefore make no further reference to such loops.

Combining Scripts and Movies

The examples just given illustrate typical patterns of use of the control structures in ActionScript. Similar examples can be found in almost any introductory programming text on almost any language. The principles of using variables and assignment within sequences, selections and iterations are largely independent of any particular language. Scripts in Flash have another level of structure, though, which distinguishes them from conventional programs: they are attached to frames of a movie, or to instances of button or movie clip symbols.

In this context, variables are often used to remember events. The action triggered in response to an event will be a script that assigns values to one or more variables that can later be used in other scripts to find out what had happened earlier during the playing of the movie. As a trivial example, the following script could be attached to a button:
```
on (release) {
    ++hits;
}
```
Provided hits was initially set to zero, its value at any time will be equal to the number of times the mouse has been clicked on the button.

A complicated movie that included a help facility could make use of such code. Suppose that in a frame used as a form for data entry (which we will see examples of in

simple scripting

the next chapter) there is a button labelled Help, which transfers users to a frame with outline instructions on filling in the form. If a user asks for help three times, they are probably confused and so they could be shown a more detailed explanation. The following action attached to the help button would accomplish this:

```
on (release) {
    if (++helps < 3)
        gotoAndStop ("help");
    else
        gotoAndStop ("more help");
}
```

The frame labels help and more help will be attached to the parts of the movie that give the outline and detailed help, respectively. At the end of the help there will be some means of returning to the form. Assuming that helps is set to zero to begin with, the third time a user asks for help, the condition in the if statement will be false and they will be sent to the detailed help page.

The value of any variable such as helps used in a button action will be available to scripts attached to other buttons and frames in the same movie or clip, so these can discover how many times the button in question was activated. This could provide a crude (too crude, really) method of allowing users to select items to purchase from a Flash-based on-line shop. Items could be represented by buttons carrying a suitable icon, thumbnail or text label, attached to each of which was a script like the one above that simply incremented a variable — a different variable name would have to be used for each item. To order an item, the user would click on its button. To order several of the same item, they would just click the corresponding number of times. A script that processed the order could inspect the values of these variables to determine how many of each item was required.

Clicking on buttons is not usually the best way of entering numbers, although it might be suitable for movies intended to be used on portable devices that do not have keyboards, or by users with physical disabilities that make typing difficult. An improvement over repeated clicking as in the example outlined in the previous paragraph is to arrange buttons in the form of a numeric keypad such as you find on a calculator. Figure 3.1 shows such a keypad being used as part of a loan repayment calculator.

The ten digits on the left are used to enter an amount to borrow, then one of the three buttons on the right is used to select a repayment term in months and calculate the monthly repayments. An obvious and serious shortcoming of this movie is that it

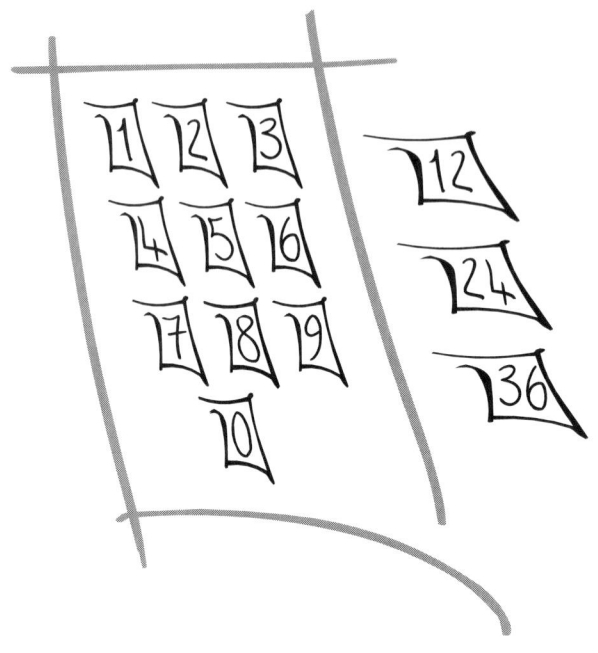

Figure 3.1 *A repayment calculator.*

provides no feedback to the user to indicate the amount that has been entered via the keypad. This is because we have not yet looked at the necessary features in Flash, and the deficiency will be rectified in the next chapter. However, the input and calculation parts of the movie work fine.

There are only two frames in this movie: the one shown in Figure 3.1, where data is entered, and one other in which the calculation is performed and the result will be displayed. The following script is attached to the first frame.

var amount = 0, period = 0;
stop ();

The variable amount will hold the amount to be borrowed, while period records the term of the proposed loan. Every time one of the buttons on the keypad is pressed, a new value is computed for amount to correspond to the number formed by appending the new digit to those entered so far. This is achieved with scripts such as the following (for the button labelled 7):

```
on (release) {
    amount = 10*amount + 7;
}
```

The buttons' scripts differ only in the digit added to the end of amount (except for the zero button, which has the obvious optimization). Similarly, the scripts attached to each of the three buttons for selecting the loan period closely resemble each other. For example, the 36 month button has the following:

```
on (release) {
    period = 36;
    gotoAndStop ("Calculate");
}
```

The other selection buttons' scripts just assign a different value to period. The period is thus set to correspond to the button's label, and the playhead is moved to the second frame.

The script attached to this second frame calculates the total amount that must be paid back, using compound interest calculated monthly. That is, we pretend that the loan is being held for the full length of the period, and work out the total that is obtained by adding interest at a fixed monthly rate each month. Then we divide that total by the number of months to arrive at a monthly repayment. (It should be stressed that this example should not be used for making any financial decisions. Interest can be calculated in many different ways, and I do not claim to understand all the subtleties employed by banks and other lending institutions.) There is a simple formula for this calculation, but since we are using a computer not a slide rule, it is as easy to work out the amount by brute force in a loop that adds the interest accrued each month. We need to know the monthly interest rate. A deceptively modest sounding value (three quarters of a percent per month) has been embedded in the code as the value of a variable rate, on the assumption that it will change relatively rarely. (A better approach would be to obtain the current rate dynamically — see Chapter 7.)

```
var rate = 0.0075;
```

The main calculation is a loop, this time a for loop. Before it starts, a variable must be initialized to hold the total amount after interest.

```
var total = amount;
```

Paraphrasing this initialization, after no months all that is owed is the original amount borrowed.

The loop is executed for a number of times equal to the period of the loan. Each time, the amount of interest incurred during the month on the total owed is added to produce a new total for the next month.

```
for (var t = 0; t < period; ++t)
    total = total * (1+rate);
```

When the loop exits, the monthly repayment can be discovered by dividing the total by the period over which the loan is taken out.
repayment = total/period;
We must wait until Chapter 4 to break the news to the prospective borrower, since we do not yet know how to display this result in the movie.

Variables and Clips

A target name can be considered as, in some ways, a kind of variable. Instead of holding a value belonging to one of the primitive data types (numbers, strings and Booleans) it can hold a movie clip. This is an over-simplification, but it will suffice for the moment. In the previous chapter we saw how methods could be called through a clip. In addition, a clip can be assigned to another variable. The effect is not the same as assigning a primitive value, though. In the cases we have been considering, assigning a string, for example, to a new variable has the effect of copying the string. Any changes made to the copy do not affect the original. Movie clips behave differently: a variable can only ever hold what is called a *reference* to a movie clip. A reference is just something that stands in for the clip — it refers to it, but it isn't the clip itself. The reason is that a movie clip is a large complicated thing that is difficult to store and inefficient to copy, so a simpler thing, the reference, is stored instead. When a clip is assigned, the reference is copied to the new location, not the clip itself. That means that we end up with two references to the same clip, which means in turn that operations affecting one copy will also affect the other.

To see how this works, consider a very simple example. Suppose I place a movie clip on the stage in a movie consisting of a single keyframe, and give it the instance name the_clip. Now suppose I add the following code to the frame:
var c = the_clip;
The assignment in the frame script does not create a new clip, it just assigns the reference to the_clip. Now suppose I add two buttons, with the following scripts attached to them:
on (release) {
    c.play();
}
and
on (release) {
    the_clip.stop();
}
Both of these buttons will control the playback of the_clip, even though the target name does not appear in the script attached to the button that causes it to play. Because c

holds a reference to the same clip, calling methods through c has the same effect as calling them through the_clip.

Using variables in this way means that targets can be specified dynamically. As in the examples that were given earlier, a variable can be used to remember some event that determines the target to be used subsequently. To see how this works, let us return to the movie player example from Chapter 2, which, you will recall, suffered from having only a single movie clip that could be controlled.

As a first step towards making the player more flexible, suppose we now place three different clips in the first frame of the movie. Assume that they all have a blank frame at the beginning, so that all three can be placed in the main movie without being seen at first. Each clip will, of course, be an instance of a movie symbol, and each needs its own instance name. Suppose that they are called clip_1, clip_2 and clip_3. Now suppose that three extra buttons, labelled 1, 2, and 3 are added to the frame in addition to the VCR controls that were defined previously. The intention is that these new buttons are to be used to select one of the three clips to be controlled by the VCR buttons. So, for example, if a user clicks on 1, then on the play button, the clip_1 will start to play. This will be implemented by attaching an action to each of the selector buttons that sets a variable the_choice to the name of the corresponding clip, like the frame action just shown. The VCR buttons are then rewired to use this variable instead of the constant instance name used previously.

The scripts are very simple. The 1 button, for example, has this code attached to it:
```
on (release) {
    the_choice = clip_1;
}
```
and the other selectors are the same apart from the specific value assigned to the_choice. Modifying the controls is equally simple. The Play button, for example, now has the following script attached to it:
```
on (release) {
    the_choice.play ();
}
```
The other controls are modified similarly, by simply replacing the *target* name the_clip with the *variable* name the_choice.

Movie Clip Properties

Every movie clip (including the main movie and any movies loaded into higher levels) has a set of *properties,* which are values that describe its state. These include its x and y coordinates, its angle of rotation, its visibility and transparency, and its instance name. As we will see in Chapter 6, properties are really just variables whose values reflect and alter the state of the clip. You can access properties by using their names in expressions. You can assign new values to some properties in order to modify the state of a clip. All properties have names beginning with an underline character; by convention, such names are only used for properties.

To obtain the value of a property of the current movie clip (i.e., the clip in which the script that is being executed is defined), you use the property name as if it was a local variable. Table 3.2 lists the available properties. If you use a property name in an action associated with a button, it is taken to refer to the movie containing the button (cf. the implicit target of methods such as stop() in buttons.) If you wish to refer to a property of some other movie clip, you prefix the property name with the clip's target name, and a dot, in the same way as you call methods using a clip's target name to control one clip from another, and the same way as we have accessed properties of the Math and String objects.

Another contrived example will help clarify matters. Suppose an extra button is added to the original single-movie player example, with the following script attached to it.

```
on (release) {
    trace ("Location = (" + _x + "," + _y + ")");
    trace("Total frames = " + _totalframes);
    trace ("The clip has " + the_clip._totalframes + " frames");
    the_clip._y += 20;
}
```

When this button is clicked, the output window will display the messages:

Location = (0, 0)
Total frames = 1
The clip has 60 frames

The first two properties whose values are reported here are those of the main movie. It makes no difference where the button is placed, the reported coordinates will always be (0,0). Only if the button was in a movie clip within a movie would a different value be produced — in that case, the location of the origin of the clip containing the button. The last trace statement reports the number of frames in the_clip, because the property is prefixed with its target name (the_clip._totalframes).

Table 3.2   *Movie Clip Properties.*

Property	Meaning	Read/Write
_alpha	Transparency value between 0 and 100	rw
_currentframe	Number of frame where playhead is	r
_droptarget	See Chapter 4	r
_framesloaded	Number of frames that have been streamed so far	r
_height	Height of clip or movie in pixels	rw
_name	Instance name of clip	rw
_rotation	Number of degrees of rotation applied to clip	rw
_target	Full target path of clip	r
_totalframes	Number of frames in clip or movie	r
_url	URL from which SWF was loaded	r
_visible	Boolean indicating whether clip is visible	rw
_width	Width of clip or movie in pixels	rw
_x	x coordinate of clip in coordinate system of its parent	rw
_xmouse	x coordinate of mouse cursor in clip's coordinate system	r
_xscale	Percentage horizontal scaling	rw
_y	y coordinate of clip in coordinate system of its parent	rw
_ymouse	y coordinate of mouse cursor in clip's coordinate system	r
_yscale	Percentage vertical scaling	rw

After the trace output is produced, a new value is assigned to the_clip's _y property. The new value is reflected in the corresponding physical quantity: the clip moves 20 pixels down the screen. If instead the assignment had been
_y += 20;
everything would move down 20 pixels, because the unqualified property is taken to belong to the movie.

There are some additional complications concerning the _x and _y properties. The coordinates they hold are those of the movie clip's *reference point*. This is normally its centre, although it can be changed to some other point using the Modify>Transform>Edit Center command when it is placed on the stage. More importantly, the coordinates are measured relative to the origin of the movie that encloses the clip. If the clip is part of the main movie, its coordinates are measured relative to the top left hand corner of the stage, but if the clip is within another clip, the coordinates are measured relative to the enclosing clip's origin, whose precise position will depend on how the elements of the clip were originally placed on the stage.

For example, suppose a clip A is placed inside a clip B, with its reference point 120 pixels to the right and 40 pixels below the origin of B, which we will assume is at its top left hand corner. Then the _x and _y properties of A will always hold the values 120 and 40, no matter where on the stage B is placed. In fact, these values will be the same, even if B is rotated or scaled within the main movie. If, for example, B is rotated through 90° and scaled up by 200%, A's _x property will still hold 120, though this will now be the vertical distance from what is now B's top right corner, divided by two (see Figure 3.2). While this may sound confusing, it often simplifies scripts, since they need never worry about any transformations applied to enclosing movie clips. (An example will be given in Chapter 4.)

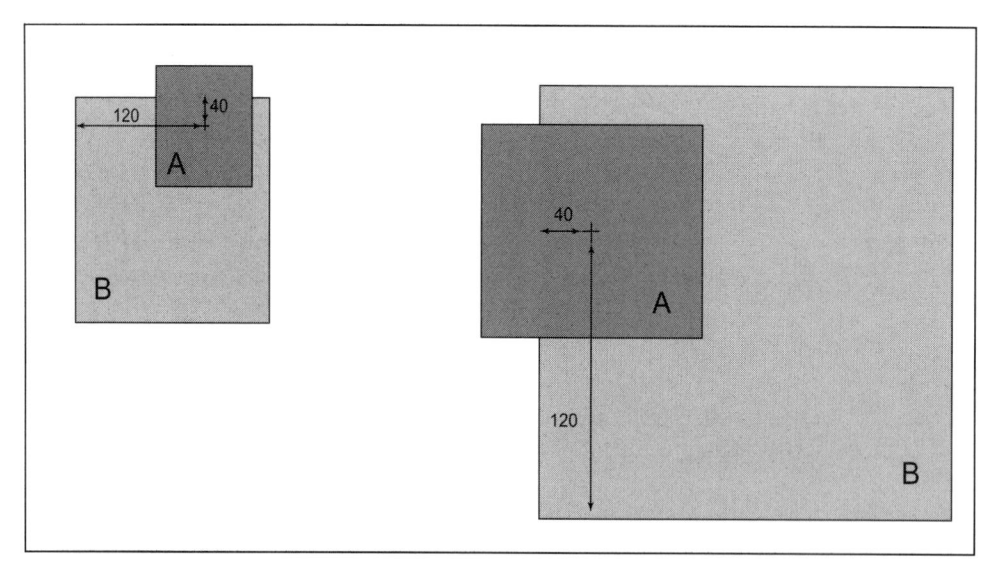

Figure 3.2 *Clip coordinates.*

A common Flash idiom that makes use of movie clip properties is the 'preloading' movie. SWF movies are often *streamed* over networks. That is, the player does not wait for the entire movie to arrive before it starts playing it, but plays frames as they arrive. This is fine if the time it takes a frame to load is less than the time it takes to display it, but otherwise playback will be jerky as the player has to wait for data. It is quite common for certain frames to contain much more data than others. For example, if a movie uses a lot of symbols and tweening, the first keyframe in which the symbols are used will contain all their definitions. Subsequent frames will only contain the information about where they should be placed, and so on. Event sounds, which are typically very bulky, must also load entirely in the frame they have been attached to.

A common ruse to ensure smooth playback despite such factors is to begin the movie with a short loop that only requires a small amount of data. This loop can be as simple as a message asking the user to wait a moment, or it may be a small purely vector-based animation without sound. The idea is that this loop will play, hopefully maintaining the user's interest, while the rest of the movie loads. For this ruse to succeed, a means of determining whether the remaining data has arrived and breaking out of the loop when it has is needed. The _framesloaded property provides the means. It always holds the number of frames that have been loaded. Since it is a movie clip property, you can access it through a target name to find out how much of a particular clip instance has been loaded; alternatively, you can use it undecorated to find out how much of the main movie has loaded.

Suppose that you wish to delay the start of your movie until it has all been loaded into the player. This can be done by comparing the value of _framesloaded with that of _totalframes. To be precise, suppose that the first frame of your movie is labelled begin, and that it is followed by a lightweight animation that you want to loop until the rest of the movie is ready. Assuming that you want the loop to play at least once, the following script can be attached to its last frame (the one before the movie proper begins):

```
if (_framesloaded < _totalframes)
    gotoAndPlay("begin");
```

There are more sophisticated variations on this technique. If you know that the bulk of the data lies before a certain frame, you can start playing as soon as that frame is loaded instead of waiting for the entire movie. (You can use the bandwidth profiler when testing your movie to determine where the bulk of the data is.) You can also use the ratio of _framesloaded/_totalframes to display a progress bar, to give the user some indication of how long they have to wait. (See Exercise 10.)

Arrays

It is often convenient to be able to treat a collection of values as a single entity. For example, suppose you are collecting statistics about the different software that visitors to a Web site use in their work. You could keep a count of the number using each program in a different variable, such n_flash, n_livemotion, and so on, but this makes it awkward to compute such things as the mean number of users of each program, or the most popular program. *Aggregate data structures* allow us to combine a set of values, giving the collection a single name, and to access the individual ones in a simple, uniform way.

The simplest aggregate data structure is the *array*, which is a sequence of values, each of which can be identified by a numerical *index*, which is its position in the sequence. The individual values are the array's *elements*. The process of extracting an individual element using a number is called *indexing*. If a is the name of an array, and e is an expression that evaluates to a number greater than or equal to zero, a[e] gives the value of the element stored in the array at the corresponding position. That is, a[0], a[1], a[2],… are the first, second, third, … elements of the sequence. Notice that the index values start at zero, not one, even though we invariably refer to the first element, and so on. This is a prolific source of stupid programming errors — but so is using one as the first index.

Arrays must be created explicitly. The expression new Array() can be used for this purpose: it returns a new array, that can be assigned to a variable. Unlike some other languages, ActionScript does not require you to specify how many elements there are in the array when you create it; it will grow as necessary as soon as you assign a value to an element. You can, if you like, pass an argument to Array to specify an initial number of elements. Space for that many will be allocated straight away. The array can still grow beyond this first allocation, but if you know how big it is, setting the size will make your script more efficient. Note that the argument specifies the number of elements, but that array indices start at 0, so if an array a has n elements, the highest element is at a[n-1]. The number of elements in a is stored in a.length, so a[a.length] is always a free element beyond those that are occupied.

Arrays as Mappings

Numerically indexed arrays are the oldest form of aggregate data structure, and have been used in programming since the earliest days, for a range of purposes. Many of these purposes are concerned with numerical computations and are unlikely to be needed in Flash scripts. One way of using arrays, though, is to provide a mapping from numbers to some other sort of value, often strings, and this can be necessary in Flash. Months provide a commonly encountered example. If you wish to find out the date six months from now, for instance, it is easiest to represent months by numbers (0 for January, 1 for February, and so on). The built-in Date object uses numbers for months in this way, allowing us to work out such things as the data at the end of a loan's repayment period arithmetically. When displaying the result, it is often better to use the month's name. In particular, because of the different conventions used in the United

States and in Europe for writing dates numerically, using the name avoids some ambiguity. An array can be used to turn numbers into names.

Since there is no pattern to the names of the months, the array has to be set up by a sequence of assignments.
```
var month = new Array(12);
month[0] = "Jan";
month[1] = "Feb";
month[2] = "Mar";
```
and so on.

If variables d, m and y hold the numerical values of the day, month and year of a date, respectively, and period holds the number of months over which a loan is to be repaid, it is simple, but a bit tedious, to calculate the date at which the loan will have been paid off. (I have assumed that the value for m is zero-based, like the numbers used for indexing month.)
```
var p_years = Math.floor(period/12);
var p_months = period%12;
var final_month = m + p_months;
if (final_month >= 12) {
    final_month -= 12;
    ++p_years;
}
final_year = y + p_years;
```
At the end of this sequence, d, final_month and final_year hold the numerical values of the day of the month, month and year of the day after the period ends. If the array month has been initialized in the way indicated above, the date can be assigned to a variable cleared_date in an unambiguous (although inelegant) format in the following way:
```
cleared_date = d + " " + month[final_month] + " " + final_year;
```
(This produces dates like 1 Apr 2000. Inserting st, nd or th is left to you.)

Arrays and Random Numbers

Arrays can be profitably used in Flash movies in conjunction with random numbers. A common requirement is to play a series of movies or movie clips in random order. This can be used to produce an animation that plays for a long time without repeating itself, even though it is built up from only a few elements. Animations made in this way can be quite elaborate, with clips playing at random positions for random periods of time in randomly chosen groups. To illustrate the role of arrays and random numbers in such a movie, we will consider it reduced to its essentials: when a user clicks on a button, a movie chosen at random from an available set is played.

Before looking at how this can be achieved, you need to know something about how random numbers are generated in ActionScript. Like other mathematical operations, ActionScript's random number generator is a method of the Math object. Math.random() returns a random number greater than or equal to 0 and less than 1. To be accurate, it returns a pseudo-random number. Since computers are deterministic devices, a program cannot generate true randomness, but there are well-known ways of producing a sequence of numbers in which the relationship between each one and the next is so complex that they appear to be chosen at random, and satisfy the statistical criteria that are generally held to correspond to our idea of randomness.

Often, what you want is not a random number between 0 and 1, but a random integer between 0 and some maximum value. The expression Math.floor(n*Math.random()) returns an integer lying between 0 and n-1 inclusive. If this expression is used to index an array with n elements, it chooses a random element. The following script shows how this works, and also illustrates another common way of using arrays: they can be used to keep count of the number of occurrences of some particular value.

```
var a = new Array(n);
for (var j = 0; j < n; ++j)
    a[j] = 0;
for (var i = 0; i < 50000; ++i) {
    var r = Math.floor(n*Math.random())
    ++a[r];
}
```

In this case, every time we generate a random integer, one is added to the array element with that number as its index. At the end of the loop, the array holds a tally of the number of times each number was generated. By looking at the values recorded, you can see just how random the random numbers are. (The values should all be the same, but in practice they won't be exactly.)

Returning to random movies, we will use the method of choosing random array elements in conjunction with the loadMovie operation, introduced in Chapter 2, to load a randomly chosen movie on top of the main movie. What needs to be done is to choose a URL at random and pass it to loadMovie. This is easily done if the set of URLs from which to choose is stored in an array. This can be set up using a series of assignments, as in the case of the arrays of months. The URLs can be absolute or relative.

If relative URLs are used, and the movies are all kept in the same directory, the initialization of the array will look something like this:

```
var url = new Array(max_url + 1);
url[0] = "red.swf";
url[1] = "green.swf";
url[2] = "blue.swf";
url[3] = "indigo.swf";
```

and so on. The variable max_url is also needed to hold the index of the highest element of the array.

The following script attached to a button in the movie will cause a random movie to be loaded into level 1 whenever it is clicked on.

```
on (release) {
    n = Math.floor((max_url+1)*Math.random());
    loadMovie(url[n], 1);
}
```

Since we can only generate random numbers, the array is used to map these to the random URLs that are needed.

Iterating Over Arrays

It is often the case that you need to access the value of each element of an array in turn. This is best done using a for loop in which the loop variable ranges from 0 to the highest element. You have already seen this sort of loop, in the code used to set the counts of random numbers to zero. In general, it can use the length property of the array as the upper limit of the loop variable, like this:

```
for (var i = 0; i < a.length; ++i)
```

Loops with headers of this form can be used for any task that computes some function of every array element or applies some operation to every element. For example, adding them all up, computing their average, setting them all to zero, adding one to them all, and so on.

Arrays, like movie clips, are potentially large complicated things, so, like movie clips, they are manipulated via references. This means that if you assign an array to a variable, only the reference gets copied, not the array elements, so if a is an array (or, strictly speaking, a variable containing a reference to an array), an assignment like b = a creates a synonym for a, not a copy of the array it refers to. If you do want to copy an array, you must use a loop to assign a copy of each element explicitly, like this:

```
for (var i = 0; i < a.length; ++i)
    b[i] = a[i];
```

Arrays of Arrays

The elements of an array can themselves be arrays, which allows you to simulate matrices and other two-dimensional tabular structures. For example, the following script constructs a 4 × 4 identity matrix,

$$\begin{bmatrix} 1 & 0 & 0 & 0 \\ 0 & 1 & 0 & 0 \\ 0 & 0 & 1 & 0 \\ 0 & 0 & 0 & 1 \end{bmatrix}$$

```
var a = new Array(4);
a[0] = new Array(4);
a[1] = new Array(4);
a[2] = new Array(4);
a[3] = new Array(4);

for (var i = 0; i < 4; ++i)
    for (var j = 0; j < 4; ++j)
        a[i][j]  = i == j? 1: 0;
```

The elements are accessed using a double indexing, as in a[i][j]. Since a[i] is an array, it makes sense to index it in this way. Matrices are widely used in numerical computation, which is perhaps not likely to be of much concern to Flash programmers, but they can also be used as a way of representing connections in networks of various sorts. For example, if you had a collection of Web pages, you could allocate a number to each one, and then set up a matrix of Booleans such that a[i][j] was true if there was a link from the page whose number was i to the one whose number was j, and was false otherwise. Well known algorithms can be applied to such a matrix to determine, for example, whether it is possible to get from a certain page to some other by following a sequence of links. Consult any good book on data structures and algorithms for the details of how two-dimensional arrays can be used for such tasks.

The Array Object

A good book on data structures is probably also your best source for inspiration on using the methods of the built-in Array object. Just as Math and String provide the higher level operations that are normally found in mathematical and string libraries, so Array provides higher level operations on arrays. These include concat for joining arrays together, end to end, reverse for turning an array back to front, and sort for placing the elements in order. A collection of methods, push, pop, shift and unshift let you simulate linear data structures, such as stacks and queues using arrays. Perl programmers will feel at home with these operations; we will see some of them at work in Chapter 5. Also useful is the join method, which converts all the elements of an array to a string, and then concatenates the string, inserting a separator, which you can specify as an argument, between the elements. By default, if you don't specify a separator, a comma is used. Thus, if month is my array of names of the months, month.join() would be the string "Jan,Feb,Mar,Apr,May,Jun,Jul,Aug,Sep,Oct,Nov,Dec", while month.join('\n') would be

Jan

Feb

Mar

.

.

.

Dec

Full details of the methods of the Array object can be found in the *ActionScript Reference Guide*.

Exercises and Experiments

1. If the variable x has the value 0, what is the value of
   (a) x > 0 && 1/x > 1
   (b) x > 0 & 1/x > 1 ?
2. What is the value of
   (a) "512" + (512 + 512)
   (b) ("512" + 512) + 512
   (c) "512" + 512 + 512?
3. Code such as the following is distressingly common:
   ```
   if (the_flag == true) {
       ...
   }
   ```
   Explain why the comparison is redundant.
4. Rewrite the first script fragment on page 57 to use a for loop instead of while.
5. Extend the same script (either the original or the version you just wrote) to count the occurrences of the target, ignoring the case of the character. (For example, if source was "Ashtabula one-piece crankset" and target was "a", occurrences should end up with the value 4; likewise if target was "A".)
6. Rewrite the second script on page 57 without using break, but in such a way that it still stops looking as soon as it finds an occurrence of the target.

7. Implement a movie along the lines suggested on page 59, in which a user may click on buttons to indicate a selection, and the number of clicks on each button is remembered in a variable. Add an extra button that causes the playhead to move to a different frame, where a trace statement is used to show how many times each button has been clicked.
8. In the movie player with selection controls, what happens if a user clicks on a selection button while a movie is playing? If you consider the result undesirable, how would you prevent it?
9. Write a script, suitable for attaching to a button in the movie player, that toggles the visibility of the_clip, i.e., if the clip is visible it hides it, if it is invisible it reveals it.
10. Make a preloading movie that displays a progress bar, by scaling a suitable movie clip using _framesloaded/_totalframes to provide a visual indication of the proportion of the frames that has been loaded.
11. A naive programmer tried to improve the script on page 70 by making the loop more compact like this:
    ```
    for (var i = 0; i < 50000; ++i)
        ++a[Math.floor(n*Math.random())];
    ```
    Explain why this was a bad idea.
12. Write a script that transposes a two-dimensional array. That is, the value of a[i][j] after the transposition should be equal to the original value of a[j][i]. (You will have to initialize the array first in order to test the script.)
13. If the elements of an array are arrays, they do not all have to be the same length, nor do the elements of the elements all need to be of the same type, which opens up many possibilities. Suppose an array site is constructed in the following way: each element is an array, whose first element is a string, and whose remaining elements are integers. The meaning is that the name is a directory or file name, and the following numbers identify the elements for directories or files contained in that directory. (Files will just be represented by arrays of length one.) Set up an array with this structure for some Web site you are familiar with, and experiment with scripts for constructing URL strings, checking that all files are reachable from the root, finding how many levels deep in the hierarchy a file is, ... Don't omit to use the methods of the Array object if they save you some work. See whether your experiments suggest a better way of representing the same information, and if they do, implement it.

user interface elements

Input Elements and Forms

In the preceding chapter, buttons were used to provide a crude way for users to enter data that could be processed by a script. On Web pages, a more usual way for data to be entered is by filling in HTML *forms*, which contain specialized controls such as checkboxes, radio buttons, pop-up menus, scrollable lists and text fields. You will find the same controls appearing in dialogue boxes in any system based on a graphical user interface. Collectively, they are called *input elements*. Later in this chapter, we will see that buttons, movie clips and scripts can be used to create most of these familiar interface elements. The exception is text fields, which are provided by Flash as a separate type of object that can be placed on the stage.

The use of input elements is governed by certain conventions. Chief among these is the rule that they are for input only: they enable the user to select options or enter data, but they do not cause things to happen. That is the prerogative of buttons and menu or keyboard commands. Thus, typically, input elements are arranged within a frame that also contains a button which causes values taken from the input elements to be used elsewhere. Most often, the frame is arranged as a *form*, with the button being labelled Submit. The associated pattern of usage is that the form is displayed, the user fills it in using the input elements, and then clicks on Submit to cause their input to be processed. In Flash, the movie containing the form will be stopped until the form is submitted. The Submit button will cause a script to be executed to process the input and transfer the playhead to a different frame, which may display the results produced by the script. Often, much of the processing will be carried out on a remote server, by means which will be described in Chapter 7. These conventions governing the use of input elements are no more than conventions though, and are regularly flouted. However, it is a good idea to stick with them, because computer users have come to expect certain sorts of behaviour from interactive systems, and may become confused or irritated when systems behave differently.

Similar remarks apply to the appearance of input elements. Here the picture is confused by the different conventions followed on different platforms. Flash movies and Web pages must be platform-independent, which makes it hard to design input elements that will feel familiar to users on all platforms. One possibility offered by Flash is to design these elements to fit in with the overall appearance of the movie, forgetting about the conventional elements of any platform's normal interface. However, it is still necessary to ensure that it is clear to users what the purpose of the input elements is, and how to use them.

Editable Text Fields

Sometimes, what the user needs to enter is text, and sometimes scripts need to be able to display text that has been generated dynamically (such as the value of the loan repayment in the example in the last chapter). Neither of these requirements can be met by any of the Flash features we have seen so far, but both of them are catered for by a new one: *text fields*.

Creating Text Fields

Text fields are created on the stage using the type tool. Clicking on the stage with this tool selected creates a resizable rectangular field, into which text can be typed. The Text Options panel lets you specify (via a pop-up menu) whether the field contains *static* text, *dynamic* text or *input* text. Static text is entered in the Flash authoring environment and displayed in the movie like any graphic element. Dynamic text is created and displayed when the movie plays, as a result of computation carried out by scripts. Input text is like dynamic text, but may also be typed in by the user when the movie plays; its value may then be passed in the other direction to scripts that perform some computation using it.

A range of typographical properties can be specified via the Character panel, including the font, type size and colour. Text may be italicized or bold, and tracking and leading (line spacing) can be specified. Using the Paragraph panel, paragraphs may be centred, justified or left or right aligned and margins and indents may be set. All these properties can be applied to text of any of the three sorts.

Text is passed between a field and a script by associating a variable with the field. The association is set up in Flash in the Text Options panel, shown in Figure 4.1. If a variable name is entered into the box labelled Variable (which is only displayed when dynamic or input text has been selected), then when the movie plays, any value that is assigned to that variable will be displayed in the text field, and conversely, any text typed into the field will be assigned to the variable. (If you are familiar with Perl, you will see an

editable text fields

analogy with 'tied variables'.) More accurately, the value of the variable is displayed in the text field on entering any keyframe containing the field, and is updated at the end of any action that changes its value.

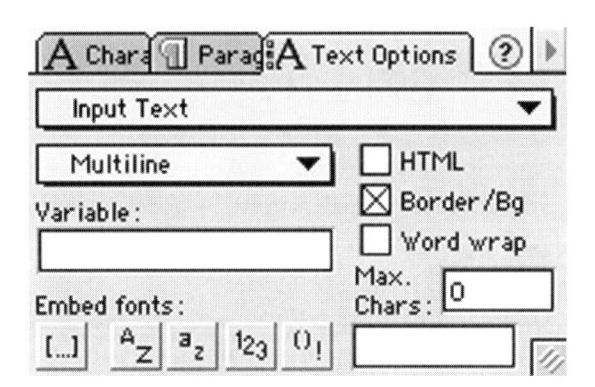

Figure 4.1 *The Text Options panel.*

Various options can be set in the Text Options panel to modify a field's behaviour and appearance. Checking the Border/Bg box causes the field to be displayed with a border and background, so that it stands out from its surroundings. Turning this option off is appropriate if the editable text field is there to allow dynamically computed strings to be inserted into fixed text. A pop-up menu allows you to choose between Single Line, Multiline and Password. Multiline allows users to enter text including newlines, whereas Single Line restricts their input to one line. Checking the Word Wrap option that appears when Multiline is selected makes the field behave like a word processor and automatically insert newlines when the text reaches the right hand edge of the field. The Password option is used when a field is provided for users to type a password or other confidential information. Instead of displaying the text as it is entered, the field shows asterisks; the text is still assigned to the field's associated variable.

If a value is entered in the box labelled Max Chars, then users will only be allowed to enter strings less than or equal in length to that value; any further characters will be discarded. This option may be used to provide a crude form of input validation. The restriction does not apply to dynamic text. An option that does apply to dynamic text is Selectable. If this is not checked, users are prevented from selecting (and thus copying and pasting) text from the field.

For dynamic and input text, typographical effects and layout can be applied using HTML tags, if the HTML box in the Text Options panel is checked. With this option selected, any HTML tags in the string stored in the text field's variable will be interpreted when the text is displayed. So, for example, text between `<b>` and `</b>` will be emboldened. This doesn't work quite as you might expect with input text: tags typed by the user are treated as part of the text and not interpreted (`<` and `>` signs are converted to the character references `&lt;` and `&gt;`), only those inserted by scripts are treated as markup. Flash only understands a few basic HTML tags: `<b>`, `<i>` and `<u>` can be used to apply boldface, italic and underline styles; the `<font>` tag, with attributes color, face and size provide control over font characteristics; `<p>` creates paragraphs, and `<a>` inserts hyperlinks.

The remaining text options are concerned with the way fonts are incorporated in the movie, and are of no relevance to our present concerns with scripts.

Using Text Fields for Output

A dynamic text field can be used to add the missing feedback to the repayment calculator example from Chapter 3. By adding a text field to the first frame of the movie, and setting its variable to amount, the amount entered with the keys will be displayed. No change to the script is necessary. The field is updated every time an assignment is made to amount, with the numeric value being converted to a string. Since the script attached to each key computes a new amount equal to the old amount with the corresponding digit appended, the digits will be displayed as they are on a calculator, provided the text field is right aligned. For example, if, at some point, amount has the value 97, and the button labelled 4 is pressed, the script

```
on (release) {
    amount = 10*amount + 4;
}
```

will be executed, and the text displayed will change to 974, shifting to the left, to reflect the assignment.

Moving on to the second frame of this movie, a first attempt at displaying the results of the repayment calculation might be to add two dynamic text fields and a piece of static text to the frame, as shown in Figure 4.2.The first field (which is wide enough to hold two digits) is associated with the variable period, the second with repayment. The intention is that, after the script has calculated the repayment amount and assigned it to the variable, a summary such as

12 repayments of £91.06

should be displayed. As Figure 4.3 shows, this isn't quite what happens.

The problem is that the variable repayment is stored as a floating point number to many digits of precision. When it is converted into a string for displaying, these digits

editable text fields

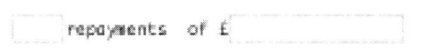

Figure 4.2 *Text fields to display the result of a computation.*

Figure 4.3 *Badly formatted output.*

are preserved and as much of the string as will fit into the editable text field is displayed. This is not what is required, since the repayment can only be made in amounts of whole pence, so the string should be displayed to two significant figures only. Restricting the length of the whole text field doesn't help, because we can have no idea how many digits there are before the decimal point.

Most languages provide library functions (such as C and Perl's sprintf) to control the format of string conversions, specifying the number of digits before and after the decimal point, whether leading and trailing zeros are suppressed, and so on. ActionScript has no such function. You have to do the formatting of numerical strings yourself. (Or not. But if you think Figure 4.3 shows acceptable output, you may find your career in Flash is a short one.)

The following code provides a quick and nasty solution to the display problem in this particular instance.

```
var i = String(Math.floor(repayment));
var f = Math.round((100*repayment)%100);
f = f < 10? "0" + f: String(f);
repayment = i + "." + f;
```

The numerical value of repayment is split into its integer and fraction parts: the first assignment takes the integer part, converts it to a string and stores it in i; the floor method of the Math object truncates its argument to the integer below. The second assignment multiplies the repayment by 100, so that the leading two digits move to the left of the decimal point, then takes the remainder on division by 100 to get rid of all the digits to the left of the second. By using Math.round to round to the nearest integer, we end up with a one or two digit integer, depending on whether the first digit after the point in the original value was 0. If we were just to convert this to a string, then leading zeros would be lost, so the next statement explicitly inserts the character 0 in front of any value of f that is less than ten — i.e., a single digit — which converts it to a string as a side-effect; two-digit values are just converted to strings. Finally, the strings in i and f are concatenated, with a decimal point in between them to produce the required string representation of repayment, formatted with two digits after the decimal point.

Because Flash lacks any built-in support for formatting numbers, almost any numerical output will require some such manipulation before it can be displayed in a text field. Text strings, however, can usually be adequately formatted using the typographic controls associated with the text field when it is created, or by inserting HTML tags.

Editing Text

Simple editing operations are available in input text fields, and dynamic text fields with the Selectable option. Characters can be selected by dragging, words by double-clicking; selections can be extended using the arrow keys with the shift key held down. The usual cut, copy and paste operations can then be used. More detailed editing of text fields can be performed using the built-in Selection object.

There is only one such object, because it always refers to the currently 'focussed' text field: the one the text cursor is in. The most useful methods belonging to Selection are getBeginIndex and getEndIndex, which return the offset of the beginning and end of the selection, respectively, thereby allowing you to extract the corresponding substring from the text field's variable. The offsets start at zero, to be consistent with substring, and refer to the text displayed on the screen. For HTML text, this is not the same as the string held in the variable, because that contains HTML tags. (In Chapter 5, you will see how to compensate for this.)

As a simple example, suppose you want users to be able to convert selected text to uppercase. If the text field's variable is called tt, the following script performs the operation:

```
var b = Selection.getBeginIndex();
var e = Selection.getEndIndex();
var before = tt.substring(0, b);
var during = tt.substring(b, e);
var after = tt.substring(e);
tt = before + during.toUpperCase() + after;
```

Using the values returned by Selection's methods, the string is split into three sections: the part before the selection, the selection itself, and the remainder (before, during and after, respectively). It is then put back together, with the selection converted to upper case using the appropriate String method. The reconstructed string is assigned back to tt so that the displayed text reflects the modification.

If you attach the script above to a button as the body of a release handler it won't work. This is because, as soon as the user clicks on the button, the text field loses the focus, and the values returned by Selection's methods are both defined to be -1 under those circumstances. Selection provides another method, setFocus, that takes a string holding the name of a text field variable as its argument and gives the corresponding text field the focus. Unfortunately, in so doing, it resets the selection to the entire field.

You could decide to trigger the change in the text field using a keyboard command (see the final section of this chapter), which works in a straightforward way, but if you decide to stick with a button you need to make use of an ingenious little trick,[1] and yet another method of the Selection object. The trick is to remember the selection when the button receives a rollOver event. This will certainly happen before a click, and there is no harm in the handler executing when the cursor just happens to roll over the button.
```
on (rollOver) {
    var b = Selection.getBeginIndex();
    var e = Selection.getEndIndex();
}
```
The release event handler must restore the selection after it has given the focus back to the text field. Selection.setSelection is provided for that purpose. The handler thus becomes:
```
on (release) {
      Selection.setFocus("tt");
      Selection.setSelection(b, e);
        splice tt as above
}
```

Checkboxes and Radio Buttons

Checkboxes are conventionally used to select options that can be either on or off, such as 'play sounds' or 'animate GIFs' in a Web browser's preferences. A checkbox is usually a hollow box, with a label near to it indicating the option it controls. When an option is selected, a check mark (usually a cross or a tick) appears in the corresponding box, to indicate that the option is on. Checkboxes are a direct analogue of the boxes you have to tick when filling in questionnaires or declining to receive news of exciting special offers after registering some software. They are usually arranged in groups of related options, any number of which may be on or off. Usually, the initial state of an option is off, so that checkboxes are displayed as empty boxes, but it is sometimes more

---

1. Originally devised in a combined effort by Kim Markegard, Phillip Kerman and Gary Grossman, I am reliably informed.

convenient to invert the sense of the option and use on as the default, so any implementation of checkboxes must allow them to be initialized to either state.

Radio buttons are similar to checkboxes, except that they always occur in groups and only one of the group may be on, the rest must be off. The name 'radio button' derives from the analogy of the preset station selection buttons on a car radio — you can only be listening to one station at a time, and if you push in a button, the one that was previously pushed in jumps out. Radio buttons often look like small circles, with a large dot appearing in the middle when they are selected.

Implementing Checkboxes

A checkbox can be easily implemented as a movie clip symbol with two frames — both keyframes — corresponding to the two possible states of the box. The first keyframe is labelled off state, the second on state. Each contains an instance of a button symbol. The one in the off state is an instance of a check off button, which looks like an empty box; the one in the on state is an instance of a check on button, which looks like a box with a cross in it. When a user clicks in the box, it should change state. To make this happen, all that is required is for the button in the off state to have the following script attached to it:

```
on (release) {
    gotoAndStop ("on state");
}
```

while the button in the on state has the inverse script:

```
on (release) {
    gotoAndStop ("off state");
}
```

Thus, mouse clicks in these buttons cause the movie clip to switch between its two frames, so the box appears to be checked or unchecked by the clicks.

Placing a button inside a movie clip so that it can receive events is a frequently employed technique. in Flash 4, it was the only way for movie clips to receive events, but in Flash 5, clips can receive events themselves, making it possible to do away with the intermediary button. However, it is often less convenient to handle mouse-related events directly in clips, because they are sent to every clip, whereas they are only sent to the button that is under the cursor at the time. In the case of a checkbox, it would be necessary before executing the gotoAndStop statement in a handler for the mouseUp event to examine the _xmouse and _ymouse properties of the checkbox clip to determine whether the mouse was actually over it (see Exercise 2).

checkboxes and radio buttons

A variable can be used to record the state of the checkbox. It is most convenient to assign a value of true or false, to indicate whether the box is checked or not, that is, whether it is in the on state or the off state. Since the movie clip enters the frame on state whenever the box is checked, the assignment can be made in a script attached to the frame:

is_set = true;

A script attached to the off state frame assigns false to the is_set variable, so that it always reflects the state of the checkbox, as displayed by the graphic in the current frame. To complete the checkbox symbol, a stop action must be added to the first frame to prevent the movie playing, and thus changing state spontaneously.

Figure 4.4 shows the implementation of the checkbox symbol in schematic form.

```
off state                              on state
is_set = false                         is_set = true

        on (release) {
            gotoAndStop("on state")
        }

        on (release) {
            gotoAndStop("off state")
        }
```

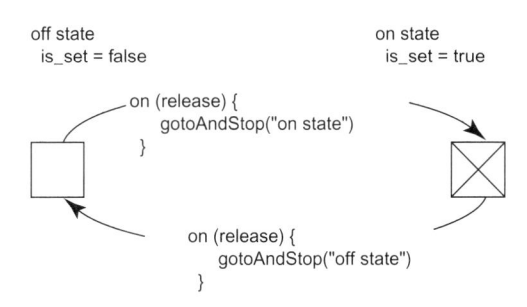

Figure 4.4   *A checkbox.*

To use a checkbox in a movie, it is merely necessary to create an instance of the checkbox symbol. In order for scripts in the enclosing movie to be able to determine whether the checkbox is selected or not, the instance must be given an instance name. For example, a checkbox that is used to allow a user to choose whether or not to receive email announcements from a company might be given the name email_declined. Assuming the company makes the usual unreasonable assumption that you want to receive their email unless you explicitly decline it, it would be necessary to check the box to decline mail. A script attached to the frame containing this checkbox instance would be able to test the variable email_declined.is_set to determine whether or not the user had done so.

If the meaning of the checkbox was inverted, so that checking it indicated that mail announcements *were* accepted, then a company that assumed it was accepted until declined would want this checkbox to be selected by default. Presumably, the form designer would change its name to email_accepted, and then add the following script to the frame containing it:

user interface elements

```
email_accepted.gotoAndStop ("on state");
```
The checkbox would be displayed with its check mark, and could then be turned off by clicking. The variable is_set would correctly be set to true as the on state frame was entered.

You may have realized that the variable is_set is superfluous, because it is possible to determine the state of the checkbox by looking at its _current_frame property. Using the variable simply makes it clearer what is going on, and makes the code for testing the checkbox's state less verbose.

Implementing Radio Buttons

It doesn't make sense to implement a single radio button, only a group, because the defining property of radio buttons is the mutual exclusion between groups of them. It is possible to define a general framework to contain an arbitrary number of radio buttons (although not with the amount of ActionScript that has been described so far), but it is easier to define separate symbols for a pair of buttons, a group of three, a group of four, and so on. Since conventional human–computer interface guidelines recommend that radio buttons should only be used in groups of between two and seven, it is not especially arduous to provide a set of symbols for each of the required sizes. The simplest case of a pair of radio buttons illustrates the technique.

A pair of radio buttons is functionally equivalent to a single checkbox (the selected and unselected states of the checkbox represent two mutually exclusive choices), so the implementation is much the same. In fact, the only difference is that each frame of the radio pair symbol contains two buttons, one showing a selected radio button, the other showing a deselected one. In the first frame, the upper button is selected, the lower deselected; in the second frame it is the other way round. Hence, if a user clicks on the unselected radio button in the first frame, the correct action is to go to the second, and vice versa. A click on a selected radio button has no effect (except, perhaps, to flash the

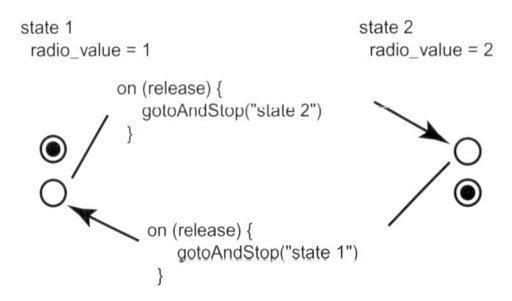

Figure 4.5 *A pair of radio buttons.*

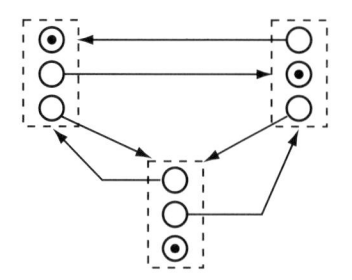

Figure 4.6 *A group of three radio buttons.*

button, which can be handled by modifying the graphic in the button symbol's Down frame), so no action need be attached to it. As with the checkbox, it is convenient to assign a value to a variable in each frame, so that the chosen radio button can be easily identified by scripts. In this case, it makes sense to assign a number to indicate whether the first or second radio button is selected. Figure 4.5 shows the structure of a radio button pair symbol.

Extending this scheme to a group of three radio buttons is simple. Because of the mutual exclusion, only one extra frame is needed: each frame corresponds to one of the buttons being selected. In every frame, it is possible to identify which frame to go to when any unselected button is clicked. Figure 4.6 shows the transitions between states of a set of three radio buttons. Implementing a symbol that behaves in accordance with this diagram is simple if slightly tedious. Extending the scheme to groups of four or more buttons is just as simple, and only slightly more tedious.

It is worth noting that the framework for radio buttons remains the same, no matter what the buttons themselves look like. Once you have created a movie clip symbol that behaves as a group of three radio buttons that have a conventional appearance, if you want to create a group of three translucent pulsating radio buttons, all you need to do is duplicate the clip, create two new button symbols (one for a selected radio button and one for a deselected one), and replace the instances of the old buttons in your clip with the new ones. (You can do this just by changing the instances' definitions in the Instance panel — click on the leftmost icon of the row at the bottom —you don't even need to create new instances.)

Pop-up Menus

Radio button groups become unwieldy for more than a few options. An alternative input element, that is suitable for roughly five to twelve choices, is the *pop-up menu*.

There is considerable variety in the appearance and behaviour of pop-up menus on different platforms, and in different programs, but the general principle is always the same: an icon or some text indicates a location where pressing and holding the mouse will cause a menu with a set of options to appear. A selection is made by dragging over the menu and releasing the mouse button when the cursor is over the chosen menu item.

Implementing pop-up menus in terms of Flash buttons and movie clip symbols is trickier than implementing checkboxes and radio buttons, and less easy to do in a way that can be conveniently reused. This is inevitable, since pop-up menus will differ in the number of items, the width needed to accommodate the items, and the text used to label them. A general-purpose reusable pop-up menu can only be produced in the form of a 'smart clip' — a movie clip abstraction that is parameterized in some way. We will look at this important generalization of movie clips separately in Chapter 6. For now, we will consider making a specific pop-up menu in order to illustrate the mechanics of popping up and selecting items.

A menu is always in one of two states, it is either open or closed. Hence, it is naturally implemented as a movie clip with two keyframes. Precisely what goes into those frames depends on the desired appearance and behaviour of the pop-up menu. To show the necessary implementation techniques, we will look at one of the simpler but less elegant variations on the pop-up menu idea. The closed and open states are shown in Figure 4.7. When the menu is closed, the triangle icon indicates its presence, and the text box shows the current value of the option associated with the menu. When it is opened, by pressing the mouse while the cursor is over the icon or the text box, the set of possible selections is displayed in menu form below the text box. When the mouse button is released, the menu is closed and the text of the item that was underneath the cursor is displayed in the text box as the new current value.

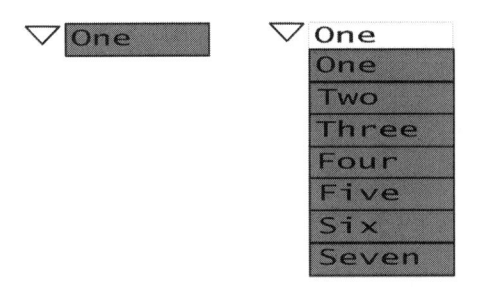

Figure 4.7   *Closed and open states of a simple pop-up menu.*

pop-up menus

The menu is built out of menu items, which are instances of a button symbol. The simplest design for a menu item is a rectangle, although any design may be used to provide unusual menus, where that is felt to be appropriate. The Over frame of the button would usually be shaded or coloured to provide the normal feedback to show the user which item will be selected if they release the mouse button. The Down frame may be differently shaded, so that it flashes in confirmation of the menu selection. The menu item symbol does not have any text on it — this will be added separately, so that each menu item can be an instance of the same symbol. A separate symbol is used as the icon — in this example, a simple triangle — that indicates the presence and nature of the pop-up menu.

The movie clip symbol that is the menu proper is constructed on three layers. One layer is reserved for actions. Although there is no requirement to give actions their own layer, it helps keep things organized. The next layer holds buttons. In the first frame of the movie clip, which will be labelled Closed, there is one instance of the pop-up triangle, and one instance of the menu item symbol. This will hold the current selection. The top layer holds text fields, which are laid over the menu items, so that their text labels the items. In the first frame, the text corresponding to the default selection is placed in a text field over the menu item. A stop action is attached to this frame, to prevent the menu opening as soon as the movie starts to play.

In the second frame, labelled Open, the buttons and text field from the first are repeated. Below the menu item, a sufficient number of extra menu items is added to the layer of buttons to accommodate all the options on the menu. Text fields are placed on top of all these menu items, containing the appropriate label.

Three things are needed to make this movie clip behave as intended. First, all the menu items must be modified so that they are tracked as menu items instead of as buttons. Recall from Chapter 2 that this means that any button will receive a release event if the mouse button is released with the cursor over it, even if it was pressed while the cursor was over some other button. This is necessary, because we wish to be able to open the menu by pressing the button with the cursor over the pop-up icon or the menu selection item, and keep it open until the button is released over the item for the new selection.

Second, actions must be attached to each of the menu items. In the first frame, both the icon button and the menu item have the same script attached:

```
on (press) {
    gotoAndStop ("Open");
```

}

Hence, as required, the menu will open when the mouse button is depressed with the cursor over either of these objects. In the second frame, each menu item has a script of the following form attached:

```
on (release) {
    menu_choice = "Two";
    gotoAndStop ("Closed");
}
```

where Two is the text on the second menu item, and so on. The two elements repeated from the first frame do not perform any assignment, they just go back to the first frame, leaving the selection unchanged.

Finally, to make the user's selection appear in the sole menu item in the closed frame, it is only necessary to set the variable associated with the text field on top of that item to menu_choice. When the playhead returns to the closed frame, the text field will be updated with the value that had been assigned when an item was selected from the menu.

The only drawback of this design is that, if a user decides not to make a choice from the menu, and moves the cursor away from it before releasing the mouse button, nothing will happen. No button will receive the release event, and the menu will stay open. The solution to this problem lacks elegance.

An extra button symbol — let's call it a Closer — must be created, consisting of a filled rectangle the size of the entire stage. When an instance of the menu symbol is placed on the stage, an instance of the Closer symbol must also be added, on a layer underneath the one containing the menu. That way, any events occurring anywhere on the stage outside the area of the menu will be passed to the Closer. By setting the alpha value of the closer to zero, it can be made invisible, but will still receive the events. In particular, it will receive release events that occur when the cursor is moved off the menu. In response to these, it should close the menu, so the Closer must make the menu instance go to its closed frame. The menu instance must, therefore, have an instance name. If this is my_menu, the Closer would have this script attached to it:

```
on (release) {
    my_menu.gotoAndStop ("Closed");
}
```

(The menu instance is necessarily in the same movie or clip as the Closer button, so its instance name can be used as a relative target name.)

pop-up menus

This arrangement with a separate Closer symbol is far from satisfactory, but there is little alternative (see Exercise 4).

This pop-up menu symbol is nothing like as easy to reuse as the checkbox and radio button groups. Every menu you use must be an instance of its own symbol, with the right number of items, labelled appropriately. To create a menu, a standard menu symbol can be duplicated, so that the framework does not need to be recreated, but the distinctive elements of the particular menu must be added. Only then, can an instance of the symbol be placed on the stage. The new symbol is completely separate from the original, but it will use the same menu item symbols, so some changes to the appearance of menus can be made globally just by editing the menu item symbol.

The changes that can be made when creating a new pop-up from a standard one based on the ideas described above can go further than simply changing the number of items and their labels. (That can be automated with a smart clip, as we will see.) Although we are used to menus arranged as a column of rectangular items, and although most operating systems' APIs only provide a few variations on that layout, Flash lets you use much more adventurous menus. Figure 4.8 shows an example. This menu was created in a few minutes just by editing the menu item symbol and moving the individual items in the open frame of the menu clip. Such unconventional menus should be used with discretion, and their behaviour may need some thought. In this example, the menu opens on a rollOver event, since users are inclined to release the mouse button when the items do not pop up next to the place they pressed it.

Figure 4.8 *A fancy pop-up menu.*

Scrolling Lists

The number of entries that can sensibly be included in a pop-up menu is limited — if you have a lot of fonts installed on your system you will know how awkward it is dragging up and down the long font pop-up menu in Flash, for example. For more than about a dozen selections, a scrolling list is a better input element.

A scrolling list is like a small window, fitted with up and down arrows, in which the items are displayed. There will be more items than can fit into the window at once. By pressing the arrows, the list can be made to scroll up or down. When the required selection is among those visible, the user can click on it.

It would be very easy to make a scrolling list in Flash if the items only had to move up or down one at a time every time the user clicked on one of the arrows, but that isn't how scrolling is supposed to work. The usual arrangement (one might almost say the correct arrangement) is that the list continues to move as long as the mouse button is held down over one of the arrows. This is more difficult, but can be achieved with a little ingenuity.

The difficulty arises because buttons can only react to discrete events: actions are executed *when* something happens, like the mouse button being pressed, not *while* some condition holds, like the mouse button being down. This is reflected in the syntax: we can say on (press), but not something like while (pressed). What we must do therefore, is use the press event to set a flag that indicates that the list should be scrolled, and the release event to clear it, and use frame actions in an enclosing movie to make the items scroll. Even this is not entirely straightforward, as you will see shortly.

The scrolling list will be constructed as a symbol, which will be called a Scroller, made up of several elements. First there are the up and down arrows, which are instances of button symbols with a suitable appearance. Next comes an outline to define the window within which the scrolling items appear. This is just a decoration, really. Finally, the scrolling items themselves. One way of making them move in the desired fashion is to use tweening. This is done by defining a movie symbol, Scrolling list. In the first frame, all the items are arranged in a column. If the items are to be selectable, each must be a button. Most likely, each item would be an instance of the same button, with the item's text placed in a text field on top of it, in the same way as menu items were constructed for the pop-up menu. Enough extra frames are then added to the movie symbol to ensure that the list will move smoothly — the correct value depends on the font size used for the text, and the length of the entries — with a second

scrolling lists **91**

keyframe at the end. In this last keyframe, the list of items is moved up, so that the final item is in the position that was occupied by the first item in the first keyframe. A motion tween is created between these two keyframes, so when the movie plays, the items slide smoothly up the screen.

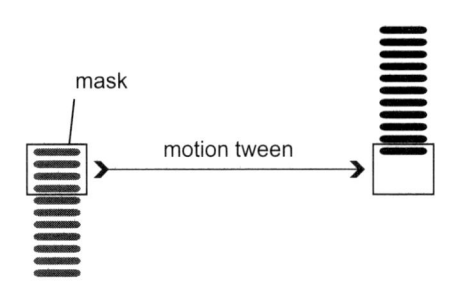

Figure 4.9 *Creating the scrolling effect.*

To create the effect of scrolling within a window, a mask layer is created above the items, consisting of a rectangle that matches the outline used in the Scroller symbol. Now, when the movie is played, the items appear to scroll within that rectangle (see Figure 4.9). However, we don't want the movie to play spontaneously, so a stop action is added to its first frame. The items are going to be made to scroll by calling movie clip methods to make the Scrolling list movie step forwards or backwards through its frames. An instance of Scrolling list, called the_list, is placed in the Scroller inside the outline. Figure 4.10 shows the construction of a Scroller. It is now time to look at the scripts that will make it work.

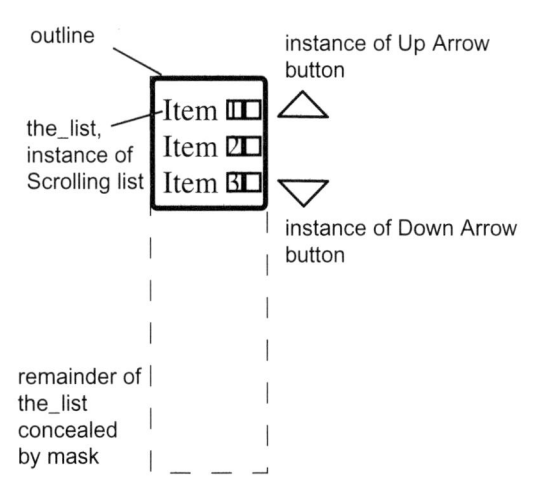

Figure 4.10 *Construction of a scrolling list.*

As explained, the up and down buttons can't actually make the list scroll, they just set flags to indicate that scrolling is required. The up button uses the following script:
```
on (press) {
    scrolling_backward = true;
    scrolling_forward = false;
}
on (release, releaseOutside) {
    scrolling_backward = false;
}
```
The variables scrolling_forward and scrolling_backward indicate the direction in which the playhead must move through the Scrolling list. Conventionally, scrolling arrows indicate the direction in which the window moves relative to its contents, so the up arrow actually makes the items in the scrolling list move down. To make this happen, the movie clip must play backwards. The script attached to the down button is similar, with the roles of the two flags interchanged.

It should be evident that the following script will send the playhead one frame in the appropriate direction whatever the values of the two flags.
```
if (scrolling_forward)
    the_list.nextFrame();
else if (scrolling_backward)
    the_list.prevFrame ();
```

We need to arrange for that script to be repeatedly executed as long as the scrolling list is displayed. This can be done by making the Scroller movie loop through a frame to which the script is attached. Sadly, using a single frame and an action that makes it go to itself doesn't work: the actions attached to a frame that is looping are only executed once, the first time the playhead enters the frame. To force them to be repeatedly executed, it is necessary to leave the frame and come back to it. Accordingly, the Scroller movie clip needs two frames. The script that targets the Scrolling list is attached to the first. The second has the same contents as the first (i.e., it is not a keyframe on any of the layers containing graphics), and has a script attached to it that jumps back to the first frame.

Although scrolling has been presented here as a way of making an input element, the same general approach can be used to scroll things other than lists of buttons within a sub-window. In particular, text fields can be made to scroll. The variable associated with a field is not simply a string, it has two other properties: scroll holds the line number of topmost line of text that is visible within the field; maxscroll holds the value that scroll would have if the bottom line of text was just visible at the bottom of the field. Input text fields scroll automatically as the user types if the text becomes too long to fit in the field, and the properties are updated by Flash to reflect the current state. Text that scrolls out of the top of the field disappears (like text on an old-fashioned VDU screen); to get it back, you must assign a new value to the scroll property. The conventional way to do this is to use scroll arrows. It is trivial to implement arrows that scroll one line up or down each time they are clicked. To make continuously scrolling arrows, the technique just described in connection with scrolling lists can be adapted (see Exercise 6).

Using Draggable Movie Clips

The ability to drag graphic objects around the screen offers a host of possibilities for user interaction. The applications of dragging can be divided into two categories: direct manipulation of objects representing entities, and the construction of controls that have draggable parts. An example of the first category would be an on-line shop in which customers could purchase items by dragging icons into a shopping basket. An example of the second category is the conventional scrollbar, where a box can be dragged up and down to scroll a document in a window. Other conventional uses of drag and drop behaviour, in particular, moving blocks of text, are not available in Flash movies.

Direct Manipulation Interfaces

Direct manipulation interfaces are quite easy to construct in Flash. The key elements are the startDrag and stopDrag methods of the MovieClip object.[1] As this suggests, only movie clip instances can be dragged, not instances of button or graphic symbols. After the startDrag method has been executed, the movie clip instance corresponding to the object through which it was called will follow the cursor around the screen. More precisely, the clip will move so that it always maintains the same position relative to the cursor. For example, if the clip is in the top right hand corner of the movie, and the cursor is moved in a circle at the bottom left, the clip will circulate up at the right in time with the cursor movement. If the optional first argument to startDrag (lock) is true, the clip will move so that its centre is always directly under the cursor, jumping to the cursor position when the drag is started if necessary.

Calling stopDrag makes the currently draggable clip no longer draggable. Only one clip can be draggable at a time (which makes sense), so a drag is also stopped if another one is started.

---

1. These methods can also be used as functions, taking a target name as their first argument (cf. loadMovie). This is just to provide compatibility with Flash 4.

Very often, you will want to arrange for a movie clip to start dragging when the mouse button is pressed with the cursor over the clip. As with check boxes, if a clip event is used to trigger the script that starts the drag, it will be necessary to include code to test the mouse coordinates to find out which clip should become draggable. An easier solution is to place a suitable button in the movie clip that you want to make draggable.

Suppose, for example, you do want to implement an interface to an online shop, in which goods are dragged off display racks into a basket or trolley. To be specific, suppose the goods are books, which are represented by thumbnail images of their covers. (See Figure 4.11.[1]) A first attempt at building the interface might be as follows.

Figure 4.11 *A direct manipulation interface to a bookshop.*

The first step is to produce a template from which book objects can be cloned. This must be a movie clip, because we want to be able to drag it. It consists of a single frame with two layers. The lower layer will contain the image of the book's cover. For simplicity, assume that a standard size is used for all the cover images. If you are actually

---

1. Which is indeed a cynical piece of product placement, justified only by the fact that I have the artwork to hand and know that I don't need to worry about copyright.

implementing this interface, it is a good idea to place a dummy cover image in the template, to act as a layout guide. On the upper layer of the template there should be a rectangular button. The easiest way to create such a button is to draw a filled rectangle that exactly covers the image on the lower layer, and then convert this to a symbol, setting its type to button. This leaves an instance of the rectangular button in the template movie. By setting its alpha value to zero, the button becomes invisible but is still able to receive events. (This would not be the case if its visibility was set to invisible.)

The intention is that books will start to drag when the mouse button is pressed while the cursor is over them, and stop (i.e., they will be dropped) when it is released. The following script, attached to the button on the upper layer, does this.

```
on (press) {
    this.startDrag();
}
on (release) {
    stopDrag();
}
```

The special object this refers, in this context, to the movie clip containing the button to which the script is attached, so it is that movie which is dragged, as required. (Strictly, this ought to be redundant here, since the containing movie would be referred to implicitly if no object was specified in the method call. Because of the way startDrag can also be used as a function, this must be used here to avoid ambiguity. We will see more conventional uses of this in Chapter 5.)

Note that, since the cursor must be over the book clip to start the drag, it is not necessary to use the optional argument to startDrag to lock it to the centre of the clip. In fact, it is better not to, because if you did, the cover would jerk as the drag started, unless the user happened to click on its exact centre.

Nice and simple, but totally useless unless something happens when a book is dropped. Exactly what this should be will depend on the particular application in which these draggable clips are being used, but, in general, we can be pretty sure that it will depend on where the book is dropped. You can discover this by examining the value of the _droptarget property of the clip after the drag has stopped. If the clip was dropped onto some other symbol instance, such as a shopping basket, _droptarget will hold its target name.

Before looking at what might happen when a book is dropped onto a shopping basket or some other object, we should consider what ought to happen if it is dropped somewhere else. This might happen by accident, or because the user was unsure what was going on. In either case, the most sensible thing to do seems to be to put the book back on the shelf where it came from. This means that the clip needs to know where it came from.

One way of achieving this is by adding a handler to each clip instance that remembers its coordinates, like this:

```
onClipEvent(load) {
    var home_x = _x;
    var home_y = _y;
}
```

These assignments will be made before there is any chance of the clip being dragged anywhere, so the values remembered in home_x and home_y will be the coordinates of the clip's original location. A clip can be sent back to where it came from by resetting its _x and _y properties to these values.

Suppose that there is a shopping basket, in the form of a movie clip whose instance name is the_basket. To find out whether or not a book has been dropped on it, we need to look at the value of the dropped clip's _droptarget property. There is a complication here: to ensure compatibility with Flash 4, the target path is stored in _droptarget as a string, using the old / notation, mentioned on page 22. To obtain a reference to the corresponding movie clip instance, this string must be passed to a built-in function called eval, whose only purpose is to convert strings to variables. (It was frequently necessary to do this in Flash 4, but it is rarely needed now.) To send movie clips that have been dropped anywhere except on the basket back to their home coordinates, the book covers' release handlers must be changed as follows:

```
on (release) {
    stopDrag();
    if (eval(_droptarget) != _parent.the_basket) {
        _x = home_x;
        _y = home_y;
    }
}
```

If a book template symbol is constructed on the lines just suggested, individual books can be produced by duplicating the template and inserting the appropriate cover image. The code does not need changing.

A detailed answer to the question of what should happen if a book is dropped on the shopping basket or some other meaningful destination must wait until Chapter 6. For now, suffice it to say that, if the value of _droptarget shows that the book has been dropped on to some named instance, then an appropriate action will be initiated.

Creating Controls With Draggable Elements

Movies with buttons in can be used to create controls such as sliders. Figure 4.12 shows an example, whose intention should be clear. By dragging the box up or down the slider, users can indicate a range of prices in which they are interested. Similar controls are commonly used for controlling the volume of sound, or the quality of compression of images. They provide a generally useful means of setting values whenever a linear representation of their range provides a helpful way of judging relative magnitudes.

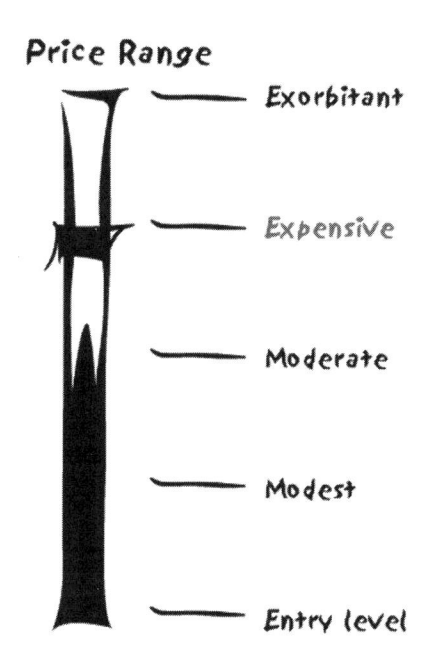

Figure 4.12 *A slider control.*

You should be able to see how a button in a movie clip can be used as the slider's box, by making it draggable in a similar way to the book covers in the previous example. There are some refinements to the implementation of the slider, though. In particular, it is necessary to restrict the area over which the box can be dragged — it would be a strange sort of slider that let you drag its box sideways off the bar. The startDrag method takes additional parameters that let you specify a rectangle to which dragging is confined, which is just what is required in this instance.

In order to see how the scripts associated with this slider work, some details of the objects it consists of need to be filled in. The slider is a movie consisting of a single frame which contains two objects, the bar and the box. (In this example, the tick marks and legend are added separately in the movie containing the slider.) The bar is really just a graphic — it isn't going to do anything, but it has been made into a movie clip instance so that we can find out its size and coordinates by accessing its properties. The box is also a movie clip instance, resembling the book covers, in that it consists of a single frame containing a button. In this case, there is no need for a separate layer to contain an image: the button is the box.

The dragging of this box must be constrained so that it only moves along the bar. An easy way of doing this would be to enter values for the left, right, top and bottom of the constraining rectangle parameters of the startDrag method corresponding to the horizontal centre and vertical extremities of the bar. Doing so would mean that if the bar was redrawn, the box's script would have to be changed, which is tiresome and error-prone. A better way of setting up the rectangle is to use the bar clip's properties. The result looks a bit complicated, but it is really quite simple.

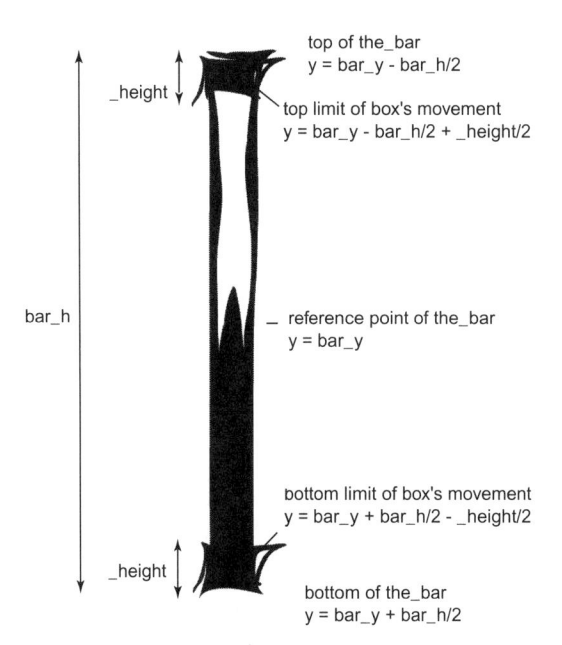

Figure 4.13 *Computing the constraining rectangle.*

using draggable movie clips

The complications arise because the properties give the coordinates of the bar's reference point, which is its centre, and because we have to take account of the finite size of the box. Figure 4.13 shows the basis of the calculation, which leads to the following scripts being attached to the instance of the box movie symbol in the slider and the button it contains. (Remember that *y* coordinates increase downwards in Flash.) A load clip event handler computes the constants (to avoid recomputing them every time).

```
onClipEvent (load) {
    var bar_y = _parent.the_bar._y;
    var bar_x = _parent.the_bar._x;
    var bar_h = _parent.the_bar._height;
}
```

The slider bar has been given the instance name the_bar. Since the bar and the box are both contained in the slider movie, the target _parent.the_bar inside these scripts refers to the correct bar. The press handler uses these values to specify the constraining rectangle when it starts the drag.

```
on (press) {
    this.startDrag (false, bar_x, bar_y-bar_h/2+_height/2,
                bar_x, bar_y+bar_h/2-_height/2);
}
```

Note that the left and right of the rectangle have been set to the same value, which constrains the box to move in a straight line.

Although slider controls are based on a metaphor of analogue devices, such as the volume sliders on a mixing desk, the way they are typically used as interface elements is essentially digital in nature. The value represented by the slider's position is quantized to one of a finite number of levels, such as a JPEG quality setting, or, in the example shown in Figure 4.12, a price level. This quantization can usefully be performed by a script when the drag of the box stops.

Because the movement of the box has been constrained, it is possible for the cursor to move away from it while a drag is in progress. This could not happen with the book covers, which always stuck to the cursor once a drag had begun. The scroll box, though, might get left behind, as it were, if the cursor moves outside its constraining rectangle. It is therefore necessary to stop the drag, not only on a release event, but also on releaseOutside and dragOut. When these events occur, the drag is stopped and the box's _y property is used to determine a price level.

```
on (release, releaseOutside, dragOut) {
    stopDrag ();
```

```
        var level = Math.round((num_levels-1)*(_y-(bar_y-bar_h/2))/bar_h);
}
```

The variable num_levels is assumed to hold the number of different values that the level can take. (In the example of Figure 4.12, this would be 5.) The expression assigned to level computes the offset of the box from the top of the bar, computes the result as a proportion of the bar height, and normalizes the result to lie between 0 and num_levels-1.

In a complete application, this level value would be used to determine the next operation. It might cause one of the titles by the slider to be highlighted, showing the user which level they had chosen. It might then be passed on to further actions, causing the movie to show goods in the chosen price range, for example.

Sliders can be used to control the sound level and stereo balance in a Flash movie. The slider's position is used to compute values to pass as parameters to methods of the built-in Sound object. The *ActionScript Reference Guide* has a detailed example.

Keys

Although working with graphical user interfaces is often characterized as 'pointing and clicking', the keys on the keyboard often play an equal role to that of the mouse in controlling the behaviour of a system. Expert users of programs that are ostensibly menu and icon driven — including Flash — invariably rely on keyboard shortcuts as a faster method of issuing commands. Specialized keys, such as the left and right arrows, and modifiers such as control and alt or command and option, according to platform, extend the utility of the keyboard; the arrow keys, in particular, provide a natural way of controlling movement that is more precise than most people can achieve with a mouse or even a pen and graphics tablet.

The drawback of using keys as controls is that they need explanation — it doesn't take much perception on the part of a user to guess that a button labelled Submit will cause a form to be submitted, but unless there are some instructions, it might be a long time before they discovered that typing S does the same. Another problem with using keys in Flash movies that might be embedded in Web browsers is that certain keys are used by some browsers for their own shortcuts, so key events caused by these will never be passed on to the Flash movie.

Keys and Buttons

The pressing of a particular key can be caught in event handlers attached to buttons. More accurately, a handler can be defined for the sending of a particular character from the keyboard, not just the pressing of any key. The event is specified as keyPress "character". A typical key press event handler looks like:

```
on (keyPress "x") {
    gotoAndPlay ("exit");
}
```

If a button needs to respond to different characters, separate handlers are needed for each key (even if the response is the same — the syntax does not allow you to combine several keyPress events the way you can combine other events). Notice that the event is associated with a character, not an actual key on the keyboard. For example, the event identified as keyPress "X" is sent if both the X and Shift keys are pressed together, and is different from the keyPress "x" event sent if the Shift key is not held down. There is no way for a button to catch the event that occurs when the Shift key alone is pressed.

If several buttons have handlers for the pressing of the same key, only one (apparently an arbitrary one) will receive the event. One way of using keyPress handlers is to provide keyboard shortcuts for buttons. In that case, it makes sense to associate one key with each button, and the handlers work as required in a natural way.

Keys and Clips

Clip event handlers for keyboard events work in a quite different way, which is more flexible but requires extra work in the handlers. There are two clip events, keyDown and keyUp, which are sent when a key (any key) is pressed or released, respectively. It is up to the handler to determine which key was pressed or released. A built-in object called Key provides some methods for finding out which key caused the event and a collection of constants for referring to certain commonly used keys, such as the left, right, up and down arrows.

Key.getASCII() returns the ASCII code for the character sent from the keyboard. This is not all that useful because when keys are used as controls you are usually more interested in the actual key or combination of keys that was pressed than in the conventional ASCII text interpretation. Key.getCode() returns the *virtual key code* for the key. Each key on a 'standard keyboard' is assigned its own virtual key code, which is just a number. Although there is some structure to the mapping, it is essentially arbitrary; you can find a list of all the codes in Appendix B of the *ActionScript Reference Guide*. To determine whether a particular key, such as the left arrow, has been pressed, you compare the value returned by Key.getCode() with its virtual key code. To avoid having to use actual numerical key codes, the Key object provides constants for some of the more commonly used keys. For example, Key.LEFT and Key.RIGHT are the codes for the left and right arrow keys.

The 'standard keyboard' for which these codes are defined is, in fact, a standard PC keyboard. Not all the keys on a Macintosh keyboard are included in the mapping, and all the named constants refer to PC keys: Key.ALT is the Alt key, but it is also the Macintosh Opt key, for example. Different keys are used for the same purpose on the two platforms: Cmd (which isn't even known to the Key object) plays the same role on the Mac as Ctl does on the PC, and Ctl is used for something different on the Mac. You need to be careful when using key codes, therefore, if you wish your movie to behave correctly and in the way users expect on both platforms.

Using Keys for Navigation

A widely understood use of the keyboard is for navigating among the elements of a form, or the cells of a spreadsheet. Suppose you are implementing some data entry system consisting of a set of input text fields arranged in a grid, rather like a spreadsheet. Flash does allow you to move between the text fields in a frame using the tab key, but the order in which tab takes you through the fields is arbitrary, and depends on the order in which the fields were added to the frame in Flash. Conventionally, tab should move on to the next cell, moving across a row and then on to the next, while shift-tab reverses this movement. Return (or enter) moves down a row within a column, and shift-return moves up. All of these wrap round when they reach the last cell. Furthermore, the right, left, down and up arrows are alternatives to tab, shift-tab, return and shift-return, in an obvious way.

To make these keys behave in the manner just described, it is first necessary to assign variables to each of the text fields, so that Selection.setFocus can be used to move between them. Following normal spreadsheet conventions, the first cell in the first row could be a1, the second cell in the first row b1, and so on, with the first cell in the second row being a2, followed by b2 and so on. It is easier to implement the desired cursor movements using a single numbering for the sequence of cells, so a mapping must be defined as an array that gives the name of the variable for each cell. This implies that we know how many rows and columns there are. Hence, if the fields were arranged in four columns of three, the following script should be attached to the frame containing the form.

```
var n_rows = 3, n_cols = 4;
var n_cells = n_rows * n_cols;
var cells = new Array(n_cells);
```

```
cells[0] = 'a1';
cells[1] = 'b1';
    similar assignments to cells[2] … cells[9]
cells[10] = 'c3';
cells[11] = 'd3';
```
(It is possible to compute the value of cells[i] for a number i using arithmetic and the character codes of the letters, if you prefer to do it that way.)

A variable current_cell will be used to remember the current cell's number. A function is defined to move the cursor to the corresponding cell, by passing its name to Selection.setFocus, and immediately called to ensure that the first frame is initially active.
```
var current_cell = 0;
function go_to_current_cell() {
    Selection.setFocus(cells[current_cell]);
}
go_to_current_cell();
```

Some simple arithmetic is used to determine which is the next cell to move to in each of the four possible directions.
```
function next_right() {
    current_cell = current_cell < n_cells - 1? current_cell + 1: 0;
    go_to_current_cell();
}
function next_left() {
    current_cell = current_cell > 0? current_cell - 1: n_cells - 1;
    go_to_current_cell();
}
function next_down() {
    var col = current_cell%n_cols, row = Math.Floor(current_cell/n_cols);
    var new_row = row < n_rows - 1? row + 1: 0;
    current_cell = col + new_row * n_cols;
    go_to_current_cell();
}
function next_up() {
    var col = current_cell%n_cols, row = Math.Floor(current_cell/n_cols);
    var new_row = row > 0 ? row - 1: n_rows - 1;
    current_cell = col + new_row * n_cols;
    go_to_current_cell();
```

}

With those definitions in place, the handler for the keyDown event becomes very simple. Since keyDown is a clip event, it is necessary to attach the handler to a clip. Any clip will do; an invisible dummy clip, for example, can be created just to have the following script attached to it.

```
onClipEvent (keyUp) {
    var the_key = Key.getCode();
    if (the_key == Key.RIGHT)
        _root.next_right();
    else if (the_key == Key.LEFT)
        _root.next_left();
    else if (the_key == Key.DOWN)
        _root.next_down();
    else if (the_key == Key.UP)
        _root.next_up();
    else if (the_key == Key.TAB)
        if (Key.isDown(Key.SHIFT))
            _root.next_left();
        else _root.next_right();
    else if (the_key == Key.ENTER)
        if (Key.isDown(Key.SHIFT))
            _root.next_up();
        else _root.next_down();
}
```

The cases corresponding to the key combinations shift-tab and shift-return use a method of the Key object that I have not yet described, although its name should be sufficient indication of what it does. If its argument is down when the event handler is invoked, Key.isDown returns true. This method can be used to determine whether a combination of keys has been pressed, as in this example.

Exercises and Experiments

1. If you did not use a variable such as is_set to record the state of a checkbox, write down the test you would have to use to determine whether or not a user had agreed to accept your email announcements by checking the box email_declined.
2. Implement a checkbox movie clip symbol without using a button. (You may find it helpful to look up the MovieClip.hitTest method in the *ActionScript Reference Guide*.)
3. An alternative to the way of implementing groups of radio buttons described in the text is to make each radio button a movie clip symbol with two frames, one for

selected and one for deselected, and just use a single frame for the group. When a deselected button is clicked, it should turn any other button that is selected off, using an appropriate method call, before changing state itself. Implement a group of four radio buttons in this way. (The advantage of this approach is that it generalizes to any number of buttons more readily, as you will see once you have read the next chapter.)

4. (a) A superficially more appealing way of closing a pop-up menu than the one described in the text is to construct a button symbol the size of the open menu and place it in the open frame of the Menu symbol so that it covers all the menu items, and then associate a `gotoAndStop("Closed")` action with this button, triggered by a `releaseOutside` event. Thus, there is no need for a separate Closer button. Why won't this work?
   (b) If a form included more than one pop-up menu, how would you arrange that whichever one of them was open was closed when the mouse button was released outside it?

5. Experiment with different shapes and placement of menu items. Consider what events are appropriate for making different designs of pop-up menu open. If possible, try out your ideas on users and see how they react. Do they know what behaviour to expect from your menus? Can they use them without being instructed?

6. (a) Implementing a scrolling list as a tweened animation is perhaps too elaborate. Re-implement the scroller using a one-frame movie for the items, with the scrolling being performed by updating its _y property.
   (b) Adapt your answer to part (a) to make a scrolling text field.
   (c) Adapt the scrolling list example described in the text to make a continuously scrolling text field.

7. What happens (and why) if one of the book covers in the direct manipulation example is dropped onto one of the others? What do you think should happen?

8. If an instance of the slider symbol is placed on the stage, rotated through 90° and stretched out to three times its original length, and no changes are made to any of the scripts, how far and it what direction will the box be able to travel? Explain your answer.

9. The scrollbars attached to document windows in conventional applications combine scrolling arrows, such as those used in the scrolling list example, and a scroll box, rather like the box in the slider. Implement such a scrollbar as a Flash movie, so that it can be used to control either vertical or horizontal scrolling of a large image in a window.

10. The built-in Mouse object has two methods, hide and show, which control the visibility of the cursor. Use these methods in conjunction with draggable clips to make the cursor change shape when it passes over different clips in a movie.

11. The left hand pane of Flash's Actions panel is an example of a type of input element, sometimes called *disclosure triangles* (although, as Flash shows, they do not have to be triangular). The Bookmarks pane in Acrobat Reader is another example. Generally, a set of links or other controls is displayed in condensed form as a set of headings; clicking on the icon next to a heading causes it to expand to display the full list for that particular heading. Clicking again closes it down. Implement this interface feature in Flash, (a) assuming that only one heading can be expanded at once, so that opening a new heading closes any that is currently open; and (b) assuming that more than one heading can be expanded at once. You do not have to deal with the possibility of headings nested within other headings, but you can if you like.
12. (a) Experiment with the interactions between clip events, button events and typing in input text fields when a key is pressed. Which has precedence?
    (b) Extend the spreadsheet example to be more realistic. Among the embellishments you might consider are the following: letting the user go to a specific cell, either by clicking in it, or by entering its name in a navigation box; providing the option of using the arrow keys for movement within the text being typed, with some modifier being employed when they are used for navigation between cells; letting the user assign keyboard shortcuts of their own choosing.
13. Implement a spreadsheet as a Flash movie, using whatever controls you consider appropriate. Don't necessarily try to copy the appearance of mainstream spreadsheets like Excel, but take advantage of the flexibility that Flash offers. (If you don't already know how to parse arithmetic expressions, you should probably restrict formulas to a single operator and its operands.)

5

abstraction

Reusing Scripts

Quite a lot is now understood about constructing conventional programs in ways that ensure they are correct and easy to maintain, from the trivial avoidance of go to statements and global variables, through the linguistic support of object-oriented languages to the fashionable use of design patterns. In comparison, constructing interactive systems around a timeline is methodologically unexplored territory. These are comparatively small systems, though, and a modicum of common sense is usually sufficient to avoid the worst pitfalls. Keeping things simple and avoiding cleverness is always the best approach.

One important principle — arguably the most important principle — of program construction is *abstraction*. A full account of abstraction would take an entire book, but for our present purposes it is sufficient to recognize it as the process that takes place whenever we take a complex idea or procedure and give it a name so that we can refer to it as if it was an indivisible entity, without worrying about its internal details. For example, *Scotland* is an abstraction, encompassing the diverse landscapes, history, people and culture of part of the British Isles — itself another abstraction. Abstraction is an absolute necessity of language: we wouldn't get very far if, instead of referring to 'Scotland', we could only point to the tangible individual elements that the abstraction encompasses. Matters are not quite so serious in programming, where it is possible to express any computation using the basic control structures enumerated in Chapter 3 and a set of primitive operations. The result is clumsy, though, and leads to a great deal of repetition. It also makes programs harder to understand, because any logical structure they may possess becomes submerged.

If the preceding discussion strikes you as itself being too abstract, consider the matter from a purely practical point of view. If you can take a computation, express it as a sequence of code in a programming or scripting language, and then give it a name so that, from then on, you can use the name instead of the sequence of code, it means that you can concentrate on that computation once, get it right, then forget about it and simply use it. And if, by some mischance, you get it wrong instead of right, you only have to mend it in one place. As a bonus your programs or scripts will be shorter, occupy less disk space and demand less bandwidth from networks.

Modern programming languages provide facilities for several different sorts of abstraction, including *functional* abstraction, where we give a name to a computation, and *data* abstraction — usually nowadays in the form of *objects* — where we give a name to a collection of values together with a set of operations that can be performed on them. ActionScript, too, provides these forms of abstraction, albeit in a relatively simple form appropriate to its character as a scripting language, instead of the more elaborate facilities supported by mainstream programming languages, such as C++ and Java.

Functions

We will see later that in ActionScript functional abstraction is tightly bound up with the way objects work, but, to begin with, it makes sense to consider functions on their own. The easiest way to think about a function is as a black box, containing some computation, with an input slot at one end and an output slot at the other. You feed values, or *arguments*, in at the input slot, computation happens inside the box (but this is an abstraction, so we don't need to worry about how that computation happens) and a result comes out of the output slot. (See Figure 5.1.) If you are an experienced programmer, you will recognize that defining a function or subroutine is a process of functional abstraction, which lets you make new functions that behave in accordance with this model. (If you are a mathematician, you will be familiar with a different definition of function. This can be reconciled with the programmer's view, but it may be easier just to think of functional abstraction and set-theoretic functions as related but different concepts.)

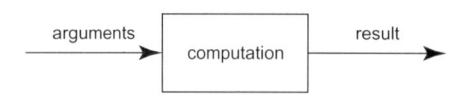

Figure 5.1 *Functional abstraction.*

In earlier chapters, you saw scripts which, to the experienced programmer, will have been crying out for abstraction. For example, on page 53 the following script was used to compute the commission on a given amount:

var commission = amount * 0.1;

if (commission < 10)

    payment = 0;

reusing scripts

```
else
    payment = commission;
```

If you frequently need to perform this computation, you would have to cut and paste this script wherever it was needed. If, however, it could be turned into an abstraction, you could just call it rake_off, say, and then use its name, as rake_off(11450) or rake_off(the_price), for example. (You have already seen a similar use of abstraction in the built-in methods and functions used in previous chapters.)

A suitable definition of such an abstraction based on the code just shown would look like this:

```
function rake_off(amount) {
    var payment;
    var commission = amount * 0.1;
    if (commission < 10)
        payment = 0;
    else
        payment = commission;
    return payment;
}
```

The definition is introduced by the reserved word function, which identifies what follows as a function definition. Next comes the name of the function, in this case rake_off. Following this, in brackets, is an identifier, which is sometimes called a *formal parameter* of the function. When the abstraction is used, the value supplied as its argument is assigned to the formal parameter. Inside the function, it is used just like any other variable.

The code enclosed between curly brackets (which are required here) specifies the computation that the function performs. It is called the *function body*. As you can see, it is quite like the original code fragment. The difference is that the value for the formal parameter amount is supplied by the argument when the function is used (or *called*, as we usually say), whereas on page 53, I had to assume that a value had been assigned to it somewhere else. The other difference between the function body and the original script is that I have declared payment, and after I have assigned the result to it, I have used it as the value of the return statement at the end of the function body. This value will be the result of the abstraction (the value that comes out of the output slot).

When I write rake_off(11450), the body of the function is executed, with the formal parameter amount set to 11450. At the end of the computation, payment will hold the

value 1145, which is returned as the value of the function call. A function call can be used as part of an expression, wherever any other value can be used. For example,
var year_total = 12*rake_off(11450);
assigns twelve commissions on an amount of 11450 to year_total.

Recall that, in Chapter 3, I showed several different variations on the code for computing the commission. Suppose that I looked at these and realized that I could make my definition of rake_off substantially neater, by changing it like this:
function rake_off(amount) {
    var commission = amount * 0.1;
    return commission < 10? 0: commission;
}
I could still use the function in exactly the same way; the assignment shown earlier would behave just as it always did, because rake_off is an abstraction, so what happens inside it doesn't matter when it is used. All that matters is the relationship between its argument and the result it computes.

When you write a function in the spirit of abstraction, you do not know where it might be used. As we will see shortly, you can organize your functions into libraries that might be used in many different Flash movies, possibly by people you have never met. This means that you need to think carefully about any assumptions that your code embodies about the arguments, and arrange to cope with any any values that do not conform to them — or, if that does not seem possible, at least to document the assumptions clearly. For example, the rake_off function works on the assumption that its argument is a number. What if it isn't? In this case, the value NaN (not a number) will propagate through the arithmetic and be passed back as the result, which is probably the correct thing to do, but the fact ought to be documented. A comment at the head of the function definition is the conventional place for such documentation.

A second example based on code you have already seen should help consolidate the idea of functional abstraction. The following code was used in Chapter 4 to format an amount of money:
var i = String(Math.floor(repayment));
var f = Math.round((100*repayment)%100);
f = f < 10? "0" + f: String(f);
repayment = i + "." + f;
Again, this cries out to be made into an abstraction; it is an operation that any movie dealing with monetary quantities might well use several times. If I just wrap it up in a function definition, with repayment replaced by a formal parameter name, it will go

wrong if it is passed a negative argument, or something that is not a number, or an infinite number. The following function definition attempts to deal with these cases.

```
function format_fp(n) {
    if (isNaN(n) || !isFinite(n)) return n;
    var sign = "";
    if (n < 0) {
        sign = "-";
        n = -n;
    }
    var whole_part = String(Math.floor(n));
    var fraction = Math.round((n*100)%100);
    var fraction_part = String(fraction);
    if (fraction < 10) fraction_part = '0' + fraction_part;
    return sign + whole_part + '.' + fraction_part;
}
```

The first thing to notice is that the function's name, format_fp, reflects what it actually does, which is format any floating point number, not just an amount of money. Although a function's name is irrelevant to ActionScript (you could call this function invert_matrix and it would still format floating point numbers), it helps people reading your scripts if you use names that are somewhat meaningful. The function begins by dealing with difficult arguments: if the argument is not a number or is infinite, it is just passed straight back to the caller. This is not an ideal solution (what could be?) but is better than letting the following code mangle the argument. Next, negative arguments are dealt with. My strategy here is not to try and make the arithmetic work correctly for numbers less than zero, but to negate the argument so I only have to think about positive arithmetic. Of course, I need to remember I have done so, in order to put a minus sign in front of the formatted string when I have finished. I do this by using the variable sign to remember what sign to insert: originally, it is the empty string, but if I have a negative argument, I reset it to the minus sign.

The next four lines are a slightly cleaned up version of the original code fragment. Finally, the string that was originally assigned to repayment is returned as the function's result, except that the sign, remembered previously, is inserted in front of it. The effect of the original code in the repayment calculator is now achieved by
repayment = format_fp(repayment);

If you have caught the spirit of abstraction, you will look at format_fp and ask yourself what is special about two places after the decimal point. Well, that's how money usually works, but in other applications we may well want to choose a different number. Just as format_fp generalized the original code fragment, from a script that formatted one particular number to a function that formatted any number supplied as an argument, we can generalize it in its turn, from a function that formats its argument to two places to one that formats its first argument to any number of places supplied as a second argument.

As a general rule, every time you abstract, you need to think about more possibilities. Now that we have two arguments, we need to consider special cases for both: the number of places supplied might be negative, infinite or not a number; it may be zero, which should be treated as a special case. As well as dealing with these new possibilities, we still have to deal correctly with the possible anomalous values for the number to be formatted that we met in the less general function. In addition, generalizing the algorithm requires additional computation. Whereas, if we know that we only need two places after the decimal point, we know that we must multiply by 100, if the number of places is passed as an argument, we must use the argument value to work out the appropriate multiplier. Similarly, previously we knew that we had to insert an extra zero after the point if and only if the fraction part was less than 10; now we need to perform some rather sordid computation to insert the appropriate number of leading zeros. You should be able to recognize the original algorithm beneath the generalization.

```
function format_float(n, i) {
    if (i < 0 || isNaN(n) || !isFinite(n)) return String(n);
    var sign = '';
    if (n < 0) {
        sign = '-';
        n = -n;
    }
    var whole_part = String(Math.floor(n));
    if (i == 0) return sign + whole_part;
    var multiplier = 1;
    for (var j = 0; j < i; ++j) {
        multiplier *= 10;
        n *= 10;
    }
    var fraction = Math.round(n%multiplier);
    var fraction_part = String(fraction);
    j = 0;
    multiplier /= 10;
    while (j < i - 1 && Math.floor(fraction/multiplier) == 0) {
```

```
        fraction_part = '0' + fraction_part;
        multiplier /= 10;
        ++j;
    }
    return sign + whole_part + '.' + fraction_part;
}
```
The task of formatting a number with two places after the decimal point now reveals itself as a special case of the general task this more abstract function performs, hence format_fp can be redefined:
```
function format_fp(n) {
    return format_float(n, 2);
}
```

As the preceding example shows, a function can take more than one argument — it can take any number of them, including zero. In that case, the brackets around the (non-existent) formal parameter in the function definition, and around the argument in a call are still required. Functions with no arguments are most often seen in the context of objects, which will be described later in this chapter.

Details

It is time to clarify some aspects of functions in ActionScript that have been left vague so far. Where are functions defined? They can only be defined as part of a script, so their definitions will be found in the same places as scripts: attached to frames or in event handlers. A function can be called before it is defined within a script (although it is usually considered better style to declare things before you use them, if this is possible). If you declare two or more functions with the same name, the latest definition is used. A function may also be called from another script, for example a script attached to different frame, provided that the frame in which it is defined has been loaded. (You can use the _framesloaded property to determine this, as shown in Chapter 3.) Functions defined in other movie clips can be accessed using dot notation, like movie clip methods.

Variables declared inside a function using var are *local* to the function. That is, they cannot be accessed outside the function body. In contrast, variables declared in a script but outside the body of a function are called *global* variables, and they can be accessed anywhere in the same movie or clip (or in other clips using dot notation). Unlike global variables declared in a movie clip, there is no way at all to get at a local variable from outside the body of the function in which it is declared. Local variables must be declared explicitly. If you just use a variable's name inside the body of a function, without declaring it first, it is taken to refer to a global variable of that name; if one has not been declared, it is created. Using global variables is a common source of program errors. (This is not the place to justify that statement, but the fact is well established.) Forgetting to declare a local variable and accessing a global by mistake will also lead to obscure errors, which will not be diagnosed by a syntax check. In general, therefore, it is good practice to make a habit of declaring all variables.

Although a function's definition includes a list of formal parameter names, you do not have to supply argument values for every one: arguments are assigned to formal parameters in the order they occur. Any formal parameters that do not receive values will be undefined in the body of the function. You can pass more arguments than there are formal parameters — the supernumerary ones are ignored.

Function arguments do not have to be numbers, of course. Exercises 1 and 2 invite you to write some functions that operate on strings. You can also write Boolean functions, though it is more common to see functions return Boolean values than take them as arguments. Additionally, you can pass arrays to functions. This works in a slightly different way from other types of argument.

Recall from Chapter 3 that when you assign an array, it is not copied, only a reference to it is assigned, creating a synonym. In the same way, when you pass an array to a function, only a reference to it is assigned to the corresponding formal parameter. This means that any assignments to elements of the array inside the function body will update the array passed as the argument from outside. A trivial example will illustrate this.

```
function add1(a) {
    for (var i = 0; i < a.length; ++i)
        ++a[i];
}
var b = new Array();
for (var j = 0; j < b.length; ++j)
    b[j] = -j;
```
At this point, b contains the sequence 0...-9.
```
add1(b);
```
Now, b contains the sequence 1...-8.

There is no way to write a function in ActionScript that changes the values of variables holding numbers, strings or Booleans by assigning to its formal parameters. (In the jargon, these types are always passed *by value*.) Only arrays and objects that are passed as references can be updated in this way. If you really feel you must update a variable defined outside a function from within it, you must access it as a global.

Higher Order Functions

From the viewpoint of abstraction, possibly the most interesting thing you can pass as an argument to a function is another function. Functions that take other functions as their arguments are often called *higher order* functions, and can be used to abstract frequently encountered patterns of computation. The technique is possibly *too* abstract for the tasks to which ActionScript is typically put, so I will confine myself to a simple example. If you find the technique compelling, you can find out more from any book on 'functional programming'.

I noted in Chapter 3 that loops that access every element of an array all have headers of the same form. Many of them also have similar loop bodies, that compute a new value for each element from the old value; that is, the new value is a function of the old. This pattern can readily be captured in a higher order function that takes as its arguments an array and a function, and loops through the array computing a new value for each element by applying the function to its old value.

```
function map(f, a) {
    for (var i = 0; i < a.length; ++i)
        a[i] = f(a[i]);
}
```

By defining various small functions and passing them to map, many simple operations can be applied to the elements of an array. For example,

```
function zero() {
    return 0;
}

function add1(x) {
    return x + 1;
}
function double(x) {
    return 2*x;
}

map(zero, an_array);
```

All the elements are set to zero.
```
map(add1, an_array);
map(add1, an_array);
```

```
map(double, an_array);
```
At the end of this sequence, all the elements are set to four.

Function Values

Notice that in a call like map(double, an_array), two identifiers are used as the arguments. We know that an_array is the name of a location that holds a reference to an array. Although double has been defined ina different way, it is not really any different. It too is the name of a location that holds a value, in this case the value is a function. In ActionScript, unlike some languages, this value can be treated like any other value held in a location. We know it can be passed as an argument to another function; it can also be assigned to a variable:
```
var twice = double;
```
creates a synonym for double. The name twice can now be used in place of double. For example, after the calls shown above,
```
map(twice, an_array);
```
will set all the array's elements to eight.

There are no operators that take functions as their operands, so all you can do with a function is call it, pass it to another function, or assign it. We will see in the next section that assigning functions is more than an entertaining curiosity. As well as assigning a function that has been defined in the way described earlier, we can also create *anonymous* functions, and assign them or pass them as arguments. If you simply leave out the function's name in a function definition, you have an expression whose value is the function being defined. Thus,
```
function(x) { return 2*x;}
```
is an expression whose value is the same function as double. You can pass this expression to a function like map, or assign it to a variable. In fact, the definition
```
function double(x) {
      return 2*x;
}
```
is precisely equivalent to
```
var double = function(x) { return 2*x;};
```

Perl programmers and functional programming experts should note that anonymous functions in ActionScript (and ECMAScript, this isn't a vagary of Flash alone) are not closures. That is, the following script
```
var x = "global";
function f() {
    var x = "local";
```

```
        return function() { trace("x is " + x) }
}
f()();
```
produces the output

x is global

Shame.

Recursion

Before moving on from the subject of functions, it is worth pointing out that ActionScript's functions can be *recursive*. That is, it is possible to call a function from inside its own body. If you are familiar with the idea, recursion will seem natural and expected; if not, it may sound as if it would lead to an endless regression. This is not the case (unless you get it wrong), and recursion allows you to produce elegant functions to perform tasks that would otherwise require awkward loops.

As an example, consider another way of formatting numbers. Usually, in manuscript, large numbers are broken into groups of three digits, separated (in English-speaking countries) by commas, as in 1,500,002. Computers rarely insert these commas, but it is easy to write a function that will take an integer as its argument and produce a string correctly formatted with commas between every three digits.

The trick in writing recursive functions is to start out assuming you have solved the problem for arguments less than a certain size, and then see how to extend it to larger arguments. You also have to identify any special cases that can be dealt with without recourse to your general algorithm. These are important, because they stop the recursion going on forever. Here, the special case is that numbers less than 1000 need no commas. If we have a number greater than 1000, it has more than three digits. If we assume that we can correctly format a number with three digits less than our argument, then we can format this argument by first formatting everything but the last three digits, inserting a comma, and then formatting the last three digits. This reasoning leads to the following function:

```
function put_commas(n) {
        return n < 1000? String(n):
                put_commas(Math.floor(n/1000)) + ',' + three_digits(n%1000);
}
```

The first case, n < 1000 needs no action except for converting the number to a string. If n >= 1000, following the scheme just outlined, everything to the left of the last three digits is passed recursively to put_commas, in the faith that it can deal with it. (Dividing by 1000 and taking the floor extracts the necessary digits.) To deal with all of n, this value is concatenated with a comma and the rest of the digits. To avoid problems with leading zeros, I need a function three_digits that will take a number less than 1000 and turn it into a string of length three, inserting leading zeros if necessary. This is trivially defined:

```
function three_digits(n) {
    return n < 10? '00'+String(n):
         n < 100? '0' + String(n): String(n);
}
```

You should be able to see that, although put_commas calls itself, it will only do so a finite number of times, because each time it does so, the argument is smaller, so that eventually the special case is bound to arise and the recursion will stop, and results will start propagating back through the chain of recursive calls to be built up into the required string.

All of that reasoning is sound, but the function is still not complete, because it cannot cope with negative arguments, or any argument that is not an integer. It would not be sensible to try and deal with these cases in the recursive function — they only occur when it is first called, and any code that handled them would be redundant once the recursion got under way. The best way is to define an extra function that checks the argument before starting off the recursion, like this:

```
function insert_commas(n) {
    if (isNan(n) || !isFinite(n) || Math.floor(n) != n)
        return "***"      // Have you got a better idea?
    return n >= 0? put_commas(n): '-' + put_commas(-n);
}
```

This pattern of using a function to stand in front of a recursive function and deal with the raw arguments is a useful one that can often simplify the structure of a script.

Objects

Object-oriented programming has established itself as the method of choice for constructing large programs out of reusable components. Although the concept is simple and intuitive, the associated terminology can be intimidating if you are not used to it. It is worth mastering the jargon because the benefits of using objects can be considerable — in any case, objects are unavoidable in ActionScript, since movie clips are objects.[1]

---

1. More or less... see Chapter 6.

The most problematical term is *object-oriented* itself. The vogue for objects has led to its being applied in different contexts, with subtly (and not so subtly) different meanings. Even in the limited realm of programming, there are at least two different legitimate ways of understanding the term — either as a metaphor for a certain kind of program organization or as a syntactical realization of ideas about data types derived from abstract algebra. Further confusion is added by the tendency to equate the abstract concept of objects with their implementation in the dominant programming language of the day — once C++, now Java.

I have no intention of offering a definition of object-oriented programming; enough nonsense has been written on the subject already. Instead, I will confine myself to describing the object-oriented features of ActionScript, pointing out where they differ from mainstream ideas that you may have come across elsewhere.

Constructors

In ActionScript, the central concept is the *object*, which is no more than a collection of *methods* (operations) and *properties* (data). As we have seen in previous chapters in the case of movie clips and other built-in objects, properties and methods can be accessed through an object, using the dot notation. There is no mechanism for protecting data from access from outside the object — the idea that objects are responsible for their own data can only be implemented by a programming discipline in ActionScript, the language will not enforce it. Although a set of objects may share common behaviour, having the same methods and properties, as, for example, all movie clips do, there is no explicit concept of a *class*, and no syntax for defining classes separately from objects. Instead, common behaviour is achieved by creating a set of objects in the same way, using a *constructor*, which is a function that is called in a special way to create an object. If K is a constructor, the expression new K() returns an object that has been initialized by K, which will assign it some methods and properties. Normally, you would immediately assign the resulting object to a variable. Since any object that is created this way will have the same methods and properties, it makes sense to say that K constructs objects belonging to the K class. I have shown K being called without arguments, but, apart from the way it is used, a constructor is just a function, so it can take arguments. Typically, these provide initial values for the object being constructed.

To clarify this, consider a simple example. Scripts in Flash movies often have to manipulate the coordinates of movie clips and other graphic entities. Instead of just treating *x* and *y* values as numbers, it would make more sense to work with objects that represented points in two-dimensional space. Some of the operations you might want to perform on such points would include moving a point down or to the right by a

certain number of pixels, moving it to the coordinates of another point, or computing its distance from another point. These operations could be implemented as methods: move_down, move_right, move_to and distance_to. The first two of these take a number as their argument, the other two take a point. To create points, the constructor Point is used; it takes an initial *x* and *y* value as its arguments. Points can be created and used in the following way:
var p = new Point(1, 10);
p.move_down(15);
p.move_right(50);
The point p is now at (51, 25).
var q = new Point(0, 0);
p.move_to(q);
Now it is at (0, 0).
var r = new Point(3, 4);
The expression p.distance_to(r) has the value 5, while p.distance_to(q) is zero. A Point is an abstraction corresponding to the geometrical idea of a point.

The constructor is the means by which this is all brought about. Syntactically, a constructor is just a function — some constructors can even be called like ordinary functions. Normally, though, a constructor is designed to be called indirectly, using a new expression, as in the examples above. When it is used this way, a brand new empty object is first created, then the constructor is called with an extra, undeclared, parameter, this, holding a reference to this new object. When a method is called, it too receives this as an extra argument, referring to the object used to call the method, so, for instance, in the call p.move_right(50), this refers to p inside the body of the move_right method. (Beware, if you are used to C++ or Java: this cannot be omitted when you access properties of the current object.[1]) In all other respects, methods, like constructors, are just ordinary functions. The constructor initializes the object by assigning values to the properties of this. Some of these values may be functions, which become the methods of the newly created object: methods are just properties whose values are functions. Constructors should not include a return statement. The constructed object is returned automatically when new is used.

A possible definition of the Point constructor is as follows:
function Point(xval, yval) {
    this.xcoord = xval;
    this.ycoord = yval;

---

1. Except sometimes if the current object is a movie clip. MovieClip objects are treated specially. See Chapter 6.

objects

```
// methods
    this.move_down = function(dy) { this.yval += dy; };
    this.move_right = function(dx) { this.xval += dx; };
    this.move_to = function(p) {
                    this.xval = p.xval;
                    this.yval = p.yval;
                };
    this.distance_to = function(p) {
                    return Math.sqrt((this.xcoord - p.xcoord)*
                                    (this.xcoord - p.xcoord) +
                            (this.ycoord - p.ycoord)*(this.ycoord - p.ycoord));
                };
}
```

The properties xcoord and ycoord remember the point's coordinates, so the constructor sets them to its arguments to establish the initial position. The methods are all anonymous functions (simply to avoid having to declare them anywhere) that are assigned to the corresponding property of the object. Note that properties do not have to be declared: they are created just by having values assigned to them. (In fact, you can add new properties to an object after it has been created.) Notice how this is used in the constructor and the methods, and how the constructor does not return anything explicitly.

Prototypes

The constructor shown above works, but it is inefficient, in that every object ends up with a reference to each of the methods. ActionScript provides a way of sharing methods (and properties) between objects created by the same constructor. The constructor itself has a property prototype, which holds a reference to an object. When the constructor is called, the value of its prototype is assigned to a property called __proto__ (there are two underline characters at each end of the name) of the object being initialized. Whenever a method is called through an object, if it cannot be found among the object's properties, it is sought among those of its __proto__ property. Thus, if methods are assigned to a constructor's prototype property, they will be available through all objects that are created by it. Thus, a better way of creating points would be like this:

```
function Point(xval, yval) {
    this.xcoord = xval;
    this.ycoord = yval;
}
Point.prototype.move_down = function(dy) { this.ycoord += dy; };
```

```
Point.prototype.move_right = function(dx) { this.xcoord += dx; };
```
etc.

Slightly confusingly, we say that the constructor's prototype property provides the values for the constructed object's prototype — the value of its __proto__ property. Any properties of the prototype are shared between all objects initialized by the same constructor. This includes data as well as methods, which provides a mechanism for defining values that are common to all objects of the same class. This can occasionally be useful, for example, if you need to keep a count of how many objects of a class have been constructed, and is commonly used to define constants that are specific to the class, and default values for properties. Generally, though, it is most useful for each object to have its own data. This is stored in its own properties, which are initialized by the constructor, like xcoord and ycoord. Figure 5.2 illustrates the relationships between a Point object, its prototype, and its constructor's prototype.

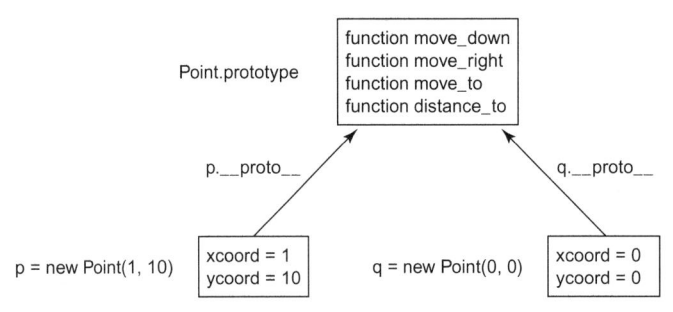

Figure 5.2 *Objects and prototypes.*

How can a constructor, which is a function, have a property like prototype? Aren't objects the things that have properties? The simple answer is that functions are objects, and in ECMAScript that is the true answer. There is a Function constructor, complete with its own prototype property, that provides some useful extra properties to all functions. In ActionScript, as it stands at the release of Flash 5.0, functions are not fully implemented as objects, and it is best to steer clear of any cleverness that involves function objects. The prototype property is simulated to make constructors behave in the way I have just described, though.

Using Objects

All this may seem a long way removed from Flash movies, so it is time for an example that uses objects within a movie. It also demonstrates a more sophisticated way of using arrays.

The example is a variation on the random movie player. Instead of playing movies at random, a set of buttons is provided, so that users can choose a movie to play, like a jukebox. To make it more like a jukebox, if a button is clicked while a movie is playing, the new selection is to be queued up and played when the current one has finished. Any other selections that are made while a movie is playing should join the queue, to be played in their turn when all the ones ahead of them have been played. This might be an appropriate organization for a kiosk presentation, where members of the public could come and select a movie they would like to see.

The movie has three frames: the first is a dummy, which has a script containing several definitions and some initialization code attached to it. The remaining two frames form a tight loop, over which the selected movie is played. Graphically, these two frames contain a row of buttons, one for each movie. These are on a layer of their own, with a keyframe in the first frame extended to the second. One of the functions defined in the first frame is called play_or_queue_up, and it does what it says: if there is no movie presently playing, it plays the one that has just been selected, otherwise it adds it to the queue. This function is called whenever a user clicks on a button. The script attached to each button calls this function with a suitable argument. For example, the first button's script is as follows:

```
on (release) {
    play_or_queue_up(0);
}
```

and the others differ only in the value passed as the argument.

The logic of play_or_queue_up is relatively simple: it adds its argument to the queue and then, if there is no movie playing, it loads the movie corresponding to the first element in the queue. In the degenerate case of no movie playing and nothing in the queue, this will be the value that was just queued up. At all times, it will be the case that if a movie is playing the value at the head of the queue will be the corresponding number. A flag will be used to remember whether a movie is playing. It must be set to false in the script attached to the first frame of the main movie.

```
var playing = false;
```

This script also sets up an array of URLs, in exactly the same way as the corresponding script in the random player in Chapter 3.

It is time to be more specific about this 'queue' that is going to be used in this movie. A queue is a data structure that is often used in programming. Its name derives from its behaviour, which resembles a line of people waiting to use a cash machine: people join it at the end and leave it to get their cash out from the front. The behaviour is usually summarized in the phrase 'first in, first out'. It is normal to describe this behaviour in terms of four operations: enqueue, which takes an argument and adds it to the end of the queue, dequeue, which removes the first element from the front of the queue, head, which returns the value of the first element, without dequeueing it, and empty, which returns true or false, depending on whether or not there are any elements in the queue.

A queue can be implemented as an object having those four operations as methods. At this point, it doesn't matter how they are implemented, so long as they are available as methods. If we know they are there, we can write the script for play_or_queue_up. Assuming that an object that implements the queue methods has been created with the name waiting, the following script implements the logic described above.

```
function play_or_queue_up(n) {
    waiting.enqueue(n);
    if (!playing) {
        loadMovie(url[waiting.head()], 1);
        playing = true;
    }
}
```

First, the argument is added to the queue. The script then tests the playing flag to see whether a movie is presently playing. If it is, the work is done. Otherwise, the head of the queue is obtained, and used to index the array of URLs to load the movie to play next into level 1. The flag is reset to reflect the fact that a movie is now playing.

When a movie finishes, we will want to play the next one in the queue, if there is one. A script attached to the final frame of the main movie determines whether or not the movie on level 1 has finished by seeing whether its current frame is equal to its final frame. If there is a movie playing and this condition is satisfied, a function called next is called to play the next movie. The playhead is sent back to the previous frame (labelled loop), because we need to perform this check repeatedly, and it is only by looping between two frames that we can force the script to be executed over and over again. (For this to work, it is important that each movie to be loaded has a stop attached to its final frame to prevent it looping, otherwise the final frame might be missed since the test is only carried out in alternate frames.)

```
if (playing && _level1._currentframe == _level1._totalframes)
    next();
gotoAndPlay ("loop");
```

The function next is defined in the first frame of the main movie. It, too, is implemented using the functions provided by the queue.

```
function next() {
    waiting.dequeue();
    if (!waiting.is_empty())
        loadMovie(url[waiting.head()], 1);
    else
        playing = false;
}
```

First it throws away the first element of the queue, which corresponds to the movie that has just finished. Next it finds out whether the queue is empty. If it isn't, there must be at least one movie waiting to be played, so the head of the queue is used to find a URL, as before. Since a movie has just stopped, playing will be true, and should be left that way. On the other hand, if the queue was empty, it must be set to false, since there is no movie to play. If that happens, next time play_or_queue_up is called, the new selection will immediately play, as required.

The queue as it has been used so far is an example of what is technically known as an *abstract data type*. It is abstract because, like a function, it can be treated as a black box that is entirely defined by its behaviour, irrespective of its inner workings. Now, however, it is necessary to implement it as an object using some real (or 'concrete') data structure. The only such structure we have available is the array, and there is a well-known technique for using arrays to provide queues. The idea is to store the elements of the queue in consecutive elements of an array, which will be a property of the queue object, and to maintain two properties, which will be called first and last to hold the index of the first element of the queue, if there is one, and of the first free array element after the last, respectively (see Figure 5.3). The first value in the array has index zero, so first and last are both initially set to zero. When a value is added to the queue, it is stored in the array element indexed by last, to which one is then added. The head of the queue is always at the index stored in first, and is removed by adding one to first. Thus, as elements are added and removed from the queue, the first index follows last down the array.

If the array is of finite size, last will eventually drop off the end. In theory, this doesn't matter in ActionScript, because new array elements can always be manufactured. However, this is wasteful, so we will insist that the array cannot grow beyond a finite size, which will be passed as an argument to the constructor and stored in a property called max_elements. Some strategy is needed to deal with the possibility that does now arise of the value of last exceeding this maximum. Since elements are usually being removed from the front of the queue as well as being added to the end, the chances are that, by the time last has become too large, first will be greater than zero — the first

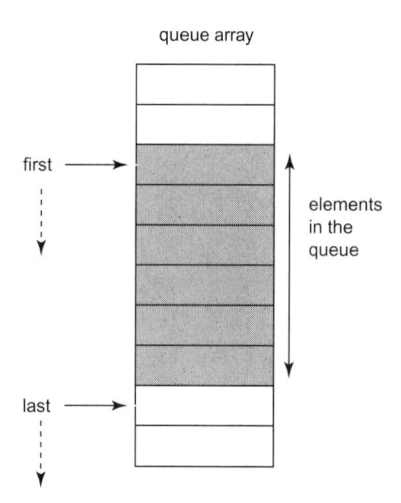

Figure 5.3 Implementing a queue using an array.

element of the array is available for reuse. Therefore, if last would become greater than max_elements, it is reset to zero. It is then possible for first to exceed the maximum in its turn, and the same strategy can be adopted. The two pointers now chase each other round, as it were in a circle.

It is still possible that an attempt will be made to queue up more than max_elements-1 values. (Imagine a small child mindlessly clicking on all the buttons in our kiosk presentation.) You should satisfy yourself that, if that happens, last will become equal to first. In that case, no more items should be added to the queue. In the jukebox, it is adequate to just do nothing if an attempt is made to add an element to a full queue, losing some selections. If this is done, so the queue is never allowed to fill up, the only time that first will be equal to last is when the queue is empty, which provides a simple implementation of the remaining queue operation.

We are now in a position to implement a queue as an object. The constructor merely initializes the properties:

```
function Queue(n) {
    this.max_elements = n;
    this.the_queue = new Array(n);
    this.first = this.last = 0;
}
```

The queue methods will be assigned as properties of Queue.prototype. Although this example only needs a single queue, the structure is a generally useful one, so it should be made into a class. We will see later in the chapter how the class definition can be made available to other movies.

Because of the way the array works as a queue, is_empty is very simple.
Queue.prototype.is_empty = function() { return this.first == this.last; };
So too is that for head. It simply obtains the value of the element of the array the_queue indexed by first.
Queue.prototype.head = function() { return this.the_queue[this.first]; }
Notice, though, that this assumes that the queue is not empty. If it is, the result will be a meaningless value. Arguably, the method ought first to test whether there are any elements in the queue, but it is not clear what to do if the test fails. Here, I will adopt the alternative strategy of asserting that the queue must not be empty when head is called, and leave it to the caller to ensure that this assertion is true. If the queue object was to be used in real applications, this assertion would be incorporated in the documentation explaining how to use it. The same assertion must apply to the dequeue operation, which is simple in the absence of any checks. It just adds one to first, wrapping it round to zero if it falls off the end of the array.
Queue.prototype.dequeue = function() { this.first = (this.first + 1)
%this.max_elements; }
The remainder (%) operation provides a slick method of performing the wrapping.

The enqueue operation is the most complex, but the complexity is caused entirely by the need to check whether the queue is about to overflow. It does not seem reasonable to pass the responsibility for this back to the caller, although this could be done by adding an is_full operation (see Exercise 7).

Since last always holds the index of the first free array element beyond the end of the list, it is safe to begin by storing the value being enqueued there. (The way this queue works, there is always one free slot in the array, even when the queue is full.)
Queue.prototype.enqueue = function(x) {
    this.the_queue[this.last] = x;
It may turn out that when last is incremented it catches up with first because there wasn't really room for a new element, so the increment will be done tentatively at first, using a different variable, new_last. This is set to one more than last, and then wrapped round if necessary, just like first was in dequeue.
    var new_last = (this.last + 1)%this.max_elements;
Next, new_last is compared with first. If they are different, the queue is not full, so the value of new_last can be assigned to last, confirming the operation. If the queue is full, last is left as it was originally — the operation fails silently, but no damage is done. Next

time a value is enqueued it will overwrite the value that was just stored, but this could never have been accessed by any queue operation.
```
    if (new_last != this.first) this.last = new_last;
}
```

The definitions of Queue and its methods are placed in the script attached to the first frame of the movie. All that remains is to create the queue:
```
var waiting = new Queue(10);
```
The value of ten is chosen arbitrarily. In a real application, you would analyse the way the object was used in order to decide upon a sensible number of elements.

Objects as Associative Arrays

When dot notation is used to access methods and properties of objects, the last component will be the actual name of a method or property. This makes it impossible to choose a particular property dynamically by using an expression. This is in contrast to arrays, where indices are usually computed dynamically. Much of the time, this doesn't matter — you generally know which property or method you want to access, or can at least use a conditional statement to access one of several depending on some computation. Sometimes, though, you really need to be able to choose a property dynamically, especially since the collection of properties of an object in ActionScript can vary dynamically.

Suppose, for example, you wanted to reverse the mapping from numbers to the abbreviated names of months that was implemented using an array in Chapter 3. You could, if you know how, do this by constructing a hash or other table in an array, but it is easier to define an object, like this:
```
function Months() {
    this.Jan = 0;
    this.Feb = 1;
    this.Mar = 2;
        .
        .
        .
    this.Dec = 11;
}
var m = new Months();
```
Now, m.Feb is 1, and so on. However, if you want to obtain the number of some month that is stored in a variable, my_month, there is no way to write an expression in dot

notation that will do this. You could write a twelve-way conditional branch, but there is an easier way.

ActionScript lets you access the properties and methods of an object using the same notation with square brackets that is used for indexing arrays. In this notation, the index is a *string* containing the name of a property. Thus, m["Feb"] is the same as m.Feb. When you use this indexing notation, though, the index can be any expression that evaluates to a string, so if my_month contains a string (perhaps obtained from a text field in a form), m[my_month] gives the corresponding number (or undefined if the string does not correspond to a property of m). Entities that behave in this way — like arrays that can be indexed by strings instead of numbers — are often called *associative arrays*. In fact, it is clear that ActionScript objects are actually implemented as associative arrays, which goes a long way to explaining their behaviour.

A special form of loop is provided for accessing each of the properties and methods belonging to an object in turn. It has the form
for (var *identifier* in *object*) *loop body*
The effect is to execute the loop body once for each property of the object, with the loop variable holding a string containing the property's name, which can be used as an index to access its value. (You don't really have to declare the loop variable, but I like to.) The following loop, which can be useful for debugging purposes, traces the values of all of an object's properties, in this case, those of my associative array of months, m:
for (var p in m)
    trace("m." + p + " = " + m[p])
The loop does not access the properties in any particular order.

Inheritance

Objects provide neat abstractions of data, but that's only part of the allure of object-oriented programming. The rest comes from the ability to reuse, extend and refine objects, using the mechanism of *inheritance*. It is a moot point whether or not there is much use for inheritance in the present state of Flash scripting. It presupposes large complex programs, or a base of generally useful classes (or objects) that can be adapted for specific purposes and shared between programmers. This all implies a mature programming culture, which, at the time of writing, Flash does not really possess. Most Flash scripts are relatively short and simple, written by a single person. Any complex computation is most often performed by programs running on remote servers, written using different technology. (This aspect of Flash programming will be described in Chapter 7.) However, inheritance is a powerful technique that is worth knowing about,

Inheritance and Prototypes

The basis for inheritance in ActionScript is the __proto__ property, which every object possesses. Earlier, I explained how this property allows objects to be grouped into classes, by adding common methods to their __proto__ properties, via the constructor's prototype. If a method or property cannot be found in an object, it is looked for in its prototype. Previously, an empty prototype was used. If, however, an object that has been constructed by some constructor, Base say, is assigned to the prototype property of a constructor Derived, all the methods of the Base object will become available to Derived objects, in addition to any extra ones that are added to Derived.prototype (see Figure 5.4). We say that the methods of Base are *inherited* by Derived. The names chosen for the classes in this illustration also reflect common terminology: a class that inherits methods is said to be *derived* from a *base class*. Although the terms originate in class-based object-oriented languages, they still make sense in ActionScript, if you understand a 'class' to be a set of objects constructed by the same constructor.

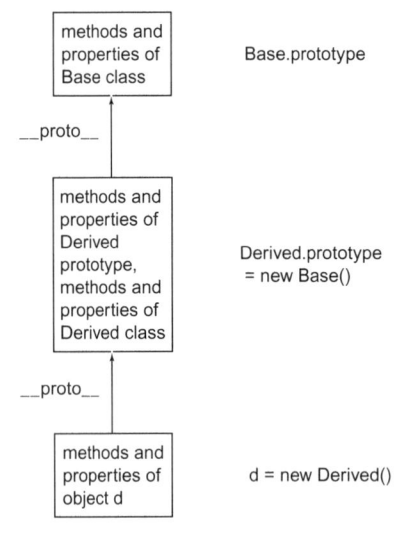

Figure 5.4 *Prototype-based inheritance.*

This is not the end of the story, though. The base constructor's prototype is an object, so it has a prototype, too, and this, in turn has a prototype, and so on. If the search for a method or property fails after looking at the object's prototype, it turns to the prototype's prototype, and then the prototype's prototype's prototype, and so on, following a *chain* of prototypes. (The chain does terminate, because any object that has not had its prototype set explicitly through being initialized by a constructor has as its prototype the built-in Object prototype object, which has a null prototype.)

If you think about this, what it means is that every object may have its own methods, unique to itself, those of its class (i.e., those added to its constructor's prototype), and those it inherits from its prototype and from further up the prototype chain. Thus, when we use an object as a prototype, we can extend its class, by adding new methods, or refine it by redefining some of those it provides. To see how this works, let us consider some objects that might be part of an ecommerce application in Flash. (We will consider integrating these objects with a direct manipulation interface in Chapter 6.)

An online store might very well sell different sorts of items that share some common characteristics. For example, several existing stores sell books, videos, music CDs and computer games. There are some pieces of information that it would makes sense to record for all of these types of item: their title, price and the number in stock, for example. Other pieces of information only apply to one type: a book has an author and publisher, a video has a director and a rating (censorship classification), and so on. Inheritance can be used to capture the common features and provide some common behaviour.

For this example, a single level of inheritance can suffice. At the base is a class Item, which holds the data common to all types of item in its properties. It also provides a method, sell, that records the selling of one or more copies of an item by adjusting the number in stock accordingly. The constructor and sell method can be defined as follows.

```
function Item(t, p, n) {
    this.title = t;
    this.price = p;
    this.number_in_stock = n;
}
Item.prototype.sell = function(n) {
    this.number_in_stock -= n;

}
```

The constructor just initializes properties that remember the title, price and number in stock, while sell subtracts its argument from the last of these. For production purposes, these functions should perform some range and type checks on their arguments, of course.

A book is a sort of item. (Inheritance typically models situations where one kind of object can be considered a sort of another kind, like this.) It has an author and publisher, but we want to record information in an Item, and we want to be able to sell it, so we will assign an Item as the Book constructor's prototype. That much is clear, but it is not clear how the properties belonging to items are going to be initialized for a book. One way is to do it by hand:

```
function Book(a, t, pub, p, n) {
    this.author = a;
    this.publisher = pub;
    this.title = t;
    this.price = p;
    this.number_in_stock = n;
}
Book.prototype = new Item("", 0, 0);
```

This will work: although each book's prototype will be the anonymous object assigned to Book.prototype and initialized by the Item constructor, and will therefore have title, price and number_in_stock properties, by assigning to these properties in the constructor, we create new, local, properties within each book object, whose values will, therefore, be found instead of the default values in the prototype.

Still, it seems a pity to duplicate the code that is already there in the Item constructor, especially since we will have to duplicate it again for videos, music CDs and games. And if new properties are defined for items, all the constructors will need updating. The following, admittedly obscure, code will call the base constructor to initialize derived objects:

```
this.base = Item;
this.base(t, p, n);
```

Functions can be assigned like any other value, so the first line assigns the Item constructor to a property of the object under construction. A function that is the value of a property is a method, so when the constructor is called in the next line, it is treated as a method of the Book object, and this is initialized to refer to the Book object, so the assignments inside the Item constructor set the values of the Book object's properties, which is what is required.

Calling the base constructor in this way makes writing the constructors for other objects simple. The video constructor is as follows, for example:

```
function Video(t, d, r, p, n) {
    this.director = d;
    this.rating = r;
```

```
        this.base = Item;
        this.base(t, p, n);
}
Video.prototype = new Item("", 0, 0);
```
Constructors for other types of item will follow the same pattern (see Exercise 10).

Objects can be created in the usual way.
```
var dmm = new Book("Nigel & Jenny Chapman", "Digital Multimedia",
                                "John Wiley & Sons", 27.95, 12);
var cpp = new Book("Nigel Chapman", "The Late Night Guide to C++",
                                "John Wiley & Sons", 29.95, 1);
var muppets = new Video("The Muppet Movie", "James Frawley", "U", 10.95,5);
var mepris = new Video("Le Mepris", "Jean-Luc Godard", "15", 16.95, 3);
```
Since all these objects are derived from Item, when we sell some, we can call the sell method, which will be found from the prototype Item object.
```
dmm.sell(2);
muppets.sell(1);
```

Multiple Inheritance

There is a school of thought which holds that requiring each class to have at most one base class is an artificial and unreasonable restriction. Starting from the observation that inheritance models the sort of relationships normally expressed with a phrase such as 'is a sort of', proponents of *multiple inheritance* argue that some objects can be described as a sort of more than one type of thing. For example, in a world where there are students and musicians, a music student is both a student and a musician. Hence, it is argued, it ought to be possible for a class to be derived from more than one base class.

The theory may or may not be sound — it has been controversial in programming language circles — but the implementation of multiple inheritance can cause problems. To take a slightly far-fetched example, suppose that our online store finds itself selling bundles comprising a video and an accompanying book. Such a bundle isn't a video, and it isn't a book, but since the two components between them have all the properties of books and videos, you might argue that it is both, so that a Bundle class should be derived from both Book and Video. Even if you believe this reasoning to be valid, you can see that problems immediately arise because both Book and Video are derived from Item. What happens if the book and video in the bundle have different titles, and the bundle itself has its own? Clearly, there are ways round such problems, by defining extra properties, but when you start doing that, the neat structure of the inheritance framework starts to break down.

These general considerations apply to multiple inheritance in any language. In ActionScript, the fact that inheritance is based on the __proto__ property, of which each object can have only one, seems to rule out multiple inheritance straight away. You can, however, simulate the effect of multiple inheritance by calling more than one base constructor. For instance,

```
function Bundle(a, t, d, pub, r, p, n) {
    this.base1 = Book;
    this.base1(a, t, pub, p, n);
    this.base1 = Video;
    this.base1(t, d, r, p, n);
}
```

The resulting Bundle object will have all the properties and methods of Book and Video, but note how the common properties are initialized twice over.

It is usually (some say always) possible to produce a simpler object without multiple inheritance, by using objects of the proposed base classes as properties. In this example, we might say that a bundle isn't a video and a book, but that it is a different sort of thing that contains both a video and a book. This makes it easy to distinguish the price of the two components, or model bundles where the two have different titles, and to provide the bundle with its own properties, such as the combined price and title.

Most of the objections to multiple inheritance disappear if the two base classes have nothing in common. If, for example, we wanted to combine the record for a book that has been described in this chapter with a movie clip of a book cover, to provide an element of the book shop interface, one way of doing so would be by using multiple inheritance. Chapter 6 shows you how to derive objects from movie clips, and also describes an alternative implementation of such combined objects.

Object Inheritance

The example of books, videos and so on shows the most typical use of inheritance to create a hierarchy of classes, in which derived classes are specialized versions of the base class. Since ActionScript uses an object-based model of inheritance, it can also be used to produce specialized versions of specific objects, in particular, the built-in objects provided by the system. Inheritance can be used to extend these objects, or to change their behaviour, if it should be found less than ideal.

Consider, for example, the Selection object, introduced in Chapter 4. There is some justification for thinking that there ought to be different objects for each text field, instead of one global object. Also, as I pointed out in that chapter, selections into text fields with the HTML option are not much use, because the selection only counts characters displayed on the screen, and the text includes HTML markup. Thus, if a variable associated with a dynamic HTML text field holds the string "Mens <i>sana</i> in corpore sano." and I select the italicized word sana, Selection.getBeginIndex() and Selection.getEndIndex() will return 5 and 9, respectively, although the actual offsets into the string should be 8 and 12 (or 5 and 16, if you include the tags). By using inheritance it is possible to construct a class of objects that overcomes both these deficiencies of the built-in Selection. Some preliminary groundwork is needed first.

It isn't terribly difficult to work out the offsets into a tagged string from the raw offsets, if you assume that the HTML is well-formed, with character entities being used where necessary, and does not include any comments. This function is one way of doing it:

```
function HTMLoffset (offset, str, before) {
    var chars = 0, cdata = 0;
    var in_tag = false;
    while (chars < str.length) {
        if (before && cdata == offset) return chars;
        if (str.substr(chars, 1) == "<") in_tag = true;
        else if (in_tag && str.substr(chars, 1) == ">") in_tag = false;
        else if (!in_tag) {
            if (!before && cdata == offset) return chars;
            ++cdata;
        }
        ++chars;
    }
    return -1;
}
```

The variables chars and cdata are used to keep count of the total number of characters, and the number of characters excluding HTML tags and attributes, respectively. The in_tag flag is toggled when a < or > character is encountered, so that it will be true if and only if the current character is inside a tag. Therefore, chars is incremented on every character as we iterate through the string, while cdata is only incremented if in_tag is false. When the value of cdata reaches the value of the raw offset, the value of chars must be the corresponding offset into the tagged string.

The flaw in the reasoning just given is that the offset into the tagged string is not uniquely defined. Since tags do not correspond to anything visible, it makes equal sense to consider the offset as being reached just before or just after a tag that immediately precedes or follows the character in the position identified by the raw offset. The argument before is used to specify which of these interpretations should be used. It affects the point at which the value of cdata is tested in the body of the loop. We will see shortly why it is better to be able to choose an interpretation when the function is called than to make an arbitrary choice once and for all.

I can now get correct offsets into tagged HTML strings by passing the offsets returned by the methods of Selection to HTMLoffset. It would be more consistent and convenient, though, if I could make a new object, HTMLSelection, which behaved like Selection, but also provides methods for obtaining the start and end indices allowing for HTML tags. This is where inheritance comes in. (I expect you were beginning to wonder.)

I will define a class of HTMLSelection objects, each of which is bound to a particular text field, and add some new methods, while inheriting all of the Selection object's methods. The binding will be done by remembering the name of the text field's associated variable inside the HTMLSelection object. Because it will be necessary to discover the value of the string stored in the variable whenever an HTMLSelection method is called, it is the name of the variable, not its value, that must be passed to the constructor, in the form of a string. The constructor just stores this string in a property:
```
function HTMLSelection(v) {
    this.variable_name = v;
}
```
If, for example, tt is the name of a variable associated with a particular text field, an HTMLSelection object could be created to go with it, like this:
```
var html_selection_tt = new HTMLSelection("tt");
```

Now for the inheritance. Remember that the object assigned to the constructor's prototype property is subsequently assigned to the __proto__ property of every object initialized by that constructor. If I merely assign Selection to HTMLSelection.prototype, then any methods I add to the prototype will be added to the Selection object. If I had wanted to do that, I could have done it directly. By assigning Selection to the __proto__ property of the constructor's prototype property instead, we can add it to the prototype chain, so that its methods and properties will be inherited, but adding new methods to the prototype will not alter the behaviour of the built-in Selection object.
```
HTMLSelection.prototype.__proto__ = Selection;
```

Next, methods can be added to the constructor's prototype (not its prototype's prototype) to define the behaviour of HTMLSelection objects. These use the methods of the original Selection object, passing the result to the HTMLoffset function to take account of the tags.
```
HTMLSelection.prototype.getHTMLBeginIndex = function() {
    return HTMLoffset(this.getBeginIndex(), eval(this.variable_name), false);
}
HTMLSelection.prototype.getHTMLEndIndex = function() {
    return HTMLoffset(this.getEndIndex(), eval(this.variable_name), true);
}
```
To get hold of the current value of the text field, the variable name is passed to eval, which, you will recall from Chapter 4 (page 96) takes a string and treats it as a variable, returning its current value. Hence, eval(this.variable_name) gives the current string in the text field. The final argument to HTMLoffset is set to false when the index of the start of the selection is being computed, and to true for the end. This way, if, for example, a word that is between a pair of HTML tags is selected, neither tag will be included in the selection.

These methods have extended the Selection object, adding new behaviour. What if you decided that you didn't want the raw selection at all when you used an HTMLSelection, but would rather have it provide the indices compensated for the HTML tags when you called the getBeginIndex and getEndIndex methods? In other words, you would like to refine the Selection object, by overwriting these methods with your own versions of them.

The way names are looked up along the prototype chain means that if you add methods to the constructor prototype, they will be found in preference to methods with the same names in Selection. The only trouble is that the methods in HTMLSelection need to call methods with the same name in Selection. In order to avoid inadvertant recursion, it is necessary to invoke methods from further back in the prototype chain explicitly, like this:
```
HTMLSelection.prototype.getBeginIndex = function() {
    return HTMLoffset(this.__proto__.__proto__.getBeginIndex(),
                      eval(this.variable_name), false);
}
```
and so on. This may look clumsy, but it does the trick, and, since HTMLSelection is an abstraction, once it has been done, you don't need to think about it again.

Libraries

One of the main benefits of abstraction is that it allows us to construct pieces of code that can be used many times. This is only an advance over cutting and pasting if there is some mechanism that allows definitions to be stored in one place and used in many others. In other words, some form of *library* is needed to accommodate definitions of functions and other reusable items.

Every Flash movie has a library, in the special sense of a collection of symbols that are used in that movie. When you are constructing a movie in Flash, you can open the library of any other movie (using the File>Open as Library... command) to gain access to its symbols. Therefore, a simple library mechanism is already available: construct a movie that consists of nothing but symbol definitions, attach scripts defining functions, constructors and methods to the frames of movie clip symbols in that movie, and then open it as a library in any other movie that needs to use those functions and so on. You can even place the movie in the Libraries sub-folder of your Flash installation, and it will be accessible by the shortcut Window>Common Libraries sub-menu.

Some of the details of this procedure are not necessarily obvious, so let's look at an example. The queue abstract data type that I used earlier in this chapter is, as I remarked at the time, a generally useful abstraction — one I might well want to use in other movies. To make this possible, I can create a movie with no content; let's call it Queue-lib.fla. With that movie open in Flash, I create a new movie clip symbol called Queue, which only needs to be a single frame. Attached to that frame is a script containing the definitions of the Queue constructor and methods shown earlier.

In any movie, such as the jukebox movie, that needs to use a queue, I open Queue-lib.fla as a library, making its symbols available in the same way as the symbols of the movie that is being worked on, so I can create an instance of the Queue movie clip symbol in this movie. It is important that this instance be available in any frame containing a script that is going to use the Queue constructor — the safest thing is to place it on a layer in the first frame, and extend that frame over the whole movie. Any scripts that use functions defined in the library must be in frames later than the first: scripts in the first frame will not be able to refer to the library instance, since they are executed as soon as the playhead enters the frame. The instance of the Queue symbol must be given an instance name; qlib might seem appropriate. Scripts can now create queues by calling the Queue constructor; since that is defined inside the qlib instance, it must be referred to as qlib.Queue. Hence, the movie jukebox's initialization script would include the following statement:

```
var waiting = new qlib.Queue(10);
```
The definitions of the Queue constructor and methods would not have to be part of the jukebox movie's script. Everything else about the script would be the same as before. Note that the methods of the waiting queue can be called as before (waiting.enqueue(n) and so on), without the qlib prefix, because the methods are assigned to properties of the waiting object by the Queue constructor.

The same technique can be used to construct libraries of functions. If a script needs to use a lot of functions or constructors from a library in a sequence of statements, the with statement can profitably be used to remove the necessity to type the library instance prefix every time.

Using movies as libraries in the manner just outlined is only a step towards reusing abstractions. The movie clip symbols are always copied into each movie that uses them. A more complete solution is provided in Flash 5 by *shared libraries*. These are organized in the same way as the libraries just described, but, instead of copying symbols into other movies, links to symbols are created. Three steps are needed to do this. First, having created the library, symbols that are to be shared must be marked for export. This is done by selecting the symbol in the library window, bringing up the Symbol Linkage Properties dialogue by choosing Linkage... from the pop-up menu in the top right hand corner of the window, and selecting Export This Symbol. Next, the library must be published, simply by creating an SWF file. Finally, any movie that is to use symbols from the library must open it as a shared library, using the appropriately named command on the File menu, instead of just opening it as a library. Symbols are then instantiated in the same way, by dragging onto the stage, but this just creates a link, it doesn't copy the symbol. When the movie is played, the shared library is downloaded. For full details of the mechanics of creating and using shared libraries, see *Using Flash 5*.

Exercises and Experiments

1. Write a function that is an abstraction of the code fragment for replicating a string on page 55. It should take a string and a repetition count as arguments, and return the replicated string as its result. Document any assumptions you make about the values of the arguments.
2. Write and test a function that takes a string as its argument and converts any upper-case letters it contains into their lower-case equivalent, and vice versa. For example, if its argument is the string "IBM-Compatible" the result would be "ibm-cOMPATIBLE".

3. (a) An alternative to the approach to formatting floating point numbers described in this chapter is to first convert the number to a string, and then to search for the position of the decimal point, and extract the appropriate substring. Reimplement the two floating point formatting functions using this approach. Assess the relative merits of the two approaches.

   (b) There is an undocumented assumption in the formatting functions in the text. What is it? Does your answer to (a) share it?

4. Under what circumstances would it be *necessary* to call a function before it had been defined?

5. Write a function that takes as its argument an array of numbers and returns their arithmetic mean.

6. Write a function that takes two arguments, an array and a function of two numbers that returns a number. Your function should use its function argument to combine all the elements of the array, returning the result. For example, if the function is called combine,

   ```
   combine(a, function(a, b) { return a + b; })
   ```

   should return the sum of all the elements of a. You can assume that the array argument has at least two elements. Devise a similar function that does not require this assumption to be made. (It won't necessarily take the same arguments as combined does.)

7. Change the implementation of the queue, so that it provides a method is_full, which returns true if the next enqueue operation would cause the queue to overflow. Modify the enqueue operation on the assumption that it is only ever called if is_full is false. Modify the jukebox to ensure that this assumption is valid. Which version of the queue is easier to use?

8. The circular array implementation of the queue is an old data structure hacker's approach. The modern (or postmodern) programmer would more likely use Array.push and Array.shift to implement the enqueue and dequeue operations. Reimplement the queue along those lines, in such a way that no script that uses a queue needs changing.

9. Extend the movie jukebox example to make it more like a real jukebox: instead of one button per movie, provide two sets of buttons, one labelled with letters, the other with numbers, so that a movie can be selected by pressing one of each, C5 for indigo.swf and so on. (You should provide some means of displaying the list of movies and their codes.) To finish the jukebox, make it play a movie chosen at random if no selections are waiting in the queue.

10. Finish the example of objects for a book, video, record and game store by adding constructors for objects, derived from Item, representing music CDs and computer games, with appropriate properties characteristic of these items.

exercises and experiments

11. Add a setFocus method to the HTMLSelection class, which takes no arguments, but sets the focus to the text field with which the object is associated.
12. Create a library of useful functions that convert numbers to strings according to a specified format. One of your functions could be your answer to Exercise 3(a). Others should format a number in a field of a given size, padding it with spaces or other characters to left or right, or print numbers in accountants' format (negative in brackets), and so on. Use this library to reimplement the loan repayment output in the example from Chapter 4.

movie clips

Using MovieClip Objects

The relationship between movie clips and objects is a slightly problematic one. Like objects, movie clips have methods and properties, as we have seen in previous chapters. The use of dot notation in target names that refer to clips within clips emphasizes the relationship between clips and objects: a clip within a clip is accessed as if it were a property of the clip object. Movie clips are not quite the same as other objects, though. Although there is a MovieClip function with a prototype property that provides a prototype for all movie clips, MovieClip cannot be called as a constructor.[1] Clips are created as instances of symbols in the library, by placing them on the stage, or by duplicating an existing movie clip, not by using new to create objects.

Movie clip objects are also special, in that they are containers for scripts. Where scripts include declarations of functions and global variables, these behave as methods and properties of the clip instance or movie in which they are declared. If you enumerate the properties of a clip using a for...in loop, you will see any such variables and functions (though you won't see the built-in methods, such as stop and play, and properties, such as _x and _y — another anomaly). Global variables and functions declared in the main movie are properties of the _level0 object. Normally, though, inside a clip, its methods and properties can be referred to without using this, as you must with any other sort of object.

All this is not quite consistent and not quite neat. It can be largely explained by the legacy of earlier versions of Flash, which lacked any objects, so that movie clips were implemented in an ad hoc manner. Nevertheless it works, usually much as expected, and so there is no point in trying to force it into the mould of some neater, more consistent system when the existing arrangement is adequate.

---

1. Well, it can, but it doesn't construct a movie clip — or even a MovieClip.

Inheritance and Movie Clips

A negative aspect of the special treatment afforded to movie clip objects is that, in the absence of a constructor, it is not possible to use the techniques described in Chapter 5 to derive specialized classes of movie clip using inheritance. It is perfectly possible to add methods and properties to individual clip instances, but the systematic construction of hierarchies of classes depends on being able to call base class constructors from inside derived constructors.

One way of getting round this is to wrap clips up in an object that is constructed in the conventional way. That is, define a constructor, MovieWrapper, that takes a movie clip object as its argument, stores the clip in a property of the wrapper, and adds to it a property that holds a reference to the wrapper object, like this:

```
function MovieClipWrapper(m) {
    this.the_clip = m;
    this.the_clip.wrapper = this;
}
```

Now, any methods that may be added to a MovieClipWrapper, including those added to objects that inherit from it, can be accessed via the wrapper property of any movie clip instance that has been wrapped. Conversely, any built-in movie clip methods and properties can be accessed from a MovieClipWrapper object via its the_clip property. The latter may be considered inconvenient (or immoral by C++ programmers), but can easily be avoided by adding methods to MovieClipWrapper.prototype with the same names as the built-in methods, which simply forward their arguments to the_clip's methods. For example,

```
MovieClipWrapper.prototype.play = function()
{ this.the_clip.play(); }
MovieClipWrapper.prototype.stop = function()
{ this.the_clip.stop(); }
```

and so on. This is tedious, but it only needs to be done once, since MovieClipWrapper would naturally be put in a library. Properties can be accessed via special methods:

```
MovieClipWrapper.prototype.getProperty = function(p)
{ return this.the_clip[p]; }
MovieClipWrapper.prototype.setProperty = function(p, v)
{ this.the_clip[p] = v; }
```

New classes of object that refine or extend the behaviour of movie clips can now be defined by inheritance from MovieClipWrapper. To see how this can be useful, we must return to some unfinished business from Chapter 4.

Recall that we left the direct manipulation interface for buying books by dragging them to a shopping basket symbol at the point where the script was capable of putting books back on the rack if they were dropped on the floor, but that nothing had really been done to handle books being dropped into the basket itself. The object-oriented approach takes the view that books and a shopping basket are sorts of thing that 'know' how to perform certain actions. In this scenario, one of the things a shopping basket ought to know is how to handle having a book dropped into it, for example, while a book ought to know what to do when a user starts to drag it or drops it.

Given the possibility of using this same interface for other types of item — CDs or games, for example — and the further possibility that we might want users to be able to drop items on other things besides a shopping basket, it is best to begin by defining some general classes of things that can be dragged and dropped to make something happen, and things that can respond to having such a thing dropped on them. I'll call them Draggable and Dropable, and since both of these will be essentially movie clips with some extra capabilities, they will both be derived from MovieClipWrapper. In the following, I will assume that the definitions of the MovieClipWrapper constructor and methods are in a library, and that an instance of the clip in which they are defined called mcw is placed in the main movie in which the new classes are defined, so as to be available to the defining scripts.

Dropable is the simpler of the two new classes, at least to begin with. It uses the technique of inheritance described in Chapter 5 to set up a MovieClipWrapper. It then adds a method called handle_drop, which will be called with a Draggable object as its argument when such an object is dropped on it. In general, we have no idea what to do then, so the method does nothing — any classes derived from Draggable must provide a handle_drop that does something if there is anything to be done.
```
function Dropable(mc) {
    this.base = _root.mcw.MovieClipWrapper;
    this.base(mc);
}
Dropable.prototype = new _root.mcw.MovieClipWrapper(_root.mcw);
Dropable.prototype.handle_drop = function(d) { }
```
We will see in a moment that the null handle_drop is not entirely useless. Contrary to usual practice, I have used an absolute target name for the mcw clip. This is necessary, because we do not know what context the Dropable constructor may be called from. It imposes a requirement on any movie that uses Dropable to ensure that the clip with the MovieClipWrapper constructor is called mcw and is in the root movie. The use of mcw as the argument to MovieClipWrapper when constructing the prototype is just a

convenience — some clip is needed, and we know that that one must be there. Nothing will ever be done with it.

I can be less vague about Draggable objects. I will want them to behave like the clips that were dragged about in Chapter 4 and go back to their initial position when they are dropped anywhere except on a Dropable object. This means that they must remember their initial positions; this time, the constructor can do that, instead of a clip event handler.

```
function Draggable(mc) {
    this.base = _root.mcw.MovieClipWrapper;
    this.base(mc);
    this.home_x = this.getProperty("_x");
    this.home_y = this.getProperty("_y");
}
Draggable.prototype = new _root.mcw.MovieClipWrapper(_root.mcw);
```

The code to return an object to its original position can be made into a method.

```
Draggable.prototype.go_home = function() {
    this.setProperty("_x", this.home_x);
    this.setProperty("_y", this.home_y);
}
```

Note that other objects can now tell a draggable object to put itself away by calling its go_home method.

Another method, end_drag, is designed to be called when a Draggable object is dropped. It examines the drop target to see whether it knows how to handle a drop, by seeing whether the type of its handle_drop method is defined. (It has to check the type, because all functions evaluate to undefined in a Boolean context. It must also check first whether the target object is undefined, since this is the value that the main movie target evaluates to.) If the target cannot handle the drop, the Draggable object is sent home, as before, but otherwise, the target's handle_drop method is called, with the dropped object passing itself as the argument.

```
Draggable.prototype.end_drag = function() {
    this.stopDrag();
    var dt = eval(this.getProperty("_droptarget"));
    if (dt == undefined || typeof(dt.wrapper.handle_drop) == "undefined")
        this.go_home();
    else
        dt.wrapper.handle_drop(this);
}
```

To lend any point to these definitions, it is necessary to create some movie clip symbols. Like the book covers in Chapter 4 (which will shortly reappear), a draggable clip can be constructed as an instance of a movie clip symbol containing a button. The desired effect is achieved by attaching the following script to the button.

```
on (press) {
    this.wrapper.startdrag();
}
on (release) {
    this.wrapper.end_drag();
}
```

For this to work, any instance created from such a symbol must be wrapped in a Draggable object. This can be done by attaching the following script to the first frame of the symbol:

```
new _root.Draggable(this);
```

(assuming that the Draggable constructor is defined in the main movie. If it was in a library, its absolute target name should be used.) It doesn't matter that the Draggable object is not assigned to any variable, it will only ever be accessed indirectly through its clip's wrapper property. Dropable clips can be wrapped in the same way.

Note that the scripts in any clip used in this way are exactly the same. This means that new movie clip symbols with the same behaviour but a different appearance can be made by duplicating a template and changing the graphics, without altering any script. This permits a division of labour between programmers and designers, which will usually result in better scripts and better artwork.

The Draggable and Dropable classes provide a framework for implementing direct manipulation interfaces, in terms of these abstract objects that can be dragged and dropped, and can handle a drop. To make a concrete system, it is necessary to construct some objects that extend these capabilities with specific properties and methods relevant to some objects in the real world — books in a bookshop, for example. The interface that was partially developed in Chapter 4 can easily be reimplemented in this way, and combined with the record objects from Chapter 5.

Since the point of using abstract classes and inheritance is to reuse code, all the definitions of the various classes that will be used in this example would naturally be in libraries. Suppose then that the definitions of the MovieClipWrapper constructor and methods are in one library, and those of Draggable and Dropable in another. Similarly, suppose that Item is defined in a library, and the different sort of item records, in particular Book, in another. Some care is needed in organizing the movie so that no attempt is made to use a library before it is loaded. A safe method is to use a separate layer for libraries, and place instances mcw and item_lib of the most abstract libraries in the first frame, and instances dd and record_lib of the libraries that depend on them in the second, and then extend the second keyframe over the rest of the movie. (This is not the only possible organization: mcw could be inside dd, for example. The 'flat' organization seems to be the simplest for purposes of exposition.) Similarly, objects should not be created before the definitions of their constructors are loaded, and objects that encapsulate movie clips should not be created before the clips are loaded.

Hence, it is only in the third frame of the movie that the following scripts, defining a class of objects that are draggable book covers can be placed.

```
function BookDrag(m) {
    this.base = _root.dd.Draggable;
    this.base(m);
    this.quantity_in_basket = 0;
}
BookDrag.prototype = new _root.dd.Draggable(_root.dd);
BookDrag.prototype.set_record = function(a, t, pub, p, n) {
    this.book_record = new _root.record_lib.Book(a, t, pub, p, n);
}
```

BookDrag is derived from Draggable, which incorporates much of the code used to drag and drop book covers in Chapter 4. It extends its base class with two new properties: quantity_in_basket, which records the number of instances of the book a BookDrag object represents, and book_record, which holds the details of the book, using a Book object, as defined in Chapter 5. The record is not initialized in the constructor, since it is not going to be possible to ensure that the information is available when the object is constructed, so a separate method, set_record is provided to allow this to be done separately.

Since a BookDrag is a sort of Draggable, which, in turn, is a sort of MovieClipWrapper, they must be initialized with a movie clip instance. In order for them to work as intended, these must be instances of clip symbols with the same structure as any draggable clip in this scheme: a movie containing an invisible button, with the handlers shown on page 147. So a sensible strategy for any project using these classes would be to make a general draggable template symbol containing just those elements, and make more specific templates, such as a book template by duplicating and altering it. A book template could have an extra layer under the button to contain a thumbnail image of the cover, and have the script attached to its first frame changed to:

```
new _root.BookDrag(this);
```

using movieclip objects **149**

Cloning this template and adding the correct image is all that is needed to create symbols which can be instantiated for display and dragging to the shopping basket.

If instances called cpp, perl and dmm are created, and placed in the movie's fourth frame they will be able to use the definitions of BookDrag and all the libraries it depends on. In the next frame, then, their book records can be initialized:
cpp.wrapper.set_record("Nigel Chapman", "The Late Night Guide to C++",
"John Wiley & Sons", 29.95, 1);
perl.wrapper.set_record("Nigel Chapman", "Perl: The Programmer's Companion",
"John Wiley & Sons", 24.95, 15);
dmm.wrapper.set_record("Nigel & Jenny Chapman", "Digital Multimedia",
"John Wiley & Sons", 27.95, 12);

The basket is treated slightly differently. There is only going to be one such object, so instead of deriving a class of baskets from Dropable, a single dropable object can be constructed, to which the extra methods and properties necessary for the working of a shopping basket are added. A movie clip symbol can be created by duplicating the general-purpose dropable symbol and adding a picture of a shopping basket to it. Like the book covers, this is placed in frame 4, to ensure that all the necessary definitions are available. The clip will automatically be wrapped in a Dropable object. Code added to frame 5 extends this object to make it into a shopping basket. First, it is given extra properties: an array called contents to hold references to any books dropped into it, and a counter, num_in to record the number of items it contains.
var bb = the_basket.wrapper;
bb.contents = new Array();
bb.num_in = 0;

Next, the default drop handler is replaced by one that does something. All it really needs to do is update the quantity_in_basket property of the object that has been dropped on it, and, if it has not been dropped before, add it to the contents array. However, in order for such an interface to preserve the intuitive feel that is the strength of direct manipulation, something must be left in the basket to show what has already been collected. One way (by no means the only way) of making this work is with a method that we have not used so far. duplicateMovieClip creates a copy of a movie clip dynamically, that is, when the action is executed within a script. It takes as a parameter a string to serve as the instance name of the newly created copy. The new clip is created in the same context as the original; you cannot specify a new target name that puts it into a different clip or movie. A second parameter is used to specify the level at which

the new clip is stacked in the frame, that is its z-ordering. To make a copy of a book cover that has been dropped into the basket, the following statements could be used.
var new_clip = "m__" + String(++this.num_in);
d.duplicateMovieClip(new_clip, this.num_in);
Newly created clips will be called m__1, m__2, and so on, and will be stacked in the order they are dropped, so later ones appear on top of earlier ones, as expected. The new clip does not need to be as large as the original, and if it is the basket will soon get clogged up, so its size can be reduced by setting the scaling properties.
var new_movie = eval("_root." + new_clip)
new_movie._xscale = 30;
new_movie._yscale = 30;
The alpha value is also set to 70%, to make the clip look less prominent than those that are not in the basket, and its x and y coordinates are set so that the contents of the basket are arranged neatly.[1]
new_movie._alpha = 70;
new_movie._x = this.getProperty("_x") + (this.num_in-2)*10;
new_movie._y = this.getProperty("_y") + 2;
The original can be put back in its place, so it can be dragged again later.
d.go_home();
The whole drop handler is therefore defined as follows:
bb.handle_drop = function(d) {
    duplicate movie, scale etc and send original home, as above
    if (d.quantity_in_basket++ == 0)
        this.contents[this.contents.length] = d;
}

The advantages of attaching this code to the basket over the perhaps more obvious approach of adding it to each book cover's scripts begin to become obvious as the actions become more elaborate. For example, all the code for duplicating clips would have to be copied into every symbol, and in a real application there would be more than just three books. More compelling, though, is the way the scheme that I have described can be adapted to changes in the interface.

Suppose that the interface is a more elaborate one, and that books can be dropped onto other things besides the shopping basket. For example, you might be able to place them on a table, in order to read extracts, or on a writing desk to contribute a review. If the code to handle a drop was associated with the books, then every time you thought of a

---

[1]. Arranging the items in the basket is a bottomless pit of elaborate code aimed at producing ever more pleasing results. To keep matters simple, I have only shown a simple first attempt here.

new sort of thing to drop books onto, the book symbols would need modifying. This would be particularly galling if you were creating book covers by duplicating and modifying a template, because every individual cover would need modifying, or else regenerating from a modified template. With the object-oriented approach, though, no change whatsoever is needed to the book cover symbols. Provided any object onto which a book may be dropped is derived from `Dropable` and has a suitable `handle_drop` method, the correct code will be invoked by the call just shown. You could say that by providing such a function (or method), a symbol implements a suitable *interface* to allow it to have book covers dropped on it.

It is worth noting at this point that the implementation just described could be changed in many small or large respects to produce other versions at least as good. Any reasonably complex system is based, to some extent, on arbitrary decisions. There is no answer to the question, 'Why is `quantity_in_basket` a property of `BookDrag` objects, and not recorded in the basket?' for example. Either way would be as good; there is no point in looking for an ideal, perfect, right solution. The exercises invite you to look at some alternatives.

It is also worth pausing at this point to reflect on how much work would be involved in implementing this interface using Java, instead of Flash and ActionScript..

Now that there is a record of what is in the basket, we can begin to deal with completing the purchase. Actually charging credit cards and arranging to despatch goods requires communication with a server, which is the subject of Chapter 7, but presenting a summary of the contents of the basket, together with the price, can be done with the means already at our disposal.

Although it might be considered dull, the obvious approach of providing a button labelled something like `Check out` is familiar to users and easy to implement. The script on the button can be as simple as:
```
on (release) {
    gotoAndStop("check out")
}
```
where `check out` labels a keyframe with the necessary scripts. We now come to a disadvantage of keeping the records of its contents inside the shopping basket: the basket must be present in the `check out` frame — but then you do carry your basket to the checkout, don't you?

As well as the basket, the check out frame can contain a set of dynamic text fields, one for each piece of information to be displayed on the virtual invoice: the author, title and price of each title found in the basket, the quantity and the total owing for that title. Additionally, a separate field will be used to display a grand total. The variable associated with each title will be the appropriate name, with _t appended. The text fields will be filled in using one line for each title. This means that the Single Line text option must be used: multi-line fields with word wrapping might get out of synch. While this method of displaying the invoice is adequate for a demonstration, you should consider alternatives which may be more suitable for real applications. (See also Exercise 4.)

All the computation is done in a script attached to the check out frame. There is no need to use any fancy object-oriented techniques here; the necessary data is available in the shopping basket's properties and only needs displaying. The first thing to do is clear all the text fields, on the assumption that it may, in general, be possible to return to this frame more than once.

Author_t = Title_t = Price_t = Quantity_t = Total_t = "";

The grand total is initially zero. A numerical value is computed separately from a text string, since it will require formatting.

GrandTotal = ""; grand_tot = 0;

The main business of this script is to loop through the books array that was set up in the basket and copy the appropriate data to the text fields, calculating the price totals on the way. Two nested with statements are used to avoid repetition of the indexing and property accessing operations.

```
with(the_basket.wrapper) {
    for (var i = 0; i < contents.length; ++i)
        with (contents[i]) {
            Author_t += book_record.author + '\n';
            Title_t += book_record.title + '\n';
            Price_t += format_fp(book_record.price) + '\n';
            Quantity_t += quantity_in_basket  + '\n';
            grand_tot += quantity_in_basket * book_record.price;
            Total_t +=  format_fp(quantity_in_basket * book_record.price) + '\n';
        }
}
```

A newline character is added after the data, so that each book appears on its own line. The function format_fp, defined in Chapter 5 is used to format prices; it could have been taken from a library, but, for simplicity of presentation, I have shown it here as if its definition had been pasted in to this script.

using movieclip objects

To finish off the script, and this version of the movie, the grand total must also be displayed.
GrandTotal = format_fp(grand_tot);

Here, the fields of a record have been assigned to the variables associated with some text fields for output purposes. Transferring data in the opposite direction from text fields to record fields is also simple. There is indeed a natural correspondence between forms and records, which has long been exploited in database systems. Flash allows you to convert your records to XML and send them to a program running on a server for processing or storing in a database. It also allows you to receive XML data and convert it into records for processing and display on the client. These features will be described in Chapter 8.

Objects and Events

As well as facilitating inheritance, wrapping movie clips in objects makes it easy to pass on events received by the clip, or buttons inside it, to other objects. Consider, for example, the slider symbol that was described in Chapter 4. As presented there, the slider responded to user input, and computed a quantized level value, but it never did anything with it. In particular, there was no way, short of rewriting the release handler for every application that used a slider, for the slider to invoke any actions involving other objects whenever its setting was changed. By making sliders into objects this shortcoming can be rectified.

The idea is to make a Slider class, derived from MovieClipWrapper. As well as encapsulating slider movie clip symbols in objects, Sliders will maintain an array of other objects that have requested to be informed when the slider setting is changed. Every time it does — that is, every time the sliding box receives a release event, or one of the other events that signifies the end of a drag — each of these objects will be notified of the new level. This will be done by the slider calling a method called handle_slider, so every object that might want to be notified of these events must implement such a method. It must also, of course, be included on the slider's list of objects to notify, so the Slider class will provide a method called register_listener for doing this. (I have adopted the 'listener' terminology from the event handling model used by the Java AWT, stretching the meaning a bit in the process.)

The definition of the Slider constructor and the register_listener method are simple.
function Slider(m) {
    this.base = _root.mcw.MovieClipWrapper;
    this.base(m);

```
            this.listeners = new Array();
}
Slider.prototype = new _root.mcw.MovieClipWrapper(_root.mcw);
Slider.prototype.register_listener = function(obj) {
            this.listeners[this.listeners.length] = obj;
}
```

Once again, I assume that an instance, called mcw, of the MovieClipWrapper symbol from a library is kept in the main movie. It is also necessary to modify the movie clip symbol for the slider itself in a couple of places. First, a script has to be attached to its only frame to wrap it up into an object:

```
new _root.Slider(this);
```

Most of the rest stays the same, but the event handler needs to be extended to call the listeners' methods. For the sake of generality, these will be passed both the level value, and another argument that gives the actual position of the slider as a proportion of the full travel. This accommodates listeners that might need to work with the actual position instead of the quantized version. The handler thus becomes:

```
on (release, releaseOutside, dragOut) {
            stopDrag ();
            var position = (_y-(bar_y-bar_h/2))/bar_h;
            var level = Math.round((num_levels-1)*position);
            var listeners = _parent.wrapper.listeners;
            for (var i = 0; i < listeners.length; ++i)
                        listeners[i].handle_slider(level, position);
}
```

Suppose you decide you want to use a slider as a movie controller, with the levels corresponding to frames. Dragging the slider to a new position will send the movie to the matching frame. If the clip to be controlled is called the_clip, all that is needed is to create an object with a handle_slider method and register it as a listener, like this:

```
var sh = new Object();
sh.handle_slider = function(level, position)
{
            _root.the_clip.gotoAndStop(level+1);
}
the_slider.wrapper.register_listener(sh);
```

where the_slider is an instance of the slider movie clip symbol that has been wrapped in a Slider object.

The only problem with this is that the number of levels in the slider is fixed into the symbol, and may not be right for the application. The solution to this problem forms the subject of the remainder of this chapter.

Smart Clips

In Chapter 5, I described abstraction as 'the process that takes place whenever we take a complex idea or procedure and give it a name so that we can refer to it … without worrying about its internal details'. Creating a movie clip symbol is an example of abstraction: having edited the symbol once and added it to the library, you can create instances of it in a movie or within other clips, without worrying about how it was put together. Movie clips as I have described them so far differ from the other types of abstraction we have seen, though, because they do not have any parameters. Every instance of a clip symbol is identical, except for those aspects of its appearance, such as scaling and transparency, that you can change by setting its properties. If you want to create a movie clip symbol of, for example, a slider control, that encapsulates the behaviour and appearance of a slider, and then pass it arguments that define the number of levels and their labels, you need some extra technology.

Clip Parameters

Flash calls clips with parameters *smart clips*. They can be used to create reusable clips which can easily be adapted in the same way that objects can be used to create reusable scripts. The mechanism is quite simple: when you create a movie clip symbol, you can declare some parameters, which are just variables, that can be given values when an instance of the symbol is created. Since the parameters are variables, some script in the symbol must make use of them to control the appearance or behaviour of instances of the clip. A simple example will show how this works.

This time, we will construct a purely decorative clip that consists of a randomly distributed and scaled number of copies of a simple graphic element, such as a star. The first step is to create the element. It must be a movie clip symbol, because we are going to need to call methods through it. Call this movie clip symbol of a single star **StarClip**. The next step is to create a new movie clip symbol called **Stars**. For this example, **Stars** only needs a single frame. An instance of **StarClip**, with instance name star0 is created in this frame. It doesn't matter where, since it will be moved later.

The decorative effect is going to be produced by duplicating star0 a random number of times, and setting the position, scale and transparency of each new star to a random value. The minimum and maximum number of stars, and the limits to their positions will be specified as parameters max, min and size. We will consider how these are defined and given values shortly. For the moment, it is enough to know that when an instance of Stars is loaded, variables with these names will be available to scripts in the clip, with initial values that are set by the designer when the instance is created.

With that understanding, the creation and placement of the duplicate stars requires nothing that we have not seen before. It is all done by a script attached to the first frame of Stars. First, some functions are defined. The first of these is a utility function that uses some code we have seen before to generate random integers. The second takes a reference to a clip as its argument, and sets its properties to random values.

```
function random_int(max_val) { return Math.Floor(Math.random()*max_val); }
function set_properties(instance) {
    var x = random_int(size);
    var y = random_int(size);
    var scale = random_int(100);
    var alpha = random_int(100);
    with (instance) {
        _x = x;
        _y = y;
        _xscale = _yscale = scale;
        _alpha = alpha;
    }
}
```

A random number between max and min is chosen, and then the star is duplicated that many times, and the properties of each clip are set. Note the use of eval to obtain a reference to the new clip from its name.

```
var n = random_int(max-min) + min;
for (var i = 1; i <= n; ++i) {
    var new_star = "star" + i;
    star0.duplicateMovieClip(new_star, i);
    set_properties(eval(new_star));
}
```

The last thing we need to do is randomize the properties of the star that was originally placed on the stage.

```
set_properties(star0);
```

As you can see, there is nothing special about this movie clip symbol, but it is not going to work unless max, min and size have appropriate values when the script just shown runs. To ensure that this happens, two steps are required. First, when the Stars symbol is created, these variables must be declared as its parameters. Second, when an instance is created, the parameters must be given values.

The first step is performed by selecting the symbol in the library window, and then choosing Define Clip Parameters... from its Options pop-up. This brings up the dialogue shown on the left of Figure 6.1. Ignore the middle pane for now. At the top is an area for entering parameter names; the controls will look familiar if you use normal mode for entering scripts: the buttons labelled + and - are used to add and remove a parameter. When you add a parameter, a line like the second line in Figure 6.1 appears. You can set a new name by double-clicking the left field and typing it in; similarly, a default value can be set in the middle field. Double-clicking the right field brings up a pop-up menu from which you can choose a type for the parameter. These are not exactly the same as ActionScript's data types; Default is used for strings and numbers, Array and Object let you enter a collection of values, either as a numerically indexed sequence or as a set of named fields, while List lets you specify a set of values from which the parameter's value is chosen (like an enumerated data type). For the stars example, the parameter names would be set to max, min and size, with suitable defaults, and all the types would be left as the default. The bottom pane of the dialogue, labelled Description can be used to enter a helpful description of the clip, what it does, and what all its parameters are used for.

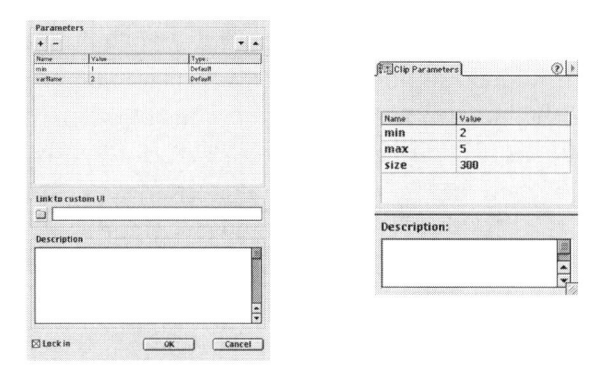

Figure 6.1 *Defining and setting clip parameters.*

Stars is now a smart clip. This is signified by the use of a subtly different icon in the libary window. What it means is that instances of it can be created with different values for the parameters. This is done by dragging the symbol to the stage in the usual way, selecting it, and opening the Clip Parameters panel. The right hand side of Figure 6.1

shows the panel as it opens for an instance of the Stars smart clip. The description that was entered when the clip was created is displayed in the lower half, so that, hopefully, anyone creating an instance will understand what it does. In the top half, new values can be entered for each of the parameters by double-clicking the appropriate cell and typing in a value. So, if a dense star burst was needed, the values could be set to, for example, 20, 100 and 50, while if just a few sparsely placed stars were needed, values of 2, 5 and 300 could be used. The parameters can be reset at any time, not just when the instance is first created.

Note that, since the duplication and randomization of the stars takes place when the script in frame 1 is executed, you don't actually see the resulting stars effect in Flash until you test or export the movie. All you see is the single instance star0, always in the same place.

Smart Interface Elements

A more typical use of smart clips is for constructing abstract versions of the input elements and controls described in Chapter 4. Consider, for example, the slider control. In describing it previously, I glibly assumed that some variable num_levels would hold the number of levels; until now, this would have had to be set in some script. You can see, though, that if the slider were made into a smart clip, the number of levels could be a parameter. We can go further, though, by including the labels on the various levels as part of the clip, and making them parameters, too instead of adding them separately as previously.

The general structure of the clip and the scripts that make it work can remain as before — or preferably, as they were modified in the previous section to allow sliders to be objects. As with the stars, what is needed for the smart clip is a script that builds the variable elements — here, the labels at suitable intervals — on the basis of the parameter values. Since this will refer to the elements of the slider, it is necessary to extend the clip to two frames, with the script in the second. The layers containing the clips that make up the whole slider are simply extended with an extra frame.

The key step in designing a smart clip is deciding what the parameters are to be. Here, the number of levels is obviously a parameter. The labels for these levels should also be something that a designer can set when an instance of the slider is created. Because we don't know how many there are until the number of levels is determined, an array is needed to hold the labels. Finally, to provide extra flexibility, the level at which the slider is set when it is first loaded should also be a parameter. This leads to a smart clip with three parameters: num_levels and initial_level will be numbers (so they use the default type for clip parameters) while labels is an array.

This is the first time we have seen an array used as a smart clip parameter. When an instance of the clip is created, values for the array elements can be set in the Clip Parameters panel; double-clicking the cell for the array value brings up a dialogue box where array elements can be added.

This smart clip's initialization script is going to work very much like that for Stars, by duplicating a clip several times and setting each new copy's properties. In this case, it will be a clip that holds a label. To do this, we need a clip to duplicate. It is an instance of a new symbol, Label, consisting of two frames containing a dynamic text field and a tick mark. The text field's variable is called the_label. The only difference between the two frames is the colour of the text: the first frame is called off and uses black, while the second is called on and uses red. A clip will be moved to the second frame when the slider is set to its level, and left in the first otherwise, so that the chosen level is highlighted. A single instance of this symbol, called label0 is added to the slider symbol at the top of the bar, at an appropriate distance from it (see Figure 6.2).

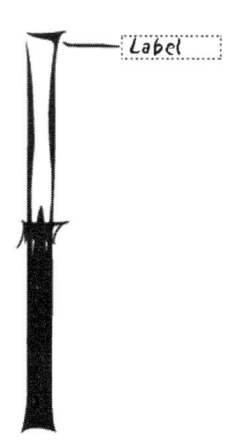

Figure 6.2 *A smart slider clip.*

All that remains to be added is the script that builds a suitable collection of labels from the values passed in the parameters when smart clip instances are created. It begins by computing the interval between labels (using the value of num_levels) and the starting y coordinate for the first label, which is also used as the initial value of a variable that will keep track of where to place each label.

```
var interval = (the_bar._height-the_box._height)/(num_levels-1);
var y_pos0 = the_bar._y - (the_bar._height-the_box._height)/2;
var y_pos = y_pos0;
```
Next, label0 is given its correct label from the Labels array, and moved to its correct position (in case it was not placed precisely when the symbol was first designed).
```
label0._y = y_pos;
label0.the_label = labels[0];
```
A loop creates copies of the label, sets each one's text from the array and places them in the correct position (the position of the previous label plus the interval just computed).
```
for (var i = 1; i < num_levels; ++i) {
    var new_label = "label" + i;
    label0.duplicateMovieClip(new_label, i);
    var new_label_clip = eval(new_label);
    y_pos += interval;
    new_label_clip._y = y_pos;
    new_label_clip.the_label = labels[i];
}
```
Note that if too few values are supplied in Labels, the missing ones will be set to the empty string (since undefined is converted to the empty string), and if too many are supplied, the excess ones will be ignored, which is consistent with the way function arguments are treated.

Finally, the slider has to be set to the specified initial value. This requires it to be placed in the right position, and its label to be highlighted.
```
the_box._y = y_pos0 + initial_level*interval;
var initial_clip = eval("label" + initial_level);
initial_clip.gotoAndStop("on");
```
As with the stars example, the final appearance of any instance of the smart slider clip will not be seen until the movie containing it is previewed or published. Figure 6.3 shows an example containing two instances of the slider symbol with different clip parameters.

Custom User Interfaces to Smart Clips

Parameterization is the essence of smart clips, but entering parameter values in the standard name/value dialogue is clumsy, and sits uncomfortably among the authoring interfaces of contemporary multimedia software. To make smart clips easier to use, Flash allows you to associate a custom user interface (UI) with any smart clip. This is just an SWF movie containing input elements appropriate to the parameters of the smart clip. It is associated with a smart clip symbol by using the middle panel, labelled

smart clips

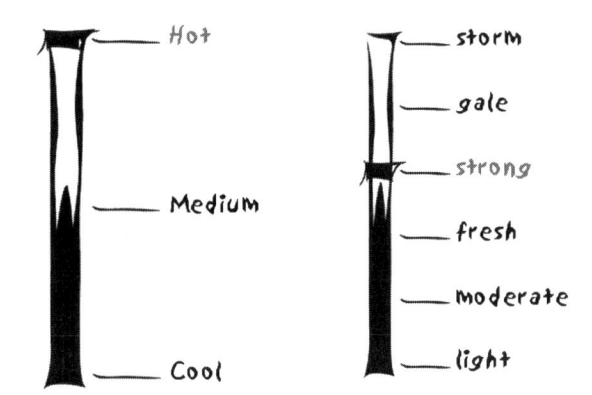

Figure 6.3 *Two instances of the same smart clip.*

Link to custom UI, of the Define Clip Parameters dialogue (refer back to Figure 6.1). A path name can be entered, or the SWF file can be selected using a standard file dialogue, which is invoked by clicking on the folder icon in the dialogue. The user interface movie linked to a smart clip is played in the Clip Parameters panel as a replacement for the standard name/value dialogue.

Smart clip UIs are, as I said, just movies, but, in order to pass the parameter values to the smart clip instance they must include a movie clip that has been given the instance name xch. The name is a contraction of 'exchange', reflecting its role in exchanging data between the UI movie and the smart clip instance. The clip parameters obtain their values from properties of xch with the same name. So, for example, if I wanted to create a custom UI for my stars, I would have to assign the values of the maximum and minimum number to xch.max and xch.min in order to set the values of the max and min clip parameters. How I obtained the values from the user, whether it was with a slider or a text field, or whatever, is irrelevant, so long as a script performs those assignments at a suitable point. This means that the smart clip's designer is free to use whatever interface conventions seem appropriate to the clip and the sort of people who are expected to use it. To see how this works in detail, we will look at some possible user interfaces to the slider smart clip.

To begin with, let's take a step backwards and start with an interface that just sets the parameters to constant values. This is a Flash movie with a single frame containing a button and an instance of an empty movie clip symbol. This instance is given the instance name xch so that it can transfer values to the smart clip. Although it doesn't really matter in this interface, it is generally a good idea to put xch on its own layer, and where there is more than one frame in the interface movie, extend it across all of them.

That way, there is no question of trying to access the clip when it is not on the stage. The following script is attached to the button:

```
on (release) {
    xch.num_levels = 5;
    xch.initial_level = 1;
    xch.labels = new Array(4);
    xch.labels[0] = "hot";
    xch.labels[1] = "warm";
    xch.labels[2] = "medium";
    xch.labels[3] = "cool";
    xch.labels[4] = "cold";
}
```

The movie is saved as an SWF file. sliderUI0.swf. (The name has no significance.) In the movie where the slider smart clip is defined, it is selected in the library, Define Clip Parameters... is chosen from the pop-up menu, and sliderUI0.swf is linked as the custom UI. Now, whenever an instance of the smart slider is selected and the Clip Parameters panel is displayed, the UI movie will run, and set the number of levels and the labels.

This, of course, defeats the object of smart clips, but, once the principle of using an exchange clip to transfer clip parameter values from the UI movie to a smart clip instance is understood, creating more useful interfaces becomes no different from creating any other interface. Provided values for the clip parameters are assigned to properties of xch, the UI movie can be anything you like. (It's not unknown for them to run little animations advertising their designer.)

A simple possibility, which is still an advance over the standard name/value dialogue, is to use a form with input text fields and other input elements for entering the parameter values. A static form with a fixed set of fields and controls is easy to set up, but it is of limited use because the number of parameter values is often a parameter itself — consider the slider smart clip, where we don't know how many labels are needed until the user has set the number of levels. Hence, smart clip UIs often need to be dynamic themselves, and use the technique of duplicating movie clips to produce a variable number of entry fields.

Figure 6.4 shows a dynamic form-based interface to the slider. Initially, it displays the current value of the number of levels and shows the labels for each level. If a number is entered in the box for the number of levels, a new set of text fields is displayed in which that many labels can be entered. Clicking on the done button causes the values of the clip parameters to be updated (by assigning new values to the corresponding properties of an exchange clip).

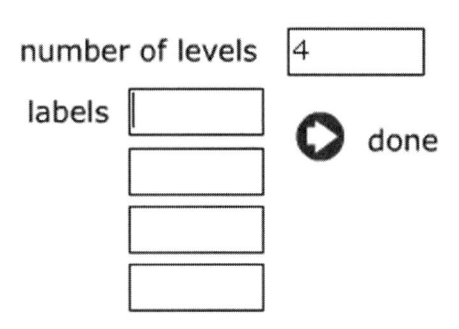

Figure 6.4 *A form-based interface to the smart slider clip.*

This interface movie is two frames long, so that scripts in frame 2 can refer to the clips that are placed in frame 1, which is extended into the other frame, as usual. The stage contains the button and static text fields seen in Figure 6.4, and two instances of a movie clip that contain nothing but a text field. One of these is used for the number of levels, the other is a placeholder that will be duplicated to make the fields for entering the labels' values. These are given the instance names n_levels and label0, respectively. The most elaborate part of this movie is a function that does the duplication of label0. By now, though, this should be familiar.

```
function create_labels(n) {
    var ypos = _root.label0._y;
    var interval = _root.label0._height + 5;
    for (var i = 1; i < n; ++i) {
        var next_label = "label" + i;
        _root.label0.duplicateMovieClip(next_label, i);
        var next_label_clip = eval("_root." + next_label);
        next_label_clip._y = (ypos += interval);
    }
    _root.num_levels = n;
}
```

As you can see, a global variable num_levels is used to record the number of levels in the current display.

The function create_labels is defined in frame 2 of the main movie, where the following initialization is also performed.

```
var num_levels = xch.num_levels;
n_levels.the_text = num_levels;
create_labels(num_levels);
for (var i = 0; i < num_levels; ++i)
    eval("label"+i).the_text = xch.labels[i];
stop();
```
This extracts the clip's current parameter values from xch and updates the display accordingly. The number of levels is remembered in num_levels, and is used to set the corresponding text field variable. Then, create_labels is called to make the correct number of label fields, which are then initialized from the labels array in xch.

When a new number of levels is typed in the text field and the user presses return, the old labels are thrown away and a new set created. The latter operation is exactly what create_labels does; removing the old set is done by repeatedly calling the built-in removeMovieClip method, which is provided precisely to remove clips that were created by duplicateMovieClip. Of course, we must not remove label0, or there will be no way of making the new label clips. However, its text must be cleared by assigning the empty string.

All this is straightforward. Getting the script to execute when a return is pressed is done in a slightly obscure way. The text field for the number of levels is actually inside a movie clip, as I said earlier. A clip event handler is attached to this clip that responds to keyPress events. When one occurs, it uses Key.GetCode to discover whether is was a return (or enter, if you prefer). If so, it needs to determine whether the cursor was in the number of levels field or somewhere else. It does this by finding where the focus was and comparing it with the target name of its own text field variable. The built-in function targetPath turns a movie clip reference into a string containing its absolute target name. Appending the name of the text field variable to the value of targetPath(this) therefore gives a string that can sensibly be compared to the one returned by Selection.getFocus(). Putting all these ideas together gives the following script attached to the n_levels instance of the text field movie clip.

```
onClipEvent(keyDown) {
    if (Key.GetCode() == Key.ENTER
        && Selection.getFocus() == targetPath(this) + ".the_text")
    {
        for (var i = 1; i < _root.num_levels; ++i)
            eval("_root.label" + i).removeMovieClip();
        _root.label0.the_text = "";
        _root.create_labels(Number(the_text));
```

```
            Selection.setFocus("_root.label0.the_text");
    }
}
```
Setting the focus to label0's text field leaves the user ready to enter the new label values.

Finally, a handler attached to the done button collects the current values and assigns them to properties of xch to pass them to the smart clip instance.
```
on (release) {
    var n = Number(n_levels.the_text);
    xch.num_levels = n;
    xch.labels = new Array(n);
    for (var i = 0; i < n; ++i)
        xch.labels[i] = eval("label"+i).the_text;
    xch.initial_level = Math.floor(n/2);
}
```
The initial level is arbitrarily set to the middle value.

This form-based interface is an advance over the standard name and value dialogue, and something of the sort will often be an appropriate way of allowing designers to set clip parameters. A more adventurous approach is to base the interface on the smart clip itself.

Figure 6.5 shows yet another interface to my smart slider clip. Once again, there is a box to enter the number of levels, but this time, doing so causes the instance of the slider clip on the left to be given the appropriate number of levels. When the slider is dragged, the corresponding level number is inserted in the legend on the lower text field, in which its label can be entered. The clip is updated, so that the designer can see how the final instance will look. Such 'bootstrapped' smart clips require a clear head, but can be very effective.

This time, in the interests of clarity, I won't bother initializing the interface using the current values of the parameters — I'll leave that to you. Instead, every time the interface clip runs, it will start afresh with a blank slider.

The movie uses an instance of the slider smart clip. It is set up using the name and value dialogue, so it starts with three unlabelled levels — an arbitrary but visually balanced number. I am going to use the slider object class described earlier in this chapter, so it will be necessary to organize this movie in the same way as the one shown on page 153, with the MovieClipWrapper in the first frame, the definitions of the Slider class's

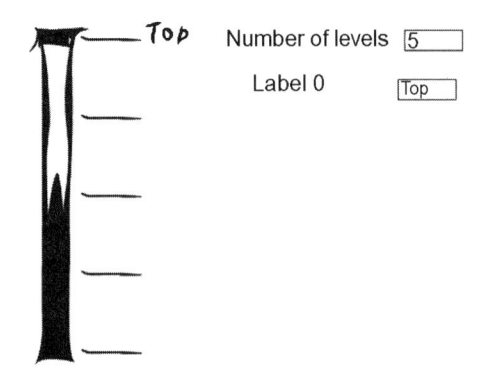

Figure 6.5 *A bootstrapped user interface to the smart slider clip.*

constructor and methods in the second, and an instance of a slider in the third, which is extended to the fourth frame, where the new scripts will be. The text fields are placed in frame 3 and 4 with the slider.

This slider is an instance of the smart slider symbol, so it has the properties that we want to be set as parameters: num_levels, labels and initial_level. We can simplify matters and save some work by using this clip as the exchange clip, so it is given the instance name xch. (Normally, using anything but an empty clip as xch is inadvisable, because it might pass unwanted information into the smart clip instance. Where the two are isomorphic, as they are here, there is no harm in it.)

The slider must be wrapped up in an object, so the first thing the script attached to frame 4 does is call the Slider constructor.
var the_slider_object = new Slider(xch);
This object is actually going to need more methods than those provided by Slider. Since there is only going to be one of it, though, these can be added to the individual object instead of to a derived class — remember, ActionScript is object-based, not class-based.

The first method sets a label at a level passed as its first argument to a string passed as its second. It also records the label in the labels array.
the_slider_object.set_label = function(i, text) {
    var mc = this.the_clip;
    mc.labels[i] = text;
    eval("mc.label" + i).the_label = text;
}
The next method is more interesting. It resets the entire slider instance by removing all its labels, setting its num_levels property to a new value passed to the method as an

argument, and creating a new empty labels array. To update the display to reflect this, it simply sends the xch clip (which the slider object is itself a wrapper for) to its first frame and plays it.

```
the_slider_object.reinitialize = function(n)
{
    var mc = this.the_clip;
    for (var i = 1; i < mc.num_levels; ++i)
        eval("mc.label" + i).removeMovieClip();
    mc.num_levels = n;
    mc.labels = new Array();
    _root.label_num = _root.sh.current_level = mc.initial_level = 0;
    this.gotoAndPlay(1);
}
```

The display and parameters need updating every time the slider is moved, so we create a listener object that does the right thing and register it with the slider object.

```
var sh = new Object();
sh.handle_slider = function(level, position)
{
    _root.label_num = this.current_level = level;
    _root.this_label.the_text = _root.the_slider_object.the_clip.labels[level];
}
the_slider_object.register_listener(sh);
```

The variable label_num is associated with the text field that displays the current level; the clip this_label is an instance of a symbol containing a text field, like the ones used in the previous interface design. Its text is updated to reflect any value that might have been set already. The property current_level of sh is a fairly convenient place to remember the level.

With all these objects and definitions in place, the only thing left for the frame script to do is clear the slider.

```
the_slider_object.reinitialize(3);
```

The text field clip in which the number of levels is entered uses the same trick as the similar field in the previous version to detect when return is pressed with the cursor inside it. If so, the slider must be reinitialized with the new number of levels.

```
onClipEvent(keyDown) {
    if (Key.GetCode() == Key.ENTER
        && Selection.getFocus() == targetPath(this) + ".the_text")
        _root.the_slider_object.reinitialize(Number(the_text));
```

}
The same trick is used yet again on the clip containing the field for entering the label text. This time, it uses the value of the current level remembered when sh handled the slider's drop together with the value in its own text field to set a label at the current level.
```
onClipEvent(keyDown) {
    if (Key.GetCode() == Key.ENTER
        && Selection.getFocus() == targetPath(this) + ".the_text")
    _root.the_slider_object.set_label(_root.sh.current_level, this.the_text);
}
```

Because the slider instance in the UI movie is itself the exchange clip, the parameter values it passes back to a new slider instance being constructed will always reflect what the designer has set up in the interface inside the Clip Parameters panel.

Exercises and Experiments

1. On page 145, I claimed that 'one of the things a shopping basket ought to know is how to handle having a book dropped into it.' You might prefer to say that one of the things a book ought to know is how to handle being dropped into a shopping basket. Explore the alternative implementation of the direct manipulation shopping interface that this view implies. Which version is going to be easier to maintain and adapt?

2. (a) Investigate the behaviour of the duplicate book cover clips that are left in the shopping basket. What happens if you drag them out, or out and in again? What if you drop a new book onto one already in the basket? Explain your observations and suggest ways of preventing any behaviour you consider undesirable.

   (b) The dynamic nature of objects in ActionScript allows you, in effect, to change the class of an object after it has been created. Make use of this capability to turn clips in the basket into members of a special class with appropriate behaviour. In particular, make it possible to remove items from the basket if you change your mind about buying them. Make sure that the basket's properties are amended so that items that have been removed do not appear on the invoice.

3. (a) You may think that all this palaver with MovieClipWrapper objects and inheritance is excessively elaborate. If so, reimplement the system in a way that seems more straightforward to you. How easy is it going to be to extend your implementation to cope with different types of merchandise? How easily can parts of it be reused? Is it possible to separate the scripting from the graphic design?

   (b) On the other hand, you may be entirely convinced of the efficacy of inheritance and want to take it further. You could argue that a BookDrag object is indeed a wrapped movie, but it is also a container for the information about the book.

exercises and experiments

>That is, instead of having a book record as a property, it should be a book record by (multiple) inheritance. Reimplement the `BookDrag` class along these lines.

4. At the very least, the text fields in the check out frame of the shop movie should have scroll bars. Alternatively, you might want to arrange long invoices over several 'pages'. Investigate possible variations on the layout of the invoice.
5. Basing your design on either the scripts in the text or your answers to Exercise 3, extend the shop so that it can sell music CDs and computer games as well as books. Choose a suitable organization for your movie that allows the design to be scaled up to a more realistic number of items.
6. There are many possible interfaces to the smart slider clip besides those described in the text. Look at alternative designs and implement any that appeal to you.
7. One possible use of sliders is to enliven the online surveys that are becoming ubiquitous. Instead of checkboxes or numbers on a scale of one to ten, users could be invited to set a slider to indicate their degree of satisfaction or whatever. Use the slider smart clip (or your own version of it) to implement such a survey. By adding suitable listener objects or otherwise, extract the response data into an object ready to be analysed.

client–server interaction

HTTP and CGI

There is little point to an interface with nothing behind it. If you are using Flash for anything more than eye-catching designs or straightforward animation, sooner or later you will find that you need to access data stored in files on disk. There are two broad requirements that can only be met by reading or writing to disk: the need to record information for future reference, and the need to use data that is already available in some database. Commonly, both these requirements arise. For example, an online shopfront would usually keep details about customers, such as their address and a history of their recent purchases, either to spare them the need to re-enter information every time they use the shop, or for marketing purposes. Such a shop would also need to refer to a database to obtain product details to be presented by Flash. Often, any data used in this way will also be used by other programs. Users' purchase histories might be analysed to help predict future demand; where an online shop belongs to an organization with conventional retail outlets, the product database will generally be shared with established systems for maintaining inventory, and so on.

In general, data files reside on a server, and must be accessed from a client that is playing a Flash movie. A couple of apparently simple methods are available for sending data to and receiving it from remote files identified by a URL. Where these do not suffice, more elaborate facilities for transferring data structured with XML are available — see Chapter 8. The simplicity of the rudimentary methods conceals some subtle pitfalls, as well as providing some opportunities that may not be immediately apparent. To fully appreciate these operations, it is necessary to understand something of how they are implemented using the HTTP protocol that is the basis of the WWW. (Readers who are familiar with the technicalities of the Web may prefer to skip the remainder of this section.)

HTTP

The passage of data between a server and a client, in any client/server application, may be likened to a ritual conversation or a catechism, in which the client asks certain questions to which the server responds in rigidly defined ways. More formally, we say that clients issue a series of *requests* to which the server sends *responses*. The rules governing the interaction are known as a *protocol*. The protocol specifies the format of requests and responses, the order in which requests may be made, and the legitimate responses that each request may elicit. It may also specify timing constraints and procedures to be taken if data appears to have been lost.

HTTP is a simple protocol, largely because it relies on the services provided by other, lower-level protocols — in particular TCP — to deal with the mechanics of ensuring that data is reliably transmitted over the network. HTTP clients and servers can behave as though they were sending streams of bytes directly to each other once a TCP connection between them has been established. This is done by the client — by definition, a server just waits for requests and cannot initiate communication. The client uses the host name part of a URL to determine the machine to which it should open the connection. (The name is translated to a real numerical IP address by the network's Domain Name Service.) We need not consider how the connection is made, nor how TCP subsequently goes about sending data packets across it. All this is transparent to HTTP.

With the connection open, the client can send a request. Every request begins with a *request line*. This has three elements. First, the *method* is a name that identifies a particular HTTP service being requested. For our purposes, only two methods are of interest: GET and POST. Next comes an *identifier*, which indicates to the server the exact resource being requested. In the case of a request for a Web page, for example, the identifier will be the path name component of its URL, which the server can translate to a path name in the directory structure on the machine on which it is running. Finally, the request line ends with a code indicating the version of HTTP that the client is using. If, for example, I were to enter the URL http://www.macromedia.com/support/flash/ in

my Web browser and click Go, the browser would open a connection to the host named www.macromedia.com (using a port reserved for HTTP connections) and then send the following request line:
GET /support/flash/ HTTP/1.1

Following the request line come a series of *headers*, additional lines that specify some parameters for the request. These are of little relevance to Flash's use of HTTP. The request is terminated by a blank line.

On receiving such a request, a server will find the requested resource and send it back, wrapped up in an HTTP response. This begins with a *status line*, comprising a version code, a numerical status code, and a short phrase indicating the meaning of the code. If all goes well, the code will be 200 and the accompanying phrase will be OK:
HTTP/1.0 200 OK

Note that the version in the response need not match that in the request — it depends on the server's abilities. On receiving this response, a client would fall back on the facilities of HTTP/1.0 to match the server.

Like a request, a response can include additional headers. Again, since Flash handles the actual HTTP interaction, most of these are of no interest. Only one is worth mentioning. The Content-type header indicates the type of data returned, using a *MIME content type*. This consists of two parts separated by a slash. The first part gives a broad indication of the type of data — whether it is text, an image, video, and so on — while the second part identifies the specific format — HTML, GIF, QuickTime, for example. The type application is used for data that must be processed by some application program or plug-in: the MIME content type of SWF files is application/x-shockwave-flash, for instance.

After the headers comes the actual data. If the server is responding to a GET request for a Web page, the HTML source of the page will be sent; if the requested resource was a Flash movie, the contents of an SWF file will be sent, and so on. Once the server has sent its response the connection is usually closed. (Only if both client and server are using HTTP/1.1 might it be kept open, if it is known that additional requests will follow, as when a page contains many images.)

CGI

Even allowing for the simplification in the foregoing description, it should be apparent that HTTP is not a very complicated protocol. However, HTTP is not the end of the story. As things stand, it can only return resources that are stored at the server end, it cannot create data dynamically by performing computation. This is a severe limitation: it makes it impossible to do something as simple as including the current date and time in a Web page, and entirely rules out such familiar devices as Web pages that include hit counters, display the results of database queries or accept user input from forms and respond to it. To produce dynamic Web content, a further mechanism is needed.

An assortment of such mechanisms is presently in use. The oldest is the *Common Gateway Interface (CGI)*, which allows HTTP servers to start up other programs, and to pass data to them. The program is identified by a URL, just as a Web page is, but the server is able to distinguish programs that should be executed from files that should be retrieved, because they are kept in a specific directory or are identified in some other way that can be specified by the server's administrator. These programs (or scripts — they are most often written in a scripting language such as Perl or Python) may carry out computation and interrogate or update databases. They then pass their results back to the server, which in turn passes them back to the client that issued the request. CGI is generally held to be inefficient, because it requires the server to create a new process for every request, and in recent years other mechanisms have begun to replace it — Apache modules, Microsoft Active Server Pages, and Java servlets are among the alternatives that avoid the excessive overhead of CGI. Unfortunately, most of these alternative mechanisms are tied in to one particular type of server, such as Apache or IIS. However, because of the extent to which CGI has been used, all its replacements present the same appearance to a Web client, which can send and receive data in the same way, irrespective of the technology being used to carry out the server-side computation. Accordingly, in what follows I will usually talk about CGI scripts, but you should understand that other mechanisms besides CGI may be used to achieve the same results.

Information always comes back to the client from a Web server in the form of an HTTP response. The client has no way of knowing whether the data in the body of a response was retrieved from a file stored on disk or generated by a program. It doesn't matter. Provided the Content-type header indicates correctly the nature of the data, and the client has been configured to deal with data of that type, there is no reason to distinguish between statically and dynamically generated responses. Problems only arise if the results of a server-side computation cannot be put into the form of an HTTP response, but the job of many CGI scripts is precisely to put the output of a database query into that form — hence the 'gateway' in the name.

HTTP requests as just described cannot send any information beyond the identity of a requested resource in the opposite direction, from client to server. Two mechanisms provided for this purpose are used by Flash. The first is the ability to add a *query string* to the end of a URL. This is separated from the URL proper by a question mark. In general, query strings may be formatted in several ways, depending on their destination, but the most common form, and the only form used by Flash, consists of a series of assignments, separated by & characters. Each assignment has the basic form *name=value*. When the server starts up a CGI script, it passes it the information in the query string so that the script can find the value that has been assigned to each name. The precise way in which the data is passed depends on the mechanism being used to execute the script, and the platform on which the server is running. The names often correspond to elements of a form, with the values being those entered by a user. Evidently, the script must be designed in conjunction with the form, so that it can use the appropriate set of names.

To ensure that query strings can travel safely over a network and not be misinterpreted by servers, the name and value are both encoded in a special way. Spaces are replaced by + signs, and characters that have significance in URLs, such as / are replaced by a % sign followed by the two characters representing their hexadecimal character code in the ISO Latin1 character set. For example, / is replaced by %2F. All + signs, %s and &s must also be encoded in this way when they occur within a name or value, and various other characters, including the underline, that are known to be subject to corruption by some network software are also sometimes encoded. (Flash is especially enthusiastic about encoding dubious characters, going as far as encoding periods and hyphens.) So, to send Digital Multimedia as the value of a parameter title, and 30/4/2000 as that of publication_date, the following query string would be appended to the URL in a GET request:
?title=Digital+Multimedia&publication%5Fdate=30%2F4%2F2000
Data in this format is said to be *URL encoded*; its MIME type is application/x-www-form-urlencoded.

The length of query string that may be passed in this way is limited to some arbitrary number of characters. The exact maximum length depends on the server, but is often 1024. A second disadvantage of sending data in query strings is that it is easily seen, so confidential information or passwords should not be sent in this way. The alternative is to use a different request, called POST. Its format is a cross between a GET request and a response, in that it consists of a request line, with POST as the method but otherwise the same as that of a GET request, followed by some headers and then the data, as in a response. An important header in POST requests is Content-length, which is used to tell the server how many bytes of data follow. The data itself is still encoded exactly the same way as in a query string. The request should include a Content-type header showing the type as application/x-www-form-urlencoded, although scripts rarely, if ever, bother to check.

If you are familiar with HTML forms, you will have encountered these concepts before. The action attribute of the <form> tag specifies a CGI script, and the method attribute determines whether the form data is sent to the server as a query string appended to the URL of a GET request (method="get") or in the body of a POST request (method="post").

Sending HTTP Requests from Flash

There are two movie clip methods that send HTTP requests. The first, getURL, sends a GET request in the manner of a Web browser. It is best suited for use in Flash movies that are playing within a browser, and will be described in Chapter 8. The loadVariables method is used for exchanging URL encoded data between a Flash movie and a remote server. It is this action that allows Flash access to data that is stored in files or generated by scripts.

loadVariables

This method takes a URL from which values are to be obtained as a parameter. The values are loaded into variables (i.e., properties) of the movie clip instance or movie (level) used to call the method. Since loadVariables can also be used to send values — from a form for instance — the method (GET or POST) is passed as a second argument in the form of a string. If no variables are to be sent, an empty string should be passed.

Calling loadVariables causes a GET or POST request to be sent to the HTTP server identified in its URL parameter. The pathname of the URL should identify either a text file that contains URL encoded data or a script that generates an HTTP response containing such data. In either case, the values are assigned to variables with the names given in the response. For example, if the response contains the data string:
author=Nigel+Chapman&title=Flash+Interactivity+and+Scripting
the string "Nigel Chapman" will be assigned to the variable author, and "Flash Interactivity and Scripting" to title. Note that the + signs have been turned back into spaces. Any other encoded characters would also have been decoded.

If either GET or POST had been passed as the second argument, the name and the current value of all the properties of the clip or movie used to call the method would have been URL encoded, and a set of assignments in URL encoded format would have been sent in the request. This would only be sensible if the URL identified a script that could handle the data.

The loadVariables method provides a straightforward way of connecting a Flash movie to files and programs running on a remote server, which works from within the Flash player or a Web browser. It is not, however, quite as simple as it appears.

When a loadVariables method is called during the execution of a script, an HTTP request is sent. Execution of the script and playing of the movie then continue *without waiting for the response*. Since data must pass over a network, and computation must occur on the server machine, some time may elapse before the response is received. When it does come, variables will be updated as just described, but until then, if the variables involved are used in an expression, the values they had before the request was sent will be obtained. In order to make use of data from a remote source, a script must wait until the HTTP response has been received. There is no explicit wait method that causes this to happen. It is necessary to put your movie into a loop that repeatedly tests for the response's arrival. There are two ways of doing this. If the method has been called from the main movie, it is necessary to look at the value of some variable that you know will be returned in the response. If the method is called via a clip, it will receive a data clip event when the values arrive, so, in that case, a handler may be used as an alternative means of responding to their arrival.

Although this may sound arcane, once the situation has been grasped, it is easy to put together movies that successfully fetch data. A simple example will show how this is done, beginning with the more direct method of testing a variable.

Loading Variables Into a Movie

The loan repayment calculator that was introduced in Chapter 3 used a value for the interest rate that was written in to the script. Since interest rates vary, this value would have to be altered, and a new SWF file generated and uploaded, every time the rate changed. This could be avoided if the value of the rate was kept in a file and loaded when it was needed. That way, only the data file would need changing when a new rate was set.

The first step is to create a file with the data. Since there is only one variable to set, and there are no special characters to encode, it looks very simple:
rate=0.0075

(There should not be a newline after the assignment.) Next, the original assignment to the variable rate in the first frame of the movie is replaced by

```
var rate = -1;
```
This will enable us to test whether a legitimate value for rate has been loaded. There seems to be no immediate risk in assuming that all legitimate interest rates will be positive.

The Calculate frame is unaltered. We will arrange to go to it only when the value of rate has been loaded. After that, the computation proceeds in the same way as ever. The button scripts must be modified so that instead of going to Calculate they move the playhead to a new frame — one of three keyframes which must be added to the movie — which will be labelled get_rate.

Relative or absolute URLs can be used as the URL argument to loadVariables to identify the data file, subject to the restriction that the file must be on a server in the same subdomain as the movie. (The subdomain is the part of the URL corresponding to the organization that maintains the servers. For example, wiley.co.uk is the domain name belonging to the UK branch of the publishers of this book. Servers with host names www1.wiley.co.uk and www2.wiley.co.uk would both be in the same subdomain.)[1] The restriction is imposed on the grounds of security.

Assuming the most simple case — a data file called interest_rate.txt in the same directory as the SWF file — the get_rate frame would have the following one-line script attached to it.
```
_root.loadVariables ("interest_rate.txt", "");
```
The apparently redundant use of _root is necessary to cause the variable to be loaded into the main movie — which is what we require since rate was global in the original version — because loadVariables can also be called as a function with an explicit target argument to maintain compatibility with Flash 4. Since, as explained, there may be some delay before the server's response is received, this frame and the following two which will be added should display some appropriate message or graphic to indicate that something is going on. A simple Please wait... text may be most suitable.

After the HTTP request has been sent from get_rate, the playhead moves on to the following frame. This will be labelled wait_for_data, and it will be the first frame of a two-frame loop that is executed until the rate arrives. It has the following script attached.
```
if (rate > 0) {
```

---

1. To be more precise, if the domain name part of a URL has only one or two components, the subdomain is the same as the domain, otherwise, the subdomain consists of everything except the final component of the domain name, so, in the example, the subdomain is wiley.co.uk.

```
        rate = Number(rate);
        gotoAndStop("Calculate");
}
```
The test will only succeed if a sensible value for rate has been received, since the variable was originally set to -1. Because the value will be set to a string when the variable is loaded from the remote file, the arithmetic that uses it will go awry: remember that + is interpreted as string concatenation, even if the string has the form of a number. Hence, the rate must be explicitly converted to a number before the playhead is moved to Calculate after which everything proceeds as in the original version. If the test fails — the data has not yet been received — the playhead moves on to the next frame, which merely loops back so that the test can be repeated.
gotoAndPlay("wait_for_data");

As you can see, the movie will continue testing until the value is received. There is no other way for it to be notified of the receipt of the response. The pattern just shown of sending a request using loadVariables, and then entering a loop that tests whether a legitimate value has been returned is always needed to retrieve data from a remote location if loadVariables is not called through a clip. An immediate implication is that, if this approach is adopted, some value that can easily be tested for legitimacy must be returned. If, for example, we lived in a more charitable world, where negative or zero interest rates could occur, the test just used would not be adequate. A sensible discipline is to require some variable that is not used for any other purpose to be returned with a suitable string as its value as part of the response to every request sent as a result of a loadVariables action. For example, you might insist that a variable called vars_loaded was set to "ok" or "not ok" in any response. If some other value, such as undefined, is assigned to vars_loaded before sending the request, it will always be possible to determine whether a response has been received, no matter what the actual useful values being returned are.

Loading Variables into Clips

Using a movie clip to perform the loading instead of doing it in the main movie has two advantages. First, it provides another form of abstraction: having once created such a clip, it is not necessary to worry too much about how it performs its function. Second, the data clip event provides a means of testing for the arrival of data without having to perform explicit checks, or insist that there is a variable among the returned data the legitimacy of whose value can be unambiguously determined.

There are many different ways of arranging the interactions between a clip and its enclosing movie, all based on creating an instance — let's assume it's called the_loader

— of some movie clip symbol, and placing in a movie. The clip itself can be anything. It might be a short animation that displayed an hour glass or watch to indicate that something was going on. Alternatively, you could not put any graphic content in the clip at all, so that it was invisible, and put a suitable message or graphic in the enclosing movie. The important thing is to attach a clip event handler to the instance. One possibility is simply the following:

```
onClipEvent(data) {
    _parent.play();
    stop();
}
```

This scheme uses the clip simply as a container for the returned values, leaving all the work to scripts in the enclosing movie. To understand why the handler is appropriate, it is necessary to see these scripts.

A two-frame sequence is used. It is vital that the same instance of the loader persists across both frames. This is most reliably ensured by placing it on its own static layer, spanning the two frames. The first of these has a script attached that calls the loader's loadVariables method, and then stops.

```
the_loader.loadVariables("interest_rate.txt", "");
stop();
```

The file name interest_rate.txt can be replaced by any relative or absolute URL in the same subdomain as the SWF file itself.

What happens when the playhead enters this frame is that an HTTP request is sent to the server. The main movie stops, while the loader clip carries on looping, as clips always do. When the server's response is received, the values are assigned to properties of the_loader with the same names as the variables in the response string, because loadVariables was called as a method of that movie clip. The clip event handler is then executed, which causes the playhead in the enclosing movie to move on to the next frame, stopping any animation in the loader clip at the same time. Hence, in the main movie, the properties of the loader can be retrieved to obtain the values sent from the server. For example, if the interest rate had been loaded in this way:

```
rate = Number(the_loader.rate);
```

Using this approach is somewhat like suspending a process while it waits for some asynchronous operation to complete. Scripts in the main movie do not need to be concerned with the arrival of the data; as soon as the playhead moves again, the data is known to be there.

A possible candidate for using this symbol is the direct manipulation interface to a bookshop that was developed in earlier chapters. The latest version, which was described in Chapter 5 required a long sequence of assignments in the first frame of the shopping basket symbol to record the details of all the books on offer. This information could be detached from the movie and recorded in a separate file, from which it was loaded when required. Apart from the minor benefit of tidying up the scripts, this arrangement means that when the price of any book is changed, only the data file needs editing, the Flash movie can be left unchanged. The disadvantage is that extra network traffic is required.

A crude way of loading the data from the remote file into the book records is first to load it into properties of the loader clip with names indicating the records and fields to which they correspond, and then extracting the values of the correct variables into the fields of the record. The data file would look something like this:
dmm_title=Digital+Multimedia&dmm_author=Nigel+Chapman+and+Jenny+Chapman&dmm_price=27.95& ... &dmm_number_in_stock=12
(all on one long line[1]). An instance of the loader symbol can be placed in the same frame as the record library, and the following can be added to the next frame's script.
the_loader.loadVariables("book_data.txt", "");
stop();
This will work as before. When the playhead moves, in response to the data clip event handler in the loader, the loader will have acquired properties such as dmm_title, dmm_author, and so on, initialized with the values taken from the data file and sent in the HTTP response. To pull them out and store them in a book record within a BookDrag object, the following method is added.

```
BookDrag.prototype.set_record_from_loader = function(prefix) {
    this.book_record = new _root.record_lib.Book();
    for (var p in _root.the_loader) {
        if (p.indexOf(prefix) == 0) {
            var prop = p.substring(prefix.length);
            this.book_record[prop] = _root.the_loader[p];
        }
    }
}
```

First an uninitialized book record is created and assigned to the object's book_record property. Next, a loop iterates through all the properties of the loader, looking for any whose first few characters match the argument passed to this method. For example, if

---

1. If your text editor can't handle very long lines, or you just prefer a more readable layout, you can use a dummy variable to absorb newlines. Just replace the & separators by &cr=*newline*&.

we are initializing the record for Digital Multimedia, the prefix "dmm_" will be passed as the argument, and all the properties beginning with that string (i.e., all the variables with values pertaining to that book) will be picked up by the test. The remainder of the property name will be a field in a book record; for example, dmm_title gives title. The substring method is used to pull that part of the name out of the property, and the result is then used to associatively index the book_record object so that the variable's value can be stored in it.

With this method in place, the sequence of calls to the set_record method of the BookDrag objects with the values of the fields wired in as literals can be replaced by:
cpp.wrapper.set_record_from_loader("cpp_");
perl.wrapper.set_record_from_loader("perl_");
dmm.wrapper.set_record_from_loader("dmm_");
Apart from a slight delay while starting up, the movie will behave exactly as before with no other changes.

The loader symbol provides a straightforward way for a movie to load variables without worrying too much about what is actually going on. It will not be suitable for all occasions, though. Sometimes, you may not wish to stop your movie while the response is awaited; you may have something useful for it to do in the meantime. In that case, you would have to tailor a script to the purpose, but it would always have to call a loadVariables method and test to see when the response arrived using one or other of the methods I have described — testing for a value or handling a data clip event.

There is one unresolved issue. What if the response never comes? Or it comes and the response code is not 200 (OK), but something that indicates an error at the server? In that case, if your movie is waiting in a loop, it will loop forever. There isn't much you can do about this: there is no way for a script in a Flash movie to get access to the actual HTTP response. The best you can do is put a counter in your loop, and, if it exceeds some reasonable value, stop the loop and go to a frame that displays an apology for being unable to complete the operation and performs any cleaning up that may be necessary. This strategy may be unduly pessimistic, but is probably safer than leaving your movie stuck or trusting to luck.

Sending Variables to a Server

So far, we have only looked at receiving data from a file. The more interesting possibility is to receive data from a program. This often entails sending data to the program first, to be used as the basis of computation. A full understanding of what is going on in such cases involves both the Flash script that sends and receives data and the program at the

sending http requests from flash **183**

server end that processes it. Usually, these will be designed together, although sometimes it may be necessary for a Flash movie to communicate with an already existing program.

To avoid vagueness, in the rest of this section I will include some actual examples of server-side code in the form of CGI scripts written in Perl, since, despite its inefficiency, CGI is the most widely understood mechanism for server-side computation. If you are not familiar with Perl, you will have to rely on the accompanying commentary to see what is happening.

The most common case is probably that of sending values obtained from a form to a script that sends back a result computed from them. We will begin with a very simple example. Many Web sites require you to register by filling in a form with your email address and a password. The password must usually be entered twice, in separate fields, to catch typing mistakes. A script associated with this form could compare the two attempts at the password and return a value indicating whether they match. At the same time, it could save the user's email address in order to send them newsletters, special offers and all the usual junk email.

The client side of this system can be fairly simple. Variables called email, password1 and password2 are associated with the three text fields, and the movie is stopped on the frame containing the form, so it can be filled in. This frame also contains a loader clip, with instance name the_loader, and the usual data event handler. This time, an invisible clip would seem to be most appropriate. The button has the following script attached to it.

```
on (release) {
    the_loader.email = email;
    the_loader.password1 = password1;
    the_loader.password2 = password2;
    the_loader.loadVariables("http://www.macavon.co.uk/cgi-bin/register.cgi",
                                                                    "GET");
    gotoAndStop ("check_result");
}
```

First, all the variables that are to be sent to the CGI script are copied into properties of the loader, and then its loadVariables method is called, with the second argument set to GET, so the URL encoded values of these variables will be appended to the URL in a GET request. The first argument identifies a CGI script.[1] The playhead is then transferred to

---

1. The URL is mythical.

a frame where the player waits for the response. This frame has no script attached to it; as soon as the loader receives its data event, the playhead will move on to the following frame. A message can be placed in the waiting frame, indicating to the user what is going on.

A typical example of the request that gets sent would be:
GET /cgi-bin/register.cgi?email=tony%40number%2D10%2Egov%2Euk&password1=RIPact&password2=RIPact HTTP/1.0
Accept: */*
Accept-Language: en-us
User-Agent: Macromedia Flash Player 4.0
Host: www.macavon.co.uk:80

Sending unencrypted passwords in a query string is not clever. Encrypting them is left to Exercise 2. Using a POST request instead of GET makes it more difficult for the data to be intercepted. If security is really an issue, Flash can make secure connections to URLs using HTTPS (HTTP–Secure). A secure approach you might wish to adopt if that is not feasible could be based on public key encryption. The movie could request a public key from the server and use it to encrypt the passwords, which could be decrypted by the server using the matching private key. However, the computation required to perform the encryption is probably more sophisticated than one would like if it had to be done using ActionScript. Flash has no facility analogous to Director's Xtras for linking to programs written in a conventional programming language to deal with complex algorithms or for accessing already existing libraries in C or some other compiled language.

After waiting in the frame labelled check_result, the playhead is moved on to a frame which has a script that uses the value of a property of the_loader called password_ok, which is sent back by the CGI script, to determine which frame to go to next. If it is "ok", the playhead is transferred to a frame labelled thankyou, where a suitable message is displayed; if it is "not ok", the user is given another chance to fill in the form.
if (the_loader.password_ok eq "ok")
    gotoAndStop ("thankyou");
else if (the_loader.password_ok eq "not ok")
    gotoAndStop ("password_error");
The password_error frame is just a copy of the original form with an error message overlaid.

What happens at the server end? To reduce the matter of passing data to and from the Flash player to its essentials, first just consider verifying that the two passwords match and returning the appropriate value in password_ok. In general, a CGI script must determine which method has been used to send variables, since they are passed to the script differently depending on the method; it must then extract the values and decode them by reversing the URL form encoding process. Nobody with anything better to do wants to do all that, but if you write CGI scripts in Perl, you don't have to. The CGI module hides all the details, and permits the value assigned to any variable to be looked up directly using a function call. In order to use this module, a Perl script must begin with the rubric:

use CGI;

The CGI module is object-oriented (as that expression is used in Perl circles), so the next thing to do is create a CGI object:

my $password_form = CGI->new;

This object provides access to all the information available about the HTTP request that the script has been called to handle, as well as methods for creating a response. In particular, the value of any of the variables passed in the request can be obtained by passing the variable name to the $password_form->param method. The next thing the script can do is extract the two passwords.

my $first_password = $password_form->param('password1');
my $second_password = $password_form->param('password2');

The arguments to param are the names of the variables used in the script in the Flash movie, and thus the names passed in the query string. It is as if the param method allowed the Perl script to reach into the Flash script and retrieve the values of variables.

Having got the values, the script now needs to compare them. I use a conditional expression to assign the value that must be returned in password_ok to a variable in the Perl script.

my $valid_password = $first_password eq $second_password ? 'ok': 'not+ok';

The script is now in a position to construct the response, and again the CGI object can be used to do so. The header method builds the response status line and headers. It may take a MIME type as its argument, for the Content-type header. Since the returned data is URL encoded, the corresponding MIME type can be used (although it doesn't really matter, because nobody is going to check).

print $password_form->header('application/x-www-form-urlencoded');

The header method actually returns a string which, as shown, must be explicitly printed in order to be passed back to the server. Finally, we also print the data.

print "password_ok=$valid_password";

That is all that is needed. The complete response is:

```
HTTP/1.0 200 OK
Content-type: application/x-www-form-urlencoded

password_ok=ok
```
(The blank line separating the headers from the body is stipulated by the protocol specification.) The response is passed back to the server, which sends it back to the Flash player, which decodes it and sets the value of the_loader.password_ok, and restarts the main movie, where the script proceeds to test it and react accordingly.

Astute readers will have realized that the passwords could have been checked on the client side. Now that the mechanism for passing data has been described, we can look at the part of the processing that can only be done on the server-side: storing the email address and password for future reference. Like most server side computation, this will entail access to some sort of database. For the present example, something very simple will suffice; a Perl module that provides the very thing is available. DB_File is one of a family of modules that allows Perl scripts to access databases managed by the Berkeley DB system as though they were associative arrays. To use it, an extra line of red tape must be added to the top of the script:
```
use DB_File;
```
The password checking can be carried out exactly as before. After it has been done, the password can be recorded in a database. This should only be done if the password was verified, of course.
```
if ($valid_password eq 'ok')
{
```
First, the database must be opened (or created if it does not yet exist). This is done by tying a 'hash' — Perl's name for an associative array — to a database file. The actual code is as follows (though the details are not very relevant to our present purposes).
```
tie %registrations, 'DB_File', 'registrations.db';
```
To simplify the description, I have omitted the error checking that a real script would have to perform in case anything goes wrong with this operation. Assuming that all goes well, the new user's email address and password can be stored in the database by assigning to an element of the tied hash, and then the database can be closed.
```
    $registrations{$email} = $first_password;
    untie %registrations;
}
```

The password is now stored permanently, so it can be used at any time in the future. The typical use of a password is to allow a registered user to log in. This can be done through a very similar Flash form consisting of two text fields and a button. The variables attached to the two text fields are called email and password; the script attached to the button is the same as the one used in the registration form, except that the URL parameter to loadVariables is changed to identify a different script, this time one that opens the database and checks whether the password that has been entered matches the one that is stored. (It still isn't very clever to be sending unencrypted passwords around in query strings.)

```
#!perl -w
use CGI;
use DB_File;
my $login_form = CGI->new;
my $email = $login_form->param('email');
my $password = $login_form->param('password');
tie %registrations, 'DB_File', 'registrations.db';
my $password_ok = $registrations{$email} eq $password;
print $login_form->header('application/x-www-form-urlencoded');
print "password_ok=", $password_ok? 'ok': 'not+ok';
untie %registrations;
```

Again, a real script would have to perform some additional error checking.

This isn't a book about CGI programming, and readers who are not familiar with Perl are probably beginning to feel alienated, so I will not go any further in showing the sort of computation that can be performed on the server side. The point that I hope has been established is that data can readily be passed to a script, which can then perform any computation using it, including accessing files and databases in order to store persistent information derived from a Flash movie. Moreover, there is nothing special about the programs that run on the server side: apart from the way in which they access the data in an HTTP request, these are perfectly ordinary Perl scripts. The same results could be obtained with perfectly ordinary C++ programs, or perfectly ordinary Python or PHP3 scripts, or any other sort of perfectly ordinary program or script. In other words, Flash movies can have access to all the power of programs, provided the programs run on the server side and provided the data that must be passed to and from them can be sent in the form of a URL encoded string of variables and values.

The preceding example used a simple type of database access to perform a simple task. More complex tasks, such as maintaining a full-blown ecommerce site, require more complex databases than Berkeley DB files, and correspondingly complex methods of accessing them. For most ambitious tasks, a fully relational database supporting SQL queries will be used. There are well established ways of connecting such databases to Web servers, either indirectly through CGI scripts or by more direct server extensions.

Relational databases and SQL are the established tools used for maintaining information in large organizations, so it is possible to use Flash to provide an attractive front end to this information, although the programming and database expertise required to provide suitable scripts to run at the server end are somewhat beyond what is needed for writing Flash scripts.

Replacing HTML Forms With Flash Movies

Since interfaces to databases have been developed using established WWW technology, particularly HTML forms, a route that avoids the need for expert programming is to use an existing script, and replace an HTML form with something more interesting or attractive using Flash and its loadVariables method. As long as the Flash version sends the same query string or POST request as the HTML form, and the form sends a suitable response, the server-side code can be left unchanged. The second half of this requirement is rarely met if the script actually sends a response — CGI scripts used with HTML forms usually send back dynamically constructed HTML pages. Many scripts don't return anything, though, or can have suitable values extracted from their response by a simple modification, so the possibility of moving from an HTML front-end to one built in Flash with minimal programming does exist. (A different way of dealing with the response is described in Chapter 8.)

All of the HTML form elements have their Flash equivalents: input elements, with type = "checkbox" or "radio" can be replaced by checkboxes or radio buttons, as described in Chapter 4; the pop-up menus and scrolling lists described in the same chapter can be used instead of select elements. Other types of input element and textarea elements have their direct equivalent in Flash buttons or editable text fields. A problem only occurs with select elements whose multiple attribute is set. This allows a user to choose more than one item from a list or menu. Each of the corresponding values is assigned to the same name in the query string sent when a form containing such an element is submitted. For example, the following HTML fragment creates a form containing a scrollable list from which several applications can be selected.

```
<p>Which digital media tools do you use regularly?</p>
<form method="get" action="cgi-bin/multiple-selections.cgi" name="software">
  <select name="select" size="5" multiple>
    <option>Illustrator</option>
    <option>Photoshop</option>
    <option>Premiere</option>
    <option>GoLive</option>
    <option>LiveMotion</option>
    <option>Dreamweaver</option>
```

```
    <option>Flash</option>
    <option>Director</option>
    <option>Fireworks</option>
  </select>
  <input type="submit" name="submit" value="submit">
</form>
```
When the submit button is pressed, a GET request is sent, with a query string similar to the following one appended to the URL.
select=Illustrator&select=Photoshop&select=Flash&Submit=Submit

Some HCI experts would argue that using a scrollable list for selecting several items is poor interface design, but HTML allows it and CGI scripts can be written to cope with it. In particular, if you use the CGI module in Perl, the param method can return a list.

The problem with trying to replace such a form by a Flash movie is that loadVariables only sends a single value for each variable in the movie or clip, including arrays (see Exercise 4). To cope with variables that may have multiple parameters, you must construct a query string yourself. (If the original form used POST as its method, and the script accesses the variables explicitly, instead of using some abstraction such as the CGI module's param method, you are stuck: there is no way of specifying a string to include in the body of a POST request.)

For example, suppose that you had constructed a scrollable list symbol, and added actions so that a user could select several items from it, with the number selected being stored in a variable number_selected, and the selections themselves in an array selection. The following script builds up a query string, assuming that the CGI script is expecting the selections to be passed as multiple values for the parameter select, as in the example above. (There is never a neat way of building up strings with separators between elements, either the first or last has to be treated as a special case. The way I have done it here looks neat, but isn't really.)
```
var selected = "", sep = "";
for (var i = 0; i < selection.length; ++i) {
    selected += sep + "select=" + selection[i];
    sep = "&";
}
```

To send the values, an expression that includes the query string is used as the URL parameter of loadVariables. The parameter indicating the query method is set to the empty string, because we don't want Flash adding another query string. An example of a suitable call is:

```
this.loadVariables ("http://www.macavon.co.uk/cgi-bin/multiple-selections.cgi?" +
                                                                    selected, "");
```
There is an important assumption behind the code just presented: the values do not contain any characters that need URL encoding. If they do — which in general they will — you will have to encode them yourself. Whereas Flash performs the encoding automatically when you send variables using one of the options to loadVariables, if you create the query string yourself, it will be sent exactly as it is. The escape function (not a method of String) is provided to perform this encoding. (Should you ever need it, its inverse unescape is also available.)

Sending Variables With loadMovie

As noted in Chapter 3, the loadMovie method and function may take an argument indicating that a GET or POST request should be used to send the values of variables to the URL from which the movie is to be loaded. This only makes sense if, in fact, the URL identifies a CGI script (or something similar) that uses the values sent in the request to choose a movie to load, or even to construct it. A trivial example, which nevertheless demonstrates the essence of the procedure, would be a script that sends a request with a variable choice set to long or short, to indicate a user's preference as to the length of movie they want to see. Assuming that the movie is to be loaded into a clip called loaded_movie, in response to a click on a button, and that the value to be sent as choice is originally stored in a variable of the same name in the main movie, the following script will take care of the Flash end:

```
on (release) {
      loaded_movie.choice = choice;
      loaded_movie.loadMovie("cgi-bin/choose-swf.cgi", "GET");
}
```

On the server, the choose-swf script could look like this:

```
#!perl -w
use CGI;
sub copy_movie {
      code to copy the bytes of an SWF file, whose name is passed as an argument
}
declare variables $short_movie and $long_movie to hold the file names of the short and
long movies
my $cgi = CGI->new;
my $choice = $cgi->param('choice');
print $cgi->header('application/x-shockwave-flash');
copy_movie($choice eq 'short'? $short_movie: $long_movie);
```

Of course, there is no point in doing this unless for some reason the identities of the two movies can only be determined at the server end. A possible reason for this is that the movies might be held on a server in a different subdomain from the movie doing the loading. The security restrictions prevent Flash from loading them directly, but it is possible to call a CGI script that is in an allowable subdomain and have it load the movies from elsewhere — it's up to you whether you trust your own CGI scripts.

As with `loadVariables`, all the variables on the timeline used for the call are sent in the request. The `data` clip event may be used to determine when the loaded movie arrives (it is sent whenever a section of movie data is received), or the `_framesloaded` property can be tested repeatedly if subsequent playback or computation depends on certain frames having been loaded.

Using Generator

You can think of `loadVariables` as providing a pipe that connects a Flash movie to a program running on a remote server. The pipe can carry values in the form of strings, but nothing else. The more complex facilities for transferring XML, to be described in Chapter 8, are also ultimately restricted to textual data. This mechanism can take you a long way, but there are some things you might want to be able to do that require other types of data to be passed to your movie. As an example, let us return once again to the bookselling movie that has been developed over the last few chapters.

In the preceding section, I showed how to add some flexibility to the system by retrieving the book information from a file, which could be updated to reflect price changes. You can probably see that the book data could equally well be retrieved from a database in response to a suitable query. From here it is only a short step to realizing that the query could be passed parameters to choose different books to display in the shop movie. The same movie could then be used to offer, for example, a weekly selection of special offers, or suggestions based on a visitor's previous purchases, or else it could be used to show the results of a search or a series of menu choices that allowed the customer to choose books by category. At least, it could be used in any of these ways, if it wasn't for the fact that the images of the book covers are embedded in the movie. What is needed is a way to retrieve the images dynamically at the same time as the author, title, and so on.

One way is to write a CGI script that writes SWF files dynamically. The equivalent of this approach is widely used with HTML, where scripts write the HTML code for a page and then send it in a server response, so that pages can be built out of dynamically computed elements. HTML code is much simpler than SWF files, though. It certainly is possible to generate dynamic Flash movies in this way, but for most purposes the programming effort will probably be considered excessive. *Macromedia Generator* provides a less demanding alternative.

It may be helpful to think of Generator as the Flash equivalent of the mail merge facility provided by many word processors. When you use such a facility, you create a document that has specially tagged variables included among the text. You also create a database, with fields corresponding to each of the variables in the document. When you invoke the mail merge, a copy of the document is created for each record in the database, with the variables being replaced by the value stored in the corresponding field of the record. The characteristic use of this facility is to produce circulars and form letters, each with an individual address and personalized salutation.

Generator works in a similar manner. Using its authoring extensions you create a *template* in Flash that includes special generator objects — which stand for elements such as GIF or JPEG images, sounds, Flash movies or symbols — and variables, analogous to the variables in your mail merge document. You also specify a *data source*, from which values for these objects and variables can be obtained. Data sources can be simple text files, or they can be generated by programs, or returned as the result of database queries. The analogy with mail merging begins to break down at this point. Instead of immediately producing many copies of the movie, you publish it as a template (SWT) file, by including Generator Template among the formats in the Publish Settings dialogue. A movie can subsequently be generated by combining the template with the specified data source. If the values produced by the data source change, a different movie is produced. So, taken over time, you generate several movies from the same template, differing only in the actual objects used to replace the Generator objects, and the values given to Generator variables. If Generator objects are used for the book cover images in the example, the covers can be selected dynamically and the movie can be used in the ways outlined earlier.

Generator can operate in two distinct modes: *online* and *offline*. In online mode, it operates in real time as an extension to a Web server to combine templates that have been uploaded to the server machine with data sources, and return them in HTTP responses. In offline mode, Generator is used from a command line to create SWF files that are stored to disk. Online mode is used to create personalized Web pages for each visitor to a site. Offline mode is used to update movies by changing data sources instead of going into Flash to change the movie itself. In our book shop example, offline processing would be suitable if the movie was being used to present special offers that were changed once a week; online processing would be needed if it was being used to offer recommendations to each customer as they arrived at the site, on the basis of their past purchasing history.

Generator Objects and Variables

In its simplest mode of operation, Generator simply provides a way of inserting images, SWF files and other objects into a Flash movie by reference, instead of actually copying them. (If you use Illustrator, it's like placing images instead of importing them.) That is, the Generator template does not contain the imported object, only a reference to it (actually, usually a URL). The object's data is only incorporated when the template is processed by Generator to produce an SWF file. This means, that whenever an SWF file is generated, it contains the current version of the object. In other words, you can edit the object (image, movie, and so on) without touching the template.

Variables allow an extra level of flexibility. They can be employed just like mail merge variables to include customized text in a movie, but they can also be used within scripts, to tailor their behaviour, and as file names, so that references placed into a template can be resolved dynamically, on the basis of the values in a data source.

The creation of templates is integrated into Flash itself. When the Generator extensions are installed, two new elements are added to the authoring interface: the Generator Objects palette[1] and the Generator panel. Generator objects are placeholders for various kinds of graphic and animated element. You add them to a movie by dragging the appropriate icon from the Generator Objects palette to the stage, the same way you create symbol instances by dragging symbols from the library.

Generator objects do not correspond exactly to Flash objects, although they can mostly be treated like clip instances. They come in several flavours, including GIF, PNG and JPEG images, Flash movies and MP3 sounds, as well as a selection of more specialized objects for displaying data. These include line, bar and pie charts, lists and tables. There is also a Generator object for a set of radio buttons, that works much like a smart clip, except that its text labels and other parameters can be set when the template is generated, not just when the object is added to the movie.

Once a Generator object has been placed on the stage, the Generator panel can be used to set various parameters. The panel is context-sensitive: different types of Generator object have different parameters. Many of them include a data source among them,

---

1. All of Flash's other palettes are referred to as 'panels'. This one, though, is always called a palette.

allowing you to associate data with the object. A data source can also be specified for an entire movie or movie clip symbol. Clicking the Generator Environment Variable icon at the top of the timeline brings up a dialogue box in which you can specify a data source. (We'll see how shortly.) This source is used to provide the values for any Generator variables that are used in the movie or clip.

As a first illustration of the mechanics of using Generator, consider a trivial example: a template for a movie containing a single GIF image. This is made by dragging the icon labelled Insert GIF file from the Generator Objects Palette to the stage. The object thus created is shown as a grey square with the icon label on it. Like smart clip instances, you cannot see the final appearance of Generator objects until you test the movie. The object can be resized, rotated and otherwise transformed like any other object on the stage.

When the object just created is selected, the Generator panel provides fields for entering the parameters appropriate to GIF image objects. The crucial one is its file name. An absolute or relative URL (which may refer to a CGI script or some other resource that performs computation) can be entered here. Another important parameter is cache, which determines whether the Generator server maintains a its own copy of the file to optimize processing of requests for the template. Other parameters are concerned with the way the image is exported to the SWF file by Generator: by default, images are converted to JPEGs and compressed.

If the file name is set to a string, when Generator processes the template the Generator object will be replaced by the actual file the string identifies. Thus, whenever the file is edited, the latest version will automatically appear in the movie. (Actually, the caching process may interfere with this, and you can take advantage of this fact to allow the file to be edited without affecting any movie until the copy in the cache is declared stale.) If the file name is set to a Generator variable, things get more interesting.

Generator variables are strings of letters and digits, begining with a letter, enclosed in curly brackets, for example {filename}. They can be interpolated in other strings, as, for example, {cover}.gif, and used in any context where a string is needed. First, we will be using variables in parameters for Generator objects, but later we will see how they can also be used in scripts. Using them introduces another level of indirection. Instead of replacing the GIF file object by a GIF file identified by a constant string, as before, Generator will first replace the variable by a value obtained from a data source, and use the resulting string as the file name.

Data Sources

Data sources must conform to one of two formats. For simple variables, they can be in 'name/value' format. The first line must be:
Name, Value
The remaining lines each consist of a variable name, followed by a comma, and then a value for that variable, for example,
cover,../GIFs/dmm-cover

For more complex data the first line must consist of a list of names, and subsequent lines consist of a list of values, one for each name. You can think of the first line as being the column headings of a table, for which the subsequent lines provide the data rows. Data in this format is easily generated from relational databases, and we will see an example of how it is used with Generator objects shortly.

For simple purposes, the name/value format is adequate. Suppose that the file name parameter for the inserted GIF Generator object in the simple GIF image movie was set to {cover}.gif, and that the data source for the movie had been set to a file containing the two lines displayed above. When the template was processed by Generator, the variable would be replaced by its value as obtained from the file, giving ../GIFS/dmm_cover.gif as the name of the GIF file to be inserted in place of the Generator object. To change the file to a different cover, all that is needed is to edit the data source file.

Data sources need not be files. They can be CGI scripts or other applications that generate the data dynamically. This enables Generator to obtain data from databases and so on. A data source may also specify a database query directly. This relies on the availability of a JDBC/ODBC compliant database. If data is stored in such a database, Generator can link to it, using a special non-standard form of URL, and pass an SQL query in the URL's query string. A data source can also be a Java class that provides a suitable method for returning data. Again, a non-standard URL is used to specify such a class as a data source, and to pass arguments to its method. For full details of these types of data source, consult the manual *Using Generator*. Evidently, using data sources of this type implies familiarity with database technology or Java programming.

Returning to simpler matters, Generator objects can be used in a shopfront application as sketched earlier in this section. The imported GIF images that were placed in the movie clip symbols for each of the books can be replaced by Generator objects, with their file name parameters set to {cover1}.gif, {cover2}.gif and {cover3}.gif. If the movie's data source is set to a file containing:

Name, Value
cover1,../GIFs/dmm-cover
cover2,../GIFs/cpp-cover
cover3,../GIFs/perl-cover

then, under the obvious assumptions about where files are on the server, the generated movie will behave just as before. When it became necessary to display a different three books in the movie, the data source file could be edited. The CGI script that returned the books' details would have to be changed in parallel to produce a new version of the shop selling different books. The data source could equally well be a CGI script too, that generated output in the form of a name/value data source for Generator. In that case, the scripts could generate covers and details for an arbitrary trio of books. The movie could actually be used in a real application. Instead of merely selling three books, it could be used to display books that matched some search criteria, or recommend books to each visitor to the site.

Using Generator Variables in Scripts

Generator variables can be used directly in scripts to make their behaviour conditional on a data source. A simple example will suffice to show how this works. Imagine a leisure centre or an adult education institution that puts on classes every day of the week. Each day there will be different classes, but every week the same classes will be held at the same time on the same day: yoga every Tuesday at 9pm, chess every Thursday and Friday at 2, and so on. Now imagine that you wanted to use Flash to display today's classes. There are, of course, many ways of doing this, but one economical way is to make a movie with seven frames, one for each day of the week labelled accordingly, plus a starting frame containing a button marked Today's Classes. (Perhaps this would be part of a menu that allowed you to display other information, too.) You could attach a release handler to the button that used a Generator variable to identify today's day of the week:

```
on (release) {
    gotoAndStop("{today}");
}
```

Remember that Generator variables are strings, and they can only be used in scripts by interpolating them into a string literal. The quote marks are needed as well as the curly brackets. If the movie is published as a template and associated with a data source containing

#name,value
today,tuesday

Generator will create a movie with the release handler:

```
on (release) {
```

```
        gotoAndStop("tuesday");
}
```
The next day, the data source can be changed so that today has the value wednesday, and the generated movie will display Wednesday's classes. The source might be a file that was edited (probably by some automatic means) every night, or a CGI script that determined what day of the week it was run on.

Displaying Numerical Data

In the examples shown so far, it has been sufficient to specify a data source for the entire movie, and use the variables it defined to make the file names of the GIF Generator objects dynamically or to change the behaviour of scripts. Some types of Generator object — mostly those concerned with displaying numerical data — require their own individual data source. Usually, these have to be in the more flexible column names and values format instead of the name/value pairs used in the earlier examples.

An example of such a Generator object is a pie chart. These are a widely used means of presenting numerical data in a graphic form. Figure 7.1 is an example. It was created by dragging the Pie Chart object from the Generator Objects palette to the stage, and, using the Generator panel to associate a data source with the object (and also to set a few parameters controlling its appearance). Each type of Generator object requires a data source with columns appropriate to the type of display it provides. Typically, some columns are compulsory, and others, which can be added to provide extra functionality of some sort, are optional. In the case of pie charts, the compulsory coumns are value and color (spelt like that). The colour can be specified in any of the formats used on the Web, including the basic HTML colour names. To produce Figure 7.1, the following data source was used:

```
#value,color
40,red
25,green
15,yellow
15,purple
5,silver
```

(It looks better in colour.) The positioning of the numbers and the apparent 3-D effect are set using parameters to the object. Additional columns can be added to the data source to add interactivity to the pie chart: GoTo and GoToLabel allow you to specify a frame to go to if the slice is clicked on, either as a frame number or a label; URL is used to associate a URL with each slice, which will be retrieved in response to a click. (See Chapter 8 for more on jumping to URLs from Flash movies.)

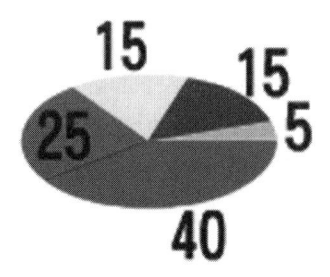

Figure 7.1 *A pie chart produced by Generator.*

Creating User Interface Elements With Generator

Smart clips provide a flexible way of constructing interface elements, and careful design and the use of dynamic text fields makes it possible to set elements such as the labels on radio buttons when the movie runs, if necessary using CGI scripts to obtain values dynamically. Generator's radio button and scrolling list objects are somewhat redundant, therefore, but they may provide an easier way of creating dynamic interfaces in some environments. As usual, a radio button object is added to a movie by dragging from the Generator Objects palette, and a data source can be associated with it in the Generator panel. For radio buttons, the only compulsory column in the data source is text, which gives a label to be attached to a radio button. When the template is processed, the Generator object is replaced by a set of radio buttons, one for each data row in the data source, labelled with the text specified. Figure 7.2 shows the radio buttons created from the following data source:

text
Mr
Ms
Mrs
Miss
Dr
Prof
Rev

The radio button object uses a slightly less than obvious way of specifying typographic properties for the labels on the button. You must create a graphic symbol containing a static text field with the Generator variable {text} in it. Any type styles that you apply to that text will be applied to the labels on the buttons in the generated movie. After this graphic symbol has been saved in the library, you set the Text Symbol parameter of the radio button object to its name. You can control the appearance of the buttons in a more obvious way, by defining graphic symbols for the on and off states and setting the On Symbol and Off Symbol properties of the Generator object to their names. Custom on and off symbols were used to make the radio buttons in Figure 7.2.

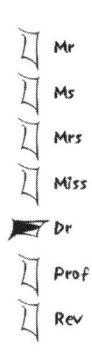

Figure 7.2 *A set of radio buttons produced by Generator.*

Full details of all the Generator objects and data sources can be found in the manual *Using Generator*, which also describes the administration and caching features of Generator.

The flexibility of templates comes at a price. Whereas Flash is averagely priced for a piece of desktop multimedia software and the authoring extensions for creating templates are free, the Generator software that combines templates and data sources is far from free. In May 2000, Generator was split into two versions: Generator 2 Enterprise Edition and Generator 2 Developer Edition. The former is intended for large corporate sites which expect many hits; it uses an elaborate caching mechanism to improve its performance. The Developer Edition does not offer the same performance, and is marketed as only being suitable for low traffic sites, prototyping and off-line use. Evidently, the full benefits of dynamic movie generation only come with the Enterprise Edition, the price of which starts (in May 2000) at $30,000. The Developer Edition was priced at a more modest $999 (less if you combine it with your purchase of Flash itself), but this is still significantly more expensive than Flash, and if you are only producing low budget sites, you may well think that smart clips and the mechanisms described earlier in this chapter provide an adequate degree of dynamism.

Exercises and Experiments

1. The way in which the details of my books are loaded from a file shown in the text is rather clumsy, with set_record_from_loader having to sift through all the variables returned from the server. Investigate ways of loading just the properties of a specific book record from a remote source. Assess the overheads, including administration, of any schemes you devise.

2. A more sensible way of handling the registration form than the one described in the text is to verify that the passwords match in the Flash movie, and then send a single encrypted version of the password if they do. Reimplement the movie in this way, using some simple password encrypting algorithm, such as rot13. Make sure that no unencrypted password is transmitted.

3. I lied to you on page 184 about the request sent from the registration form. Actually, the request line would be

    GET /cgi-bin/register.cgi?email=tony%40number%2D10%2Egov%2Euk&password1=RIPact&password2=RIPact&constructor=%5Btype+Function%5D&%5F%5Fproto%5F%5F=%5Bobject+Object%5D HTTP/1.0

    Explain.

4. The loadVariables method only sends the values of strings and numbers. Investigate ways of sending arrays and objects to a remote URL, and receiving them back. You will probably need to devise a way of encoding the properties and elements that can be decoded at either end. Try to think of ways of adding simple-to-use methods to objects, or creating objects that can perform these operations.

5. Assuming that you have access to a server (or can simulate it) you should now be in a position to implement a more or less complete shopfront using Flash and CGI scripts, or your preferred server-side technology. Extend the ideas described so far to a more realistic scale, with more products and types of products, and a back end on the server that, if not actually dealing with credit card transactions, can record sales and update the inventory accordingly. (Think carefully about the implications of people being able to access the shopfront from different places simultaneously.) This is a place to explore possibilities and look at facilities that you can provide in Flash that are not so easy with conventional Web technologies. Use Generator if you can and it seems to be useful.

6. Simulate Generator's radio button object using smart clips and CGI scripts.

flash and other technologies

HTML

Up to this point, I have considered Flash movies in isolation, implicitly assuming that the Flash Player will be used to display them. This is a viable way to work — the Player can load movies across the Internet and send HTTP requests — but, more often Flash content is displayed using a Web browser, equipped with a suitable plug-in. Again, it is possible to configure Web browsers so that they recognize SWF files and either pass them on to the Flash Player or play them in a browser window using the plug-in. More usually, though, Web browsers expect HTML files, and Flash movies are usually published to the Web by embedding them in a page of HTML, using the tags provided for that purpose.

Embedding Flash Player Movies in HTML Documents

There are two ways of embedding a Flash Player movie (and some other forms of multimedia content) in HTML: the non-standard way, which usually works, and the standard way, which usually doesn't.

The <embed> tag[1] is one of Netscape's proprietary extensions to HTML, which has been adopted by most other Web browsers, but not by the W^{3}C. It is similar to the well-known <img> tag used for embedding images: it takes an src attribute whose value is a URL identifying the location of the data to be embedded, in our case a SWF file, and width and height attributes which define the size of the box used to display the embedded content, either in pixels or as a percentage of the dimensions of the browser window. In addition, a type attribute may be used to specify the MIME type of the source file; this is a hint to the browser, which may not bother to download embedded files of types that it cannot display. Some browsers support an attribute pluginspage, whose value is a URL from which a plug-in for the embedded data may be downloaded.

---

1. The case of tags is ignored in HTML, but in XHTML they must be in lower case, so I have adopted that convention here, with an eye on the future.

If the plug-in is not installed, the user is given an opportunity to get it from the specified plug-in page.

Some other attributes are specific to Flash (although other media types, such as QuickTime movies may use attributes with the same names). These include loop, which determines whether the movie plays once or loops indefinitely; quality, which specifies the amount of anti-aliasing applied when the movie is rendered, and thus its visual quality; play, which specifies whether the movie starts automatically; and menu, which specifies whether a contextual menu is available during playback. The base attribute has as its value a URL, which is used to resolve any relative URLs used in the movie; it is similar to the <base> element that is sometimes included in the document head of Web pages, and makes it possible to separate a movie from any files it uses. (Keeping them all together tends to be a more robust solution, though.) There are some other options concerned with layout, but it is preferable to use CSS formatting for these aspects if possible. Full details of all the attributes can be found in Chapter 14 of the manual *Using Flash*, although, as we will see shortly, you may not need to be unduly concerned with them.

A typical example of the use of <embed> to place an SWF file in a Web page is the following:[1]
<embed src="slider.swf" quality="high"
bgcolor="#FFFFFF" width="550" height="400"
type="application/x-shockwave-flash"
pluginspage="http://www.macromedia.com/shockwave/download/
index.cgi?P1_Prod_Version=ShockwaveFlash"/>

The <embed> tag has never been part of any HTML standard. Instead, HTML 4 advocated the use of <object>, and this has been inherited by XHTML 1.0. The <object> tag is intended to unify, generalize and ultimately replace all the standard and non-standard HTML tags for embedding data and executable content, including <embed>, <applet>, <iframe> and even the venerable <img>.

At its simplest, <object> is like <embed>, except that it uses data as the name of the attribute that identifies the data to be embedded instead of src, and it is not an empty element. Instead, there may be HTML content in between the start and end tags <object> and </object>. There are two types of content that may be placed here. First, <param> tags may be used to pass parameters to the object, thus avoiding the need for

---

1. Again, I have adopted XHTML conventions, even though most Web pages use the less strict HTML 4 conventions (e.g., not putting quote marks around parameter values).

attributes that only apply to certain types of object. Secondly, arbitrary HTML may be included, to be displayed if and only if the browser is unable to display the embedded object identified by the data attribute. That is, the content provides something to fall back on if the desired embedding cannot be achieved. It is common to find object elements nested, with the outermost specifying some multimedia format, such as a QuickTime movie, and containing an object that specifies a still image to be displayed by browsers that can't handle QuickTime, which in turn contains some text to be displayed by browsers that can't display images.

More generally, <object> tags can be used to specify some software to process the associated data. This may be a Java applet, in which case <object> works like the better known <applet>, but it may also be a plug-in or ActiveX control, or, indeed any arbitrary executable content. The code is specified by the classid attribute. Its value may be a URL, but more often it is a special URI (Uniform Resource Identifier — a generalization of URL) beginning with a prefix that identifies the sort of code it is. For example, a URI for a Java class would begin java:, while one referring to a Python class would begin with python:. For practical purposes, the most important case is class ids that identify ActiveX controls. These begin with the prefix clsid:, which is followed by some gibberish that serves as a unique identifier for a particular control. For example, the ActiveX control for playing Flash movies is identified as
clsid:D27CDB6E-AE6D-11cf-96B8-444553540000

The codebase attribute is used in conjunction with classid, to specify the location of program libraries and so on which the program specified by the class id may require. In the case of ActiveX controls, the codebase is used to specify a location from which the control identified by classid may be obtained if it is not already installed locally. An <object> for a SWF movie looks like this:
<object classid="clsid:D27CDB6E-AE6D-11cf-96B8-444553540000"
codebase="http://download.macromedia.com/pub/shockwave/cabs/flash/
swflash.cab#version=5,0,0,0"
width="550" height="400">
    <param name="movie" value="slider.swf">
    <param name="quality" value="high">
    <param name="bgcolor" value="#FFFFFF">
  other content
</object>

The parameters that were passed to the Flash plug-in as attributes of the <embed> tag are passed to the ActiveX control using <param> tags, whose name and value attributes identify the different parameters and their values. This mechanism is arbitrarily extendible to new media types, so it is more flexible than the use of named attributes.

The Flash control uses a parameter named movie to identify the SWF file, instead of using the data attribute to <object>.

Although <object> is the method of embedding objects specified in the HTML and XHTML standards, few browsers implement it properly. On the other hand, <embed> only works for data that is interpreted by a plug-in built according to the Netscape plug-in API; <object> must be used for ActiveX controls, which are Microsoft's preferred way of extending the capabilities of Internet Explorer, at least on the Windows platform. Accordingly, to be sure your SWF movie will play on the largest possible number of browsers and platforms, you need to use both. Fortunately, the way <object> works, and the way browsers deal with tags they don't understand (by ignoring them) means that everything works if you use an <embed> inside an <object>. And that is what most people do, and it is also what Flash does when publishing HTML files.

It must be admitted that the previous paragraph is a little optimistic. Web browsers, especially the two most widely used, seem to be particularly prone to bugs, and both their manufacturers only pay attention to standards when it suits them. Older versions of both Netscape Navigator and Internet Explorer do an even worse job than more recent ones, and making a Web page (any Web page) that is guaranteed to work, or even to fail gracefully, on all version of all browsers on all platforms is a hopeless task. However, combining <object> and <embed> is a strategy that usually works with recent mainstream browsers.

Publishing And Templates

Creating HTML pages that include these tags can be approached from two different directions: from the HTML side and from the Flash side. In an environment where the main concern is the production of HTML, and SWF files are just one sort of element that may be included in a Web site, it makes sense to start from the HTML. If you write HTML by hand, you just add the appropriate tags in the same way as any others. If you use a Web authoring package, matters are even simpler. Both Macromedia Dreamweaver 3 and Adobe GoLive 5 allow you to add a Flash Player movie to a page by dragging an SWF object from one of their palettes and setting a few parameters. Both of these programs insert an <object> with an <embed> inside it, as described above. Using these programs, or writing HTML by hand in a text editor, you can easily combine Flash movies with other Web elements.

On the other hand, if you are primarily concerned with Flash itself, and regard HTML as a delivery vehicle for getting your movies onto the Web, you will probably prefer to use Flash to create HTML with your movies embedded in it. This, too, is easily done.

The Publish Settings dialogue is used to select different formats in which to export a Flash movie. For each format selected in the Formats tab of this dialogue, a tab is added in which you can choose parameters that apply to that format. If HTML is selected, in order to generate an HTML page with the movie embedded in it, the tab shown in Figure 8.1 becomes available. (Note that selecting HTML automatically causes Flash (SWF) to be selected too, since you can't sensibly produce an HTML page without also producing a movie to embed in it.)

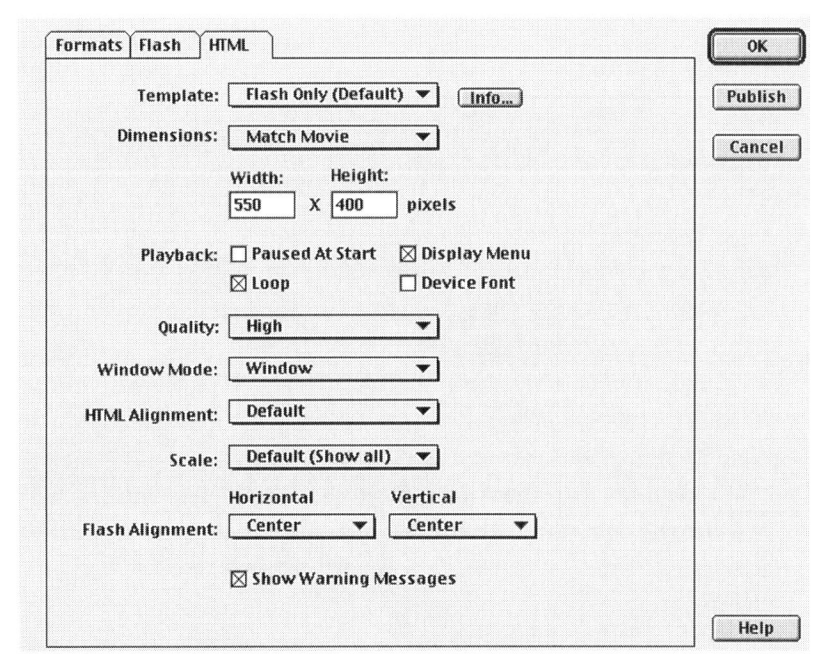

Figure 8.1 *HTML publish settings.*

Most of the options map on to parameters of the HTML tags in an obvious way. The pop-up menu labelled Template is the most interesting option here. It allows you to choose a style of HTML page in which to embed your movie. Several templates are available with Flash, and you can create your own. The mechanism for doing this is straightforward, and allows someone familiar with HTML to provide suitable boilerplate for Flash experts to use, without having to get involved with HTML. It also provides a way of creating a uniform look for all pages with embedded Flash Player movies in a particular site.

The easiest way to see how templates are constructed is by looking at an example, the default template, which just embeds a movie in an otherwise blank Web page.

```
$TTFlash Only (Default)
$DS
Use an OBJECT and EMBED tag to display Flash.
$DF
<HTML>
<HEAD>
<TITLE>$TI</TITLE>
</HEAD>
<BODY bgcolor="$BG">

<!-- URL's used in the movie-->
$MU
<!-- text used in the movie-->
$MT

<OBJECT classid="clsid:D27CDB6E-AE6D-11cf-96B8-444553540000"
 codebase="http://download.macromedia.com/pub/shockwave/cabs/
flash/swflash.cab#version=5,0,0,0"
 WIDTH=$WI HEIGHT=$HE>
 $PO
<EMBED $PE WIDTH=$WI HEIGHT=$HE
 TYPE="application/x-shockwave-flash" PLUGINSPAGE="http://
www.macromedia.com/shockwave/download/
index.cgi?P1_Prod_Version=ShockwaveFlash"></EMBED>
</OBJECT>

</BODY>
</HTML>
```

As you see, the template is just HTML[1] which includes the <object> and <embed> tags as advertised, with some names beginning with a $ sign among it. These names are *template variables*, and their function is mainly to transfer information from the HTML panel of the Publish Settings dialogue to the HTML file being published. There are nearly forty template variables, most of them having an obvious relationship to both the HTML attributes and the publish settings. For example, $WI and $HE hold the values entered in the Width and Height boxes in the HTML Publish Settings panel. They are used as the values for the width and height attributes of the <object> and <embed> tags.

---

1. This time, I have not used XHTML, but have shown the template exactly as it is supplied.

When the movie is published, the current values of these variables are substituted for any occurrences of them in the template, with the desired effect of setting the HTML attributes to the values entered in the dialogue. (You will probably see a parallel between the processing of HTML templates and Generator's processing of SWT files.) Most significantly, $MO holds the name of the movie.

Not all of the template variables are used in this way. $TT, $DS and $DF are used to document the template and pass values in the opposite direction, back to the dialogue box. $TT is the template title; its value is the string immediately following it, which appears in the Template pop-up menu to allow the template to be selected. In the example above, Flash Only (Default) is the title. $DS and $DF mark the start and finish of the template's description, which is displayed when the info... button to the right of the pop-up menu is clicked with the template selected in the pop-up. $MU and $MT hold the URLs and text strings used in the movie. Including them in a template causes all these to be inserted into the generated HTML file inside an HTML comment. This is done to assist automatic indexing programs and search engines, and to make it possible for link checking tools to ascertain whether there are any broken links. Without $MU and $MT, such programs would be unable to see any of the content of the SWF file at all.

The final noteworthy template variables are $PO and $PE, the parameters for <object> and <embed>. These provide a shorthand for referencing any parameters to these two tags that have been set to anything other than their default values. The default template shown above demonstrates the way in which they are used.

Apart from substituting values for template parameters, the HTML template is copied unaltered to the published HTML file. It is therefore simple for an HTML expert to construct new templates that add additional text or images or apply CSS formatting to impose a house style on all pages that contain embedded Flash movies. It is not possible, however, to define new template variables, nor is it possible to embed more than one SWF file in the same HTML page in this way. To do that, you must resort to an HTML authoring program.

Not all the templates supplied with Flash are as simple as the default. Some of them include code that makes some attempt to detect whether or not the user's browser is able to display Flash movies, and provide some alternative if not. This is a vexed question to which we will return later. Other templates provide hooks for adding JavaScript or VBScript that interacts with the movie, another subject which we will describe more fully later in the chapter.

ActionScript and Web Pages

When a Flash movie is embedded in HTML, new scripting possibilities arise. The getURL function can be used to load a Web page into a browser window. It takes a relative or absolute URL as its compulsory first parameter and loads it into the browser. An optional second parameter specifies a window into which the page should be loaded. This may be either the name of a window, or one of the special values _self, _parent, _top or _blank. Using a value of _self causes the new page to overwrite the current one, while _blank opens a new window for the new page. The options _parent and _top only make sense if the movie in which getURL is called is embedded in an HTML file that is displayed in a frame within a frame set. In that case, _parent specifies the frame set immediately containing the frame, while _top is the window containing the frame set, irrespective of any intermediate frames within frames. These values will be familiar if you know HTML: they are the possible options for the target attribute of <a> tags.

A popular way of using getURL in conjunction with HTML frames is to provide navigation controls for a conventional Web site using Flash. That is, one frame of a frame set is an HTML file with a Flash movie embedded in it. This uses all the facilities of Flash to provide custom controls to allow users to find their way around the site. It is possible to use the interface elements and scripting techniques that have been described in previous chapters to implement elaborate navigational interfaces, but a much simpler approach that seems to be popular with Web designers is simply to use a set of Flash buttons to select new pages. Remember that each state of a button symbol may include a movie or sound, so this is an easy way of introducing animated buttons into a Web site. (Remember also that a button doesn't have to look like a push button.)

Suppose then that you have a Web site with just half a dozen main pages, and you want visitors to the site to be able to go to any one of those pages at any time using a navigation bar at the top of the window. The site is displayed in a frame set, with the navigation bar in its own frame at the top, and the rest of the window occupied by a frame called main. The navigation bar contains a Flash movie. That is, the body of the HTML file for the site's main page contains something like the following:

```
<frameset rows="60,*" border="0" framespacing="0">
    <frame src="flash-nav.html" name="navigation" noresize scrolling="no">
    <frame src="home.html" name="main" noresize>
</frameset>
```

where flash-nav.html is the name of an HTML file generated by Flash to contain the navigation movie, which consists simply of a row of animated buttons, each with a script such as the following attached to it.

javascript **209**

```
on (release) {
    getURL("info.html", "main");
}
```
This trivial way of using getURL can be surprisingly effective if the animated buttons are well designed.

Perhaps the most common Flash Web idiom (one that is becoming a cliché at the time of writing) is used on hierarchically organized sites, divided into major topics with sub-topics. The navigation bar lists the major topics; rolling the mouse over one of these causes its sub-topics to appear. You should be able to see how this is implemented using Flash movie symbols for each of the topics, containing buttons for the sub-topics. Using Flash gives Web designers considerable scope for creating navigation bars of this sort with a distinctive appearance that can help create an identity for a site. It should be remembered, though, that alternative means of navigation should always be provided for users who do not have Flash, or who are not able to use graphical navigation controls, because of physical or cognitive disabilities.

As well as being used explicitly in scripts, getURL is also called implicitly if link elements embedded in dynamic text fields with the HTML option on are clicked. This ensures that these links behave as expected, even though they are part of the Flash movie, not the HTML page proper.

JavaScript

Modern Web sites are more than just static HTML. The use of client-side scripts to add interactivity, provide feedback and perform simple data validation has become routine. Most client-side scripts are written in JavaScript, although VBScript is also widely used, despite only working properly on Windows machines running Internet Explorer. Flash movies can interact with browser scripts, allowing them to control the browser. Browser scripts can also control Flash movies, by calling methods that provide access to MovieClip objects.

Before we look at some applications of mixing JavaScript and Flash a word of warning is in order. Two different mechanisms are used to allow Flash movies and Web browsers to interact with each other and both are propietary. Netscape's LiveConnect, which allows Java and JavaScript to work together, is used in Netscape browsers from version 3.0 upwards, on Windows and MacOS. In order for LiveConnect to work, Java must also be enabled in the browser, and any <embed> tags must have the attribute SWLiveConnect set to true. ActiveX is used in Internet Explorer on Windows. Again, it must be enabled by the user. This leaves other browsers and platforms out in the cold. To make matters worse, code that is inserted into Web pages to detect the browser type often assumes that if it detects Internet Explorer, it can use ActiveX, although the Flash ActiveX control is not used by the the MacOS version of Explorer, which uses a plug-in, like Netscape. So, if you rely on a mixture of JavaScript and Flash, it is quite likely that your Web site will not work on some browsers. On the whole, it is better to try and work entirely within Flash, but if you cannot, or if you know that your site will only ever be viewed using one type of browser (for example, if it is on an intranet that can only be accessed from machines set up in a standard configuration) the mixture can be useful.

Calling JavaScript From ActionScript

Consider first controlling a Web browser from inside a Flash movie. This is a special case of the more general function of a Flash movie controlling its *host environment*. Although it contains executable scripts, a movie is not a program, and needs some other program to act as a host — to display it and interpret any scripts it contains. The Flash Player is one possible host environment, Web browsers are another; other possibilities include Director, and the QuickTime player. Since the Flash Player code is now publicly available, other host environments may be developed. The fscommand function is provided in ActionScript to allow scripts to send messages to the host environment. It takes two strings as arguments. The first is a name that is conventionally used to identify an operation for the host to perform, the second is a parameter to that operation.

In the case of the Flash Player, there is a small fixed repertoire of commands. For example, quit, to close the player, fullscreen to determine whether the player occupies the entire screen without showing a menu bar, and trapallkeys, which determines whether special keys, such as control and alt, are used for keyboard shortcuts to control the player or are passed to the Flash movie via keyDown events. For the last two commands, which are, in effect Boolean values, the second argument to fscommand should be either "true" or "false". So, to switch the player to kiosk mode, the first frame of a movie could have the script
fscommand ("fullscreen", "true");
fscommand ("trapallkeys", "true");
attached to it. A full list of the FS commands for the Flash Player can be found in Chapter 5 of the *ActionScript Reference Guide*.

When the host environment is a Web browser, the fscommand method calls a JavaScript function defined in the HTML page in which the movie is embedded. The movie must be an identifiable document element, which means that the <embed> tag must have a name attribute, and the <object> tag must have an id attribute, providing an identifier for the element. If this is, for example, the_movie, an fscommand in the SWF movie will call a JavaScript function called the_movie_DoFSCommand, and pass it both its arguments. Typically, the_movie_DoFSCommand will use the first argument to select some other function to call, passing it the second argument.

JavaScript is, like ActionScript, an implementation of ECMAScript, but instead of the latter's built-in objects that correspond to elements of Flash movies, it provides a set of objects that model HTML documents in browser windows. The methods of these objects allow scripts to dynamically modify the page, and to perform operations on windows. One of the most common operations is the opening of a new window. Whereas a window can be opened by specifying a target of _blank for a link, or as an argument of getURL, this always opens a full-size window, with the standard controls. This is not always appropriate: smaller windows without toolbars might be preferred for providing help; they are often used for advertisements (which at least has the benefit that you can close them, unlike advertisements embedded in the page, which don't go away).

The JavaScript function open is used to open windows. It takes a URL and a window title as its first two arguments, and a string of options as its third, which specifies the window's size and other aspects of its appearance. (For details, consult a book on JavaScript or Dynamic HTML.) To open a file called help.html in a small resizable window without any toolbars, you would use the following call:
window.open("help.html","Help", "scrollbars,resizable,width=120,height=160");
But that's JavaScript. What if you wanted to open such a window in response to a click on a help button in an SWF movie inside a Web page? That is where fscommand comes in. The ActionScript end is trivial:
on (release) {
    fscommand("helpwindow", "");
}
If the movie is embedded with tags whose name and id attributes identify it as the_movie, then this will cause a JavaScript call of the_movie_DoFSCommand("helpwindow", ""). All that is needed is to define an appropriate JavaScript function in the HTML page containing the movie. The following is the simplest possibility:
function the_movie_DoFSCommand(command, args) {
if (command == "helpwindow")
    window.open("help.html", "Help", "scrollbars,resizable,width=120,height=160");
}

Generally, you may want to perform several different operations via calls of fscommand. They will all be passed to the same JavaScript function, so this will usually consist of a sequence of conditional statements that select an appropriate piece of code based on the value of the argument command. If you select Flash With FSCommand from the Template pop-up menu in the Publish Settings tab for HTML, a skeleton for the appropriate JavaScript function is written into the published HTML file, and you only need to fill in the body with the code for your specific commands.

For simple operations, there is an alternative way of calling JavaScript from inside a movie, and that is to use getURL with a URL beginning javascript:. Normally, the first part of a URL specifies a protocol, but most browsers understand the JavaScript pseudo-protocol, and interpret everything after javascript: as code to be executed. Thus, an alternative way of making a help window pop up is to attach the following script to the help button in a movie.

```
on (release) {
    getURL('javascript:window.open("help.html", "Help",
        "scrollbars,resizable,width=120,height=160")');
}
```

This does not rely on LiveConnect or ActiveX, so it is a safer way of proceeding if only simple JavaScripts need to be executed.

Flash Methods in JavaScript

Working in the opposite direction, as it were, and controlling the Flash movie using JavaScript commands is done by calling special *Flash methods* on the JavaScript object representing the embedded movie. This will be a property of the page or frame in which the movie is embedded. To be more precise, it will be a property of the page or frame in Internet Explorer, but of the page or frame's document property in Netscape Navigator. The list of Flash methods is extensive, but essentially it provides all the operations available in Flash 4 ActionScript. They are documented in a Macromedia Technical Note, *Scripting With Flash*, available from http://www.macromedia.com/support/flash/publishexport/scriptingwithflash/scriptingwithflash.html. A small example will be sufficient to convey the way in which they work.

A popular variation on the navigation bar style of Web site uses tabs on the navigation bar that can be in one of two states. The tab corresponding to the page currently being displayed in the main frame indicates the fact by being in a highlighted state of some sort. Sets of tabs like this can be implemented in Flash using the same techniques as a set of radio buttons. Each tab is a movie clip with two frames. The first clip contains a button with the following script attached:

```
on (release) {
    getURL(the_url, "main");
    gotoAndStop("selected");
}
```
The tabs can be instances of a smart clip, with the_url being a clip parameter. The second frame, labelled selected, will contain a graphic indicating that the tab is selected; it does not need a button, because it makes no sense to select a tab that is already selected.

The hard part of implementing a set of tabs is, of course, making sure the tabs that are not selected are in the right frame. You should be able to see how to extend the script to move the playhead in all the other buttons to the correct frame. Suppose, though, that you follow approved Web design practice and supplement the Flash navigation bar with simple HTML text links on the pages themselves. If a user clicks one of these links, how can you ensure that the tabs in the navigation bar are updated to reflect the new state of the display? Flash methods provide an answer.

In particular, the TGotoLabel method can be used to send the playhead to a specific frame in a movie clip. (The T stands for 'target'.) The HTML file for the navigation frame could include the following JavaScript in its document head.

```
var buttons = new Array(3);
buttons[0] = "home_button";
buttons[1] = "a_button";
buttons[2] = "b_button";

function synch(n) {
    for (var i = 0; i < 3; ++i) {
        var f = i == n? 'selected': 'not selected';
        document.navbar.TGotoLabel(buttons[i], f);
    }
}
```
You will notice that this could be ActionScript. The navigation bar movie is called navbar. To avoid cluttering the code with browser tests and conditional expressions, I have just shown the script as it would be to work in Netscape. The array buttons is initialized with the target names of all the buttons. (I have only shown three to keep the example short.) The synch function takes a number corresponding to one of the buttons as its argument, sends all the other tabs to their first frame (not selected) and the tab corresponding to its argument to its selected frame.

The HTML file for each page needs an event handler that causes this function to be called whenever the page is loaded. The handler will be executed however the page was reached, whether from the getURL call attached to a tab in the navigation bar, or from a text link in one of the other pages. The handler is set by assigning a suitable call to the onLoad attribute of the page's <body> tag. For example,
<body onLoad = "parent.navigation.synch(0)">
Here, navigation is the name of the frame containing the navigation bar. The parent object in JavaScript works with frames roughly like _parent does with movie clips in ActionScript, allowing scripts in one frame to refer to other frames in the same frame set.

Making JavaScript and ActionScript work together smoothly is not easy, and, as I remarked earlier, it will not necessarily work on all browsers. Before implementing Web sites that rely on it as the example just given does, you should think carefully. A redesign of the site that makes it work on more browsers may be more worth the effort than a clever combination of the two technologies.

Attempting to Detect the Flash Plug-in

You may prefer to try and accommodate all comers by determining whether their browsers can cope with mixed JavaScript and ActionScript, and only if they cannot falling back on a more prosaic version of your site. If you take this attitude, you must also tackle the more fundamental problem of determining whether a user's browser can even play Flash movies at all — not everyone has installed the Flash plug-in, and some people, whether through preference or because of disabilities or rudimentary access to the Internet (it is a worldwide World Wide Web, after all) use text-only browsers. This is such a common requirement that you might think it would be easy, but it is not.

To begin with, while JavaScript provides ways of finding out whether the plug-in is installed, before you can use them you need to find out whether JavaScript is enabled. The next complication is that you need to test for both the Flash plug-in and the corresponding ActiveX control. Before you can do that, you need to find out which browser the user is running and on which platform. You also need this information to cope with the major problem that faces anyone trying to write JavaScript. Because the different browser manufacturers implemented scripting support semi-independently in their version 3 and 4 browsers, the objects that represent page elements and windows are different on different browsers. The W^{3}C has now produced a standard Document Object Model but, even when all new browsers implement it this will not help with older ones. To add to the problems, there are many browser detecting scripts available on the Internet, but they don't all work properly for all browsers. (There are not, in fact, just two browsers in the world.)

So what do you do to make sure that your sites which include Flash movies work? There is much to be said for putting a pure HTML welcome page in front of your actual site, with links to the Flash version and an alternative Flashless version, and a link to the page from which the plug-in can be downloaded. However, it is not pretty, and is no help to users who don't actually know whether they have the Flash plug-in installed. If you wish to automate the process of determining whether the browser can display SWF movies, unless you are experienced with writing cross-browser JavaScript, it is best to let somebody else do the work. Several of the templates available in the HTML tab of the Publish Settings dialogue include JavaScript and VBScript code to detect the plug-in, and allow you to provide an image as an alternative to your SWF movie. The scripts in these templates will work most of the time but they are not infallible. Macromedia have made available a 'Flash Deployment Kit', which provides a set of tools and techniques for determining whether a browser can play SWF movies, allowing them to download the appropriate plug-in or ActiveX control if not, and providing alternative content to fall back on if necessary.[1] Even this is not perfect — it has, for example, a habit of trying to run VBScripts on MacOS versions of Internet Explorer. A discussion of the problem and of various strategies that might be adopted can be found in a Macromedia Technical Note entitled *How to detect the presence of the Flash Player* at http://www.macromedia.com/support/flash/ts/documents/uber_detection.htm. As far as I know, nobody has yet extended these tools to determine whether a browser is capable of supporting Flash methods and FS commands, but in principle this could be done.

XML

The mechanism described in Chapter 7 for sending data to servers was never intended to cope with structured data. The URL encoded string of name and value pairs was designed for sending data from forms, and it works admirably for that purpose. However, if you need to send an object, such as one of the book records introduced in Chapter 5, you must 'flatten' it and send each field as a separate variable. Data must be flattened in the same way if it is to be retrieved using loadVariables, as we also saw in Chapter 7. This means that either data must be stored in an awkward format, such as the one shown on page 181, or CGI scripts must do some extra work to massage it into the required form.

---

[1]. You can find a link to it in the Goodies folder on the Flash5 CD.

This situation is not unique to Flash. To avoid unnecessary duplication of effort and to allow the same data to be used by different applications, a standard format for transmitting structured data is required. XML (eXtensible Markup Language) has been widely adopted for this purpose.

As its full name suggests, XML is a markup language, like HTML, which can be used to annotate documents with tags indicating their structure. Whereas the repertoire of tags in HTML is fixed, XML allows you to invent your own tags. A *Document Type Definition (DTD)* is a formal specification of a set of tags together with their attributes and any constraints on their usage which may be imposed. In effect, a DTD defines the set of documents that are legally marked up with the tags of some markup language. For example, the XHTML DTD defines the set of valid XHTML documents. XML documents don't need a DTD, though. Any document that uses XML syntax for tags and is correctly tagged — that is, whose tags are properly terminated, and so on — is said to be *well-formed*. Software that processes XML can usually analyse well-formed documents, although it cannot determine whether they are *valid*, that is, that they conform to a DTD unless one is present and the software is sufficiently complex to perform the extra analysis. The concept of well-formed documents may seem to be lacking in rigour, but it makes it easier for programs to process XML documents efficiently, as well as making it possible to use documents that combine elements from different DTDs. Although XML uses the terminology of documents and markup, it provides a general mechanism for representing structured data in textual form. XML can be used to structure databases and as a format for exchanging data between diverse applications. Not requiring DTDs makes using XML as a data transfer format more attractive, since it is not necessary to go to the effort of defining a DTD for every type of data that may be encountered.

XML and HTML share a common ancestry in SGML, so the conventions for writing tags in XML will mostly be familiar if you know HTML. Tags are enclosed in angle brackets, and assignments to attributes may follow the tag name; entity references beginning with an & are used in a similar way. At first sight, XML looks like HTML with different tags. There are some differences, though. XML is more strict than HTML: all start tags must have matching end tags, whereas HTML allows you to omit them where context makes it obvious, and attribute values must always be enclosed in quotes. XML uses a different syntax for empty elements. Instead of just using a start tag immediately followed by an end tag, empty elements use tags with a / just before the closing angle bracket (for example, <hrule />). XHTML is a redefinition of HTML using an XML DTD, so it incorporates these differences, which will therefore soon become familiar to everyone working on the Web.

XML and Data Records

Consider the following XML document.

```xml
<?xml version = "1.0" ?>
<books>
    <book id = "cpp">
        <title>The Late Night Guide to C++</title>
        <author>Nigel Chapman</author>
        <price sterling="29.95" euro="50" />
        <publisher>John Wiley and Sons</publisher>
        <numberinstock current="1" ordered="6" />
    </book>
    <book id = "perl">
        <title>Perl: The Programmer's Companion</title>
        <author>Nigel Chapman</author>
        <price sterling="24.95" euro="44" />
        <publisher>John Wiley and Sons</publisher>
        <numberinstock current="0" ordered="0" />
    </book>
    <book id = "dmm">
        <title>Digital Multimedia</title>
        <author>Nigel Chapman</author>
        <author>Jenny Chapman</author>
        <price sterling="27.95" euro="48" />
        <publisher>John Wiley and Sons</publisher>
        <numberinstock current="12" ordered="20" />
    </book>
</books>
```

The first line is an *XML declaration*, a piece of red tape that identifies this as an XML document and indicates the version of XML being used. It should be apparent that the document proper, which follows the declaration, includes all the information required to initialize the book records for my book shop example, and more.

A little thought will tell you that there is considerable scope for choice in mapping a record structure to an XML DTD. In particular, there is no clear-cut criterion for deciding whether to use an element with an attribute to record the values of a field, or an element whose content is the value. For example,

```xml
<publisher>John Wiley and Sons</publisher>
```

or

```xml
<publisher company="John Wiley and Sons" />
```

Here, I have used a mixture: the price and number in stock are recorded using attributes; this has made it easy for me to combine two different values in both cases: the price in sterling or in Euros, the number in stock currently and in a few days time. Using attributes avoids multiplying the number of elements. On the other hand, placing the author in the content of an element has made it possible to have two author elements for the jointly written book. This would help indexing and searching software to identify the book from either author. (Sadly, it actually complicates the scripts that are going to manipulate this data in Flash, but that's the price you pay for working with a general-purpose format.) The decision to use element content to record the values of the remaining fields is somewhat arbitrary.

What has this to do with Flash? The XML class built into ActionScript provides methods for constructing and analysing tree structures representing XML documents, and for transmitting XML data to and from a server. This means that, instead of relying on loadVariables and URL-encoded data, scripts can work with structured data in XML and can communicate with other systems that use XML as a format for storing or exchanging data.

The XML support in Flash 5.0 is slightly rough at the edges, although it is usable. It is based on objects of class XML, which represent both XML documents and nodes in the *structure model* of such documents. The structure model is an abstract representation of the structure of an XML document —essentially, the way in which document elements are ordered and contained within each other. Figure 8.2 is a picture of the structure model for the books document shown earlier. Each document element is represented by a node in the model, as is each section of text. Each node corresponding to an element that is not empty has some *child nodes* representing its content; as you might expect, such a node is the *parent* of its children, and the terminology is extended to refer to *siblings*, the children of the same parent. The structure model is a tree, with each node having exactly one parent, except for the node representing the entire document, which has none.

XML Objects

It is possible to build up an XML tree using methods of XML objects. It is also possible to construct it from an XML document. Among the several ways of doing this, the most useful is the load method, which takes the URL of an XML document (or a program that generates XML documents), obtains the document, parses it[1] and constructs a

---

1. XML experts note: the Flash XML parser is a non-validating one. It can handle documents that include DTDs, but apart from doing some elementary syntax checks and storing it in the docTypeDecl property of the XML object for the whole document, it doesn't do anything with the DTD.

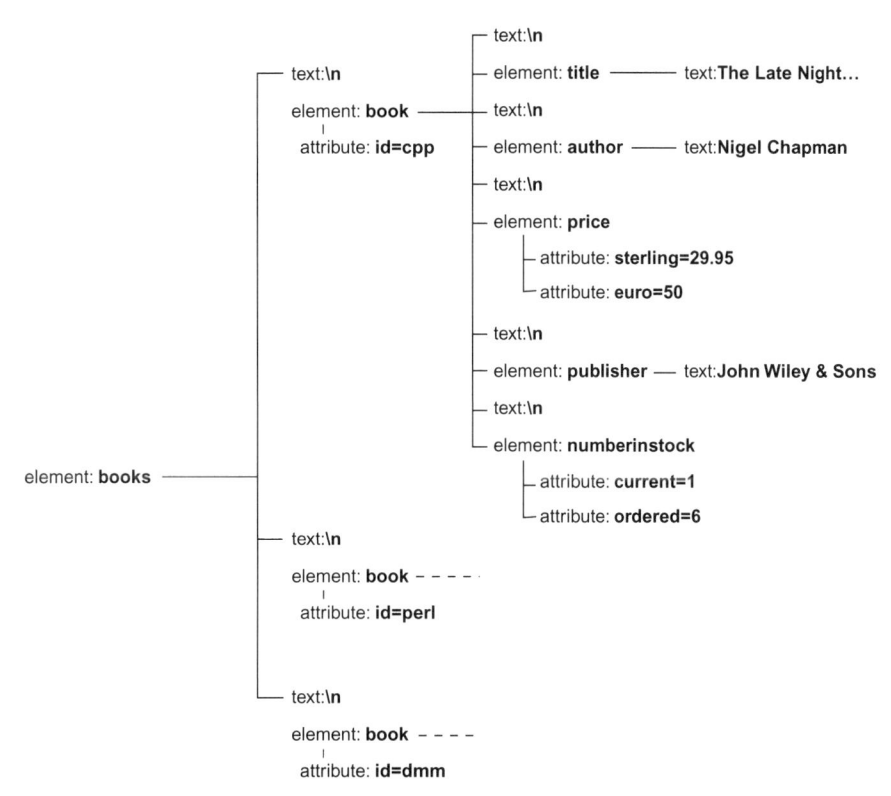

```
                                    ┌─ text:\n
                                    ├─ element: title ──── text:The Late Night…
                    ┌─ text:\n      ├─ text:\n
                    ├─ element: book ┼─ element: author ─── text:Nigel Chapman
                    │   │            ├─ text:\n
                    │   attribute: id=cpp
                    │                ├─ element: price
                    │                │      ├─ attribute: sterling=29.95
                    │                │      └─ attribute: euro=50
                    │                ├─ text:\n
                    │                ├─ element: publisher ── text:John Wiley & Sons
                    │                ├─ text:\n
                    │                └─ element: numberinstock
                    │                       ├─ attribute: current=1
                    │                       └─ attribute: ordered=6
element: books  ────┤
                    ├─ text:\n
                    ├─ element: book ─ ─ ─ ─
                    │   │
                    │   attribute: id=perl
                    │
                    ├─ text:\n
                    └─ element: book ─ ─ ─ ─
                        │
                        attribute: id=dmm
```

Figure 8.2 *The structure model for the books document.*

collection of linked XML objects that represents its structure. In order to be able to call the method, you must first create an XML object; after the call, the structure tree of the XML document is placed in this object. You might proceed like this:

var books_xml = new XML();

books_xml.load("books.xml");

Like the other methods we have seen for downloading data, load executes asynchronously. That is, once the request has been sent, the script containing the call continues and the movie goes on playing without waiting for the data. XML objects have a loaded property which can be tested to determine when the data has arrived. A more sophisticated way of dealing with asynchronous XML downloads is to assign a function to the onLoad property of the XML object which will receive the data; that is, you set the onLoad method to a handler that will be called when the download and parsing of the data is complete. So, if you have written a handler called handle_xml_loaded that will deal with the XML when it arrives, you simply assign it to the onload property, like this:

books_xml.onLoad = handle_xml_loaded;

The movie can be stopped, play a holding animation or do some useful work while the XML data is downloaded.

Structure Tree Traversals

When the handler is called, it typically extracts data from the XML object. Note that, since the handler was assigned to a property of that object, when it is called it behaves like a method, so the object is available as this. Often, it will be necessary to *traverse* the tree of the structure model, visiting all the nodes to inspect or modify the information they contain. Here is a function that performs such a traversal, building up a string representation of the tree structure. This is a useful debugging aid in itself, but the pattern it illustrates is one that can be used for any computation based on a tree traversal. Only the computation at each node will be different.

```
function dump_xml(x, indent) {
    var s = "";
    if (x == undefined) return s;
    if (x.nodeType == 3) s += (indent + '[' + x.nodeValue + ']\n')
    else {
        s += (indent + x.nodeName)
        for (a in x.attributes)
            s += (' ' + a + '=' + x.attributes[a])
        if (x.hasChildNodes && x.childNodes.length>0) {
            s += ('->\n')
            for (var i = 0; i < x.childNodes.length; ++i)
                s += dump_xml(x.childNodes[i], indent+' ')
        }
        else s += '\n';
    }
    return s;
}
```

A tree is a recursive structure (the children of a node are themselves trees) so the natural way of traversing a tree uses a recursive function. This dump_xml function shows several of the methods and properties belonging to XML objects. It also illustrates some oddities of Flash's current implementation of XML parsing.

The function takes two arguments: an object, which ought to be an XML object, and a string of spaces, which is used for indenting the nodes to show the tree structure. The local variable s is used to build up the string which will be the eventual result of the function. The first thing the function does is test whether the object it has been passed is undefined. This should never happen, but, at least in Flash 5.0r6, a bug in the XML parser means that an undefined node is added to the tree where an XML declaration is found. (Since this will presumably be fixed, in future examples tests for this undefined node will be omitted.)

There are two types of node in an XML structure model: text nodes and element nodes, corresponding to literal text and document elements (i.e., the components of the document identified by markup tags), respectively. The nodeType property records which of these types a node belongs to, using a value of 3 for text and 1 for elements. Thus, the next thing the function does is determine whether it has been passed a text node. If it has, it appends the actual text, which is held in the nodeValue property to the result string, indented and surrounded by delimiters. Otherwise, the node must correspond to a document element. It will have a nodeName property, holding its name as used in the markup tags, and an attributes property, which is an associative array giving the values of any attributes of the element. The name and attribute values are added to the result string, suitably formatted.

If a node is neither text nor empty it will have some descendants. These are kept as an array in the childNodes property. A method hasChildNodes is provided as a convenience to determine whether this property exists, but (again possibly due to a bug) it is necessary to test whether the array has any elements before concluding that there are descendants. If there are, the function recurses to dump each one in turn. When given the books document to analyse, the function produces output that begins as follows (cf. Figure 8.2).

```
null->
  [
]
  [
]
  books->
    [
    ]
    book id=cpp->
      [
      ]
      title->
        [The Late Night Guide to C++]
```

There are two important points to note about this output, and about XML objects built from XML documents. First, the existence of the null node, which is a parent to the whole tree. It is also used to record information about the whole document. For example, its xmlDecl property holds the text of any XML declaration that may be included in the file; its docTypeDecl holds the text of the DTD, if any has been included in the document. Second, there are text nodes for all the white space characters (spaces, tabs and new lines) in the XML file. Although the XML standard is a little obscure on the point, this does appear to be correct behaviour — white space can be significant, so the parser should not throw it away. However, these white space nodes are usually a nuisance. The following function detects them.

```
function is_ws_node(x) {
    if (x.nodeType == 1) return false;
    var s = x.nodeValue;
    for (var i = 0; i < s.length; ++i) {
        var c = s.charAt(i)
        if (!(c == ' ' || c == '\n' || c == '\r' || c == '\t'))
            return false
    }
    return true;
}
```

The following one removes them from a tree.

```
function strip_ws_nodes(x) {
    if (is_ws_node(x)) x.removeNode();
    else if (x.nodeType == 1 && x.hasChildNodes)
    {
        var cn = new Array(x.childNodes.length)
        for (var j = 0; j < x.childNodes.length; ++j)
            cn[j] = x.childNodes[j]
        for (var i = 0; i < cn.length; ++i)
            strip_ws_nodes(cn[i]);
    }
}
```

The removeNode method detaches a node from its parent, removing it from the tree. The function strip_ws_nodes shows the same pattern of recursion as dump_xml. The only complication arises from the fact that removeNode actually updates the childNodes array of the parent node, which can cause havoc with the iteration. To avoid this, a copy of the array is made and the loop that calls strip_ws_nodes recursively looks at the copy instead of the original.

Putting all this together, a dump of the essential structure of an XML document omitting white space can be obtained as follows.
```
function handle_xml_loaded() {
    strip_ws_nodes(this);
    trace(dump_xml(this, ''))
}

var books_xml = new XML();
books_xml.onLoad = handle_xml_loaded;
books_xml.load("books.xml");
```
which produces the following output.
```
null->
  books->
    book id=cpp->
      title->
        [The Late Night Guide to C++]
      author->
        [Nigel Chapman]
      price sterling=29.95 euro=50
      publisher->
        [John Wiley and Sons]
      numberinstock current=1 ordered=6
    book id=perl->
            details for perl book
    book id=dmm->
            details for multimedia book
```

If you have used Java or JavaScript to manipulate XML data, you will probably be aware of the W^{3}C Document Object Model (DOM), which provides a standard interface to the structure tree of an XML document. ActionScript's interface is related to the DOM, but unfortunately it does not conform to the standard. XML objects have methods and properties that combine those of the DOM's Node and Document interfaces; there is no provision for differentiating between different sub-classes of node. It is to be hoped that a future release of Flash will provide an interface to XML that conforms to the DOM standard.

Using XML Data

Scripts that traverse data structures tracing what they find are instructive, but they don't get any work done. In order to use XML to send the data records for the book shop, a suitable handler that extracts the information and puts it into book record objects is needed.

To make it easier to integrate the new data format into the existing movie, I will first store the records in an associative array (i.e., an object), loaded_books, from which they can be extracted and assigned to the BookDrag objects' book_record properties subsequently, in much the same way the values were extracted from the loader clip in the previous version. I will also assume that a function called error has been defined in the main movie in case anything goes wrong. It should be emphasized, though, that if you are really considering using Flash for ecommerce transactions, you should make strenuous efforts to ensure that all data reaching the Flash movie is correct. There are not many positive steps that a Flash script can take to rectify matters, and potential customers will not be impressed with a screen containing nothing but a brief error message.

Since we know what format the XML received by the shop movie should be in, the functions that extract the data can work down the tree to pick out the values they need. The handler begins by finding the node corresponding to the <books> tag, and then looking at each of its children, the nodes for each individual book.

```
function handle_xml_loaded() {
    if (this.status != 0)
        _root.error("An error occurred loading XML data, code = " + this.status);
    strip_ws_nodes(this);
    var books = this.firstChild;
    for (var i = 0; i < books.childNodes.length; ++i) {
        var b = books.childNodes[i];
        var brec = new _root.record_lib.Book();
        brec.set_from_xml(b);
        loaded_books[b.attributes.id+'_'] = brec;
    }
    _root.play();
}
```

The status property of an XML object is set to zero if the parse was successful; other values are used to indicate various specific types of error that may be encountered.

To make manipulating the structure easier, white space nodes are stripped out, as before. The firstChild property of an XML object gives a convenient way of finding the first child node. The book nodes are the children of the first child of the node that is loaded, and these are the nodes that are assigned to the variable b on each iteration of the loop. A new book record is created and initialized from the XML node before being stored in the loaded_books array. The key that is used to index this array is contructed by appending an underline to the id attribute of the book element. The way these attributes have been assigned means that the key is exactly the same as the prefix that was used in the previous version of this script, so that the same interface can be presented to the rest of the scripts in the movie.

A new method of the book class is used to take the values from the XML structure and assign them to the properties of a book object. It is defined like this:

```
book.prototype.set_from_xml = function(x) {
    if (x.nodeType != 1 || x.nodeName != "book")
        _root.error("An unexpected node was found in the XML tree");
    else {
        var c = x.childNodes;
        var authors = new Array();
        for (var i = 0; i < c.length; ++i) {
            var xi = c[i];
            if (xi.nodeType != 1)
                _root.error("An unexpected node was found in the XML tree");
            if (xi.nodeName == "author") authors[authors.length] =
                                                        text_content(xi);
            else if (xi.nodeName == "price") this.price = xi.attributes["sterling"];
            else if (xi.nodeName == "numberinstock") this.number_in_stock =
                                                        xi.attributes["current"];
            else this[xi.nodeName] = text_content(xi);
        }
        this.author = fix_authors(authors);
    }
}
```

It begins with some perfunctory validity checking before working its way through the node's children — the XML nodes corresponding to the book record's fields (see Figure 8.2). There are three different sorts of action to be performed. The simplest case handles the two nodes that use attributes to store the value: the attribute values can be found in the attributes array. For the nodes that store the value in the document element's content, an auxiliary function text_content is used to find the value. The author field presents a particular problem, because I decided to use one <author> element for each author, so now I need to stitch them together. To begin with, the values obtained by calling text_content are stored in an array. Another auxiliary function fix_authors is used to put them together into a string with conventional separators.

```
function text_content(x) {
    var c = x.firstChild;
    if (c.nodeType == 3) return c.nodeValue;
    else _root.error("An unexpected node (not text) was found in the XML")
}
function fix_authors(as) {
    var a = "";
    for (var i = 0; i < as.length; ++i)
        a += (as[i] + (i == as.length - 1? "":
                      i == as.length - 2? " and ": ", "));
    return a;
}
```

After this handler has executed, loaded_book contains book records in exactly the same format as before. These can be used to initialize the BookDrag objects by replacing the set_record_from_loader method used previously, with one that simply assigns the appropriate element:

```
BookDrag.prototype.set_record_from_loader = function(prefix) {
    this.book_record = _root.loaded_books[prefix];
}
```

(By using the same name, and constructing the keys as described, I avoid having to change the calls.)

Sending XML

Scripts can send XML data to the server as well as getting it. The send method of XML objects takes a URL as an argument, and sends the object to the CGI script (or equivalent) that the URL identifies. That is, it sends an XML document corresponding to the structure model embodied in the object. An HTTP POST request is used to send the data. Since it is XML and not a URL-encoded string of form data, the CGI script must analyse it using its own XML parser, rather than the simple methods such as those of the CGI.pm module that suffice for forms. XML parsers are available for most programming languages that you might use for writing server-side scripts to communicate with a Flash movie.

In many cases, a movie will need a response to any data that it sends to a server. At the least, a status code ought to be returned, indicating whether the server-side script successfully processed the data that was sent. If the response is also formatted as XML, the portmanteau method sendAndLoad can be used to send the data and get the response. (If a response comes to a request sent by send it is treated in the same way as responses to getURL calls and displayed in a browser window. The method takes an optional second argument to indicate which window: _blank, _self, and so on.) The sendAndLoad method takes a URL as its first argument, like send, and an XML object as its second. The parsed response is placed in this object after it has been received. As with load, the object receiving the response may have an onLoad handler that will be called when the data has been downloaded.

If the book shop were a real application, eventually it would have to process customers' orders. Arranging to despatch goods and take money can only be performed at the server end, so the movie should send a summary of the invoice data that it displays in the checkout frame. A script invoked by the server can then pass that data on to the shop's information processing systems to do whatever is necessary. How this is done lies beyond the scope of this book. The data can be made into an XML object and sent in that form; this would be particularly appropriate if the organization used XML to communicate between the different programs and databases that made up its information processing system. If we assume that the title and author of a book are sufficient information to identify it uniquely in these systems, a suitable layout for an order summary could consist of a sequence of <book> elements, with attributes author, title and quantity, contained in an <order> element. For example,

```
<order>
    <book author="Nigel Chapman and Jenny Chapman"
        title="Digital Multimedia" quantity="2" />
    <book author="Nigel Chapman"
        title="The Late Night Guide to C++" quantity="1" />
</order>
```

This is not, of course, adequate for placing a real order. You should be able to see how the example described here can be extended on the client side to gather information including details of a method of payment and the delivery address and incorporate it into a suitable XML document.

We don't need an XML document to send to the server, we need an XML object. We can build this by hand, using methods such as createElement, createTextNode, appendChild and insertBefore, which are described in the *ActionScript Reference Guide*. For a simple case like this, though, it is easier to build the XML document in a string, which can then be passed to the XML constructor to be parsed. (You may cringe at the idea of creating a string to convert to an object only to be converted back to a string to be sent to the server. It gets the job done, but do try Exercise 4.) The string may be built by extending the script attached to the Check out frame as follows:

```
var xml_string = "<order>";
with(the_basket.wrapper) {
    for (var i = 0; i < contents.length; ++i)
        with (contents[i]) {
            assign to text fields for display as before
            xml_string += ('<book author="' + book_record.author +
                           '" title="' + book_record.title +
                           '" quantity="' + quantity_in_basket + '" />');

        }
}
xml_string += "</order>";
```

A string of XML can be passed as an optional argument to the XML constructor, which will create an object by parsing it. We can prepare the object for sending the order in that way.

```
var xml_order = new XML(xml_string);
```

We also need an empty XML object to hold the reply, and this will need an onLoad handler to deal with it. The actual content of the reply will depend on the details of the complete system, but at the least it will have to provide some indication of whether the transaction at the server went off successfully. A minimal reply would be something like this:

```
<receipt status="ok" />
```

The status attribute might take on other values to indicate particular problems and a real reply would include extra information, such as an order number and an estimated delivery time. Just considering the status, though, a handler could display a suitable message to tell the customer what had happened. Assuming a text field has the variable thanks associated with it, the object for the reply could be created and its handler could be set as follows:

```
var xml_receipt = new XML();
xml_receipt.onLoad = function() {
    var the_receipt = this.firstChild;
    var success = the_receipt.attributes.status == 'ok';
    thanks= success? 'Thank you for your order.\nYour books will be on their way shortly':
            'Something went wrong.\nSorry you wasted all that time.\nHave a nice day.';
}
```

All that remains for the Flash end of the transaction is to indicate that something is happening and then use sendAndLoad to send the order and get back the receipt.
thanks = 'Please wait a moment.';
xml_order.sendAndLoad("http://www.macavon.co.uk/cgi-bin/process-order.cgi", xml_receipt);

XML Sockets

All the methods we have considered so far for sending and receiving XML data use HTTP to handle the actual communication. This is simple and efficient, and serves admirably when the communication takes the form of a sequence of transactions consisting of a request and its response. However, HTTP treats each such transaction as a completely separate event. The server cannot send more data to the same client without being requested to do so, and a new connection must be established for each request, which introduces delays into the interaction. For some sorts of application, this won't do. For instance, suppose you wanted to display up-to-date weather information, news, stock market data, or even just the current time according to an astronomically accurate clock in a movie. If you were to try and implement such a system using HTTP, your client (Flash movie) would have to keep sending requests to the server on the off-chance that it had some data to send back. If the data was arriving fast, and the movie only sent the requests relatively infrequently, data would pile up at the server, and would be out of date by the time it was displayed. Even if the data only changed fairly slowly, the movie would be spending much of its time sending requests.

A better way of proceeding under these circumstances is to establish a permanent connection to a custom-built server, which allows the server and client to exchange data as and when it is necessary or convenient to them. Doing things this way entails more complicated programming, especially at the server end, and may tie up network resources unnecessarily, so it is not a route to be taken casually. Sometimes, though, it is the only way.

The XMLSocket object is provided in ActionScript as an abstraction of a TCP/IP connection that allows XML data to be passed to and from an arbitrary server, without using any higher-level protocols. Since any text that doesn't contain any <, > or & characters is, technically speaking, well-formed XML, these sockets can, in fact, carry just about any character stream. The mechanism conceals most of the wearisome details of the underlying network programming. The procedure for setting up communication with a server is as follows. First, create an XMLSocket object.
var my_sock = new XMLSocket();

Next, assign it two methods, onConnect and onXML. These are event handlers, which are called at the end of the connection phase and when XML data is received, respectively. We will look at what these might do shortly. Once the handlers are in place, the connect method is called to try and establish a connection. It takes two arguments: the first is either a URL identifying a host machine or the special value null identifying the host from which the movie was loaded, the second is a port number, which the server uses for its communications. The method returns false if the connection fails immediately, and true if the first phase succeeds, so it looks as if the connection might go through. A typical call will send the playhead to a frame that displays an error message in the first case, or a holding message or animation in the second.

```
if (my_sock.connect(null, 2345))
    gotoAndStop("waitforit")
else gotoAndStop("connection failed");
```

The port number used here is arbitrary. In general, any number greater than 1024 can be used — ports lower than that are reserved for standard services such as FTP and HTTP. The number must match that used by the server, which will usually have been determined beforehand.

If connect returned true, the onConnect handler will be called when the connection process is complete. It receives a Boolean argument indicating whether the connection ultimately succeeded or not. If it did, the movie and the server can start exchanging data; if not, it's back to the error message, so a typical handler might be assigned like this:

```
my_sock.onConnect = function(succeeded) {
    if (succeeded) gotoAndStop("connected")
    else gotoAndStop("connection failed");
}
```

When a script needs to send data over an XMLSocket, it uses the send method of that object. The argument to this method may be an XML object, in which case it is converted into an XML document. A string is sent as it is, though. Whatever the data, a zero byte (i.e., eight bits of zeros) is sent after it; the server can use this value to determine where the data ends. Any response it sends must be terminated in the same way. When it arrives, it is parsed as XML and converted into an XML object. (If it is just a string of text, the object only contains a single text node.) This object is passed to the onXML handler, which is called when it arrives, like the onLoad handler of XML objects. So, if the server was sending text replies, and all that was required was to display them in a text field, the handler could have been assigned as follows:

```
my_sock.onXML = function(x) {
```

```
    their_text = text_content(x);
}
```
where text_content is the function shown on page 226. If it is also the case that the data sent to the server is the text from a text field, and that sending is initiated by a button, all that is needed to complete the Flash end is the following script attached to the button.
```
on (release) {
    my_sock.send(your_text);
    your_text = '';
}
```

The hard stuff is in the server. Since this is not a book about network programming, it is not appropriate to go into very much detail about what happens there, but if you are going to be using Flash as a client, it helps to understand a little about what the server does.

Most servers follow the same pattern. First, they create a socket, using their chosen port number. Next, they start to listen for incoming connections on that socket. They sit in an infinite loop, accepting any connections that come in, receiving and sending data, and then closing the connection. That's all, really, but generally servers are not provided with neat abstractions like `XMLSocket` but must perform much of the socket programming explicitly. For the sake of completeness, here is a rudimentary server, written in Perl, which might be used in conjunction with the Flash scripts just shown.

```perl
#!perl -w
use Socket;
my $port = 2345;
my $proto = getprotobyname('tcp');
socket(Server, PF_INET, SOCK_STREAM, $proto) or die "socket: $!";
bind(Server, sockaddr_in($port, INADDR_ANY)) or die "bind: $!";
listen(Server, SOMAXCONN) or die "listen: $!";

$/ = "\000";
while (my $paddr = accept(Client, Server)) {
    print Client "Here to serve\n\000";
    while ((my $incoming = <Client>) !~ 'BYE') {
        process($incoming);
    }
    print Client "bye too\000";
    close Client
```

}

The first block of code, although it may look obscure, is just a routine way of creating a socket and setting it up so that the server can accept incoming connections. The mysterious assignment to $/ sets the 'record separator' to a zero byte. This means that when Perl's filehandle reading operator <> is used to read a record, it will read everything up to a zero, that is, all of the data sent down an XMLSocket. The accept call causes the server process to be suspended until a client attempts to connect to it. If that connection succeeds, the filehandle Client is opened to allow communication in both directions between client and server. Every time the expression <Client> is assigned to the variable $incoming, the next chunk of data from the client is read. In order to allow the client to close the connection, this server checks for the string BYE, and if it finds it, terminates the loop. Otherwise the data is passed to a subroutine process, which does whatever the server needs to do, and sends its response. On exit from the inner loop, the server sends a final farewell message, terminated with the requisite zero byte, and closes the connection, before looping back to wait for another connection request.

Real servers are not usually quite like this. Instead of simply processing the data when it arrives, they spawn a new thread or process, allowing the parent process to go back and wait for new connections straight away. This is not something that the client needs to know about, though, so the (system-dependent) code for multi-threading the server has been omitted to keep the example clearer.

The process function of the server can do just about anything, which means that Flash can become a front end for arbitrarily complex distributed applications. In particular, the server can be used to pass data arriving through the XMLSocket connection on to other servers, thereby connecting Flash to other Internet services, such as time servers. Flash does not allow scripts to open connections to servers that are not on the same subdomain as the movie for security reasons, but a simple server can be used to provide a gateway, incorporating appropriate checks, to the rest of the Internet.

Other Media Formats

Flash Player movies (SWF files) are the only format that supports the full range of interactivity offered by Flash5, but SWF is not the only format in which Flash movies can be saved. If all you are interested in is the animation and you want to avoid the headaches associated with trying to detect the Flash plug-in, you can save your Flash movie as an animated GIF — the only file format that provides animation in Web pages without relying on a plug-in, scripting or Java.

A rudimentary sort of interactivity can be maintained without the need for plug-ins by exporting a frame as an image map in any of the three common Web image formats, GIF, JPEG or PNG. This only does anything useful if the frame in question contains buttons with `getURL` calls attached to them. In that case, a server-side image map is created, with the buttons being converted to active areas that link to their URLs. If you are creating an image map, you must also create an HTML page to contain it, implying that you must select HTML as well as one of GIF, JPEG or PNG from the Publish Settings formats. The template that you use must include the `$IM` template variable, which acts as a placeholder for the HTML `<map>` element generated from the image. It also must include an `<img>` tag with its `src` attribute set to the template variable `$IS`, which will be replaced by the URL of the image when the HTML is published. By default, Flash converts the last frame of a movie to an image map. To choose a different frame, you must attach the special frame label `#Map` to it. (If it already has a label, you can attach a second one by putting it on a different layer.)

QuickTime

Much the most interesting alternative to SWF as a format for publishing Flash movies is QuickTime. Although it is often thought of as a digital video format, QuickTime is a more general multimedia architecture, capable of supporting a wide range of digital media types. In QuickTime 4, Flash movies are among them. While QuickTime 4 does provide some facilities of its own for interactivity, they are fairly primitive and very few programs exist that allow you to add these features to QuickTime movies. Flash provides an alternative, letting you use familiar techniques to provide controls and input elements in QuickTime.

There are, broadly speaking, three reasons for combining Flash and QuickTime: mixing vector animation with video, adding interactivity to QuickTime movies, and allowing Flash movies to be played in any QuickTime-enabled application. In the first two cases, it is necessary to import a QuickTime movie into Flash, using the File>Import... command. When you do so, only the first frame of the movie is displayed. In order to show the entire movie, you must add frames to the layer on which it has been placed to match the length of the imported QuickTime. Having done so, you can then add extra layers for Flash elements, including movie clips and buttons that provide interactivity, as described in earlier chapters.

The Flash Player cannot display QuickTime, but QuickTime movies can include SWF tracks, so if you want to produce a mixture of Flash animation or interactivity with QuickTime you must save your movie in QuickTime 4 format. Although this format does support Flash interactivity, it is only at the level of Flash 3 (the same as the Basic

Actions category in the Actions panel in normal mode). Essentially, this means that you cannot use variables or any control structure based on them — a severe limitation. (It is possible that QuickTime's support for Flash interactivity will be extended in subsequent releases.) Since the QuickTime movie becomes part of the Flash movie you can control it with stop, play and gotoAndPlay/Stop actions, so it is easy to replace the standard QuickTime movie controller with something unique made out of Flash buttons. You can also add getURL calls to combine Web pages with QuickTime and Flash.

To create a QuickTime movie from Flash, you simply select QuickTime[1] from the Publish Settings formats. The options allow you to specify the size and so on, as with other formats. They also let you set the transparency of the Flash track — by making its background transparent to let underlying tracks show through you can composite your Flash elements with video. When the QuickTime movie is created, the Flash movie is placed on its own track, and the original QuickTime is copied to a separate track, with its original compression preserved.

If Flash content is combined with QuickTime video, the result will have the heavy bandwidth requirements of video, not the modest demands of Flash. It is not, therefore, a combination that can be casually used over the Internet.

SMIL

Not to be outdone, RealPlayer G2, the widely used streaming media format, can also incorporate Flash movies. Again, the newer features for interactivity are lost; RealPlayer can only handle Flash Player movies in the Flash 4 format, and sounds must be streamed; event sounds are not handled. Synchronization may be lost if scripts move the playhead. Potentially, though, this may be the most flexible format for saving Flash movies, because the RealPlayer format incorporates SMIL, the W^3C markup language for synchronized multimedia. When you publish a Flash movie in RealPlayer format, up to four files are created. First, there is the ordinary SWF file; next, a 'tuned' SWF file, which has extra information that indicates to RealPlayer the bit rate and buffer size to be used for streaming. If the Flash movie includes sound, a separate Real Audio file containing the streamed sounds is created. Finally, a SMIL file is used to specify the synchronization between sound and animation. A typical example looks like this:

```
<smil>
    <head>
        <!-- Presentation attributes. -->
```

---

1. Not QuickTime Video. This renders each frame as a conventional bitmapped frame of video, losing any interactivity. It is used for converting a Flash animation into ordinary digital video.

```
            <meta name="title"     content="Boogie" />
            <meta name="author"    content="Nigel Chapman" />
            <meta name="copyright" content="© 2000" />
            <meta name="keywords"  content="Boogie Woogie" />
            <meta name="description" content="Indescribable" />
            <layout>
                <root-layout width="550" height="400" background-color="black" />
                <region id="flashreg" left="0" top="0" width="550" height="400"
                                                                    z-index="1" />
            </layout>
        </head>
        <body>
            <par>
                <animation src="boogiet.swf" region="flashreg" fill="freeze"/>
                <audio src="boogie.rm" />
            </par>
        </body>
</smil>
```

As you can see, SMIL is XML. The overall structure of a SMIL file resembles that of an HTML document, with a head and body. In the head of this file, Flash inserts some meta-information, which is entered via a dialogue that can be brought up by clicking the button labelled Project Properties in the RealPlayer tab of the Publish Settings dialogue. Next comes some layout information; in this case, it just sets the size of the presentation to that of the Flash movie, and defines a named region to hold the movie. The body of the document contains a single par (parallel) element. This is a *synchronization element*, which specifies that the elements it contains should be played in parallel. The two elements are specified by the <animation> tag, for the Flash movie, and the <audio> tag for the streamed sound that has been exported as a RealAudio file.

There is nothing very interesting about this, it just wraps up the elements of the Flash movie into a form that RealPlayer software understands. However, there is nothing to stop you from adding other elements to the SMIL document, to combine the animation and audio with other media elements, including video, images and other animations and sounds. As well as specifying that elements should be played in parallel, SMIL allows you to specify sequences, with delays and event synchronization. Additional layout elements can be used to arrange multimedia objects in space. Since SMIL is XML, it is purely textual, so SMIL files can be edited with a text editor to create synchronized multimedia presentations. At present, there are few tools for creating such presentation in SMIL, but the format is one which is likely to grow in importance in the future.

QuickTime 4.1 also supports SMIL, though it does not support RealAudio sound, so the SMIL files published by Flash cannot be used without alteration if your Flash movie includes streamed sounds. For QuickTime, it is probably easier to write the SMIL by hand, until SMIL authoring programs come along.

Printing

All the technologies that we have considered combining with Flash in this chapter so far are digital. Flash is a computer program and its artefacts are essentially digital, but sometimes it is necessary to leave the digital world. In particular, it is sometimes useful to be able to transfer the content of a Flash movie to paper. For example, it may be necessary to provide visitors to a Web site with a form that they can print and sign — this is commonly required by online banks when you open an account, since there is as yet no universally accepted digital equivalent of a person's signature. It may also be helpful to offer a printable brochure for products in an online store, so that people can look at the goods without having to sit in front of their computers.

Computer monitors and printed media have quite different characteristics from each other. Simply printing an image of what is displayed on a screen is not likely to be satisfactory. Apart from considerations of layout and established idioms in the two media, the low resolution images and text required by computer screens look jagged when printed at high resolution. (Computer screens have a nominal resolution of 72 or 96 dots per inch; even the most modest desktop inkjet printers use resolutions of 600 dots per inch.) Flash movies, though, are basically vector graphics, and, as I explained in Chapter 1, this means that they are inherently independent of resolution. Flash makes it possible to print the vector information instead of simply dumping a rendered bitmap of the image displayed on the screen to a printer. PostScript printers can use the vector information directly, since PostScript is a vector-based page description language. Other printers' drivers convert the vectors to bit maps for printing.

Movies, or parts of them, can be printed in one of two ways. Either the user can choose the Print command from the context-sensitive menu in the Flash Player or Web browser, or a script can use the print function. The latter option provides more flexibility; in particular, it allows you to designate a movie clip as the source of the printed pages, whereas the menu command only allows you to print the main movie. In both cases, certain frames in the movie may be designated for printing, and a bounding box can be set up. Special frame labels are used for both these purposes. Any frame that has a label #p will be printed; if no frame has this label, all the frames will be printed. (As with image maps, you can place these labels on their own layer, so as not to interfere with any labels used by other scripts.) If any frame is labelled !#p, printing is disabled. A frame labelled #b may be used to specify a bounding box for printing. The way this works deserves a little extra explanation.

The bounding box of a frame is the smallest rectangle that encloses all the objects in it. By labelling a frame #b, you make its bounding box act as a mask, which the printed frames are clipped to. That is, only the parts of frames that fall within the bounding box of the specified frame are printed. Those parts are then scaled to the size of the paper. This allows you to remove extraneous elements, such as buttons or other controls, from the printed version. A simple way of defining a bounding box is to draw a rectangle of the desired size in a frame that cannot be reached by the playhead (for example, because it follows a frame with a stop) and label that frame #b. The #b bounding box is always used, if it is present, when printing is done from the context menu. If the print function is used, other options are available.

This function takes two arguments. The first is a target name, identifying the movie or clip whose frames are to be printed. The second is one of three strings, "bmovie", "bframe" or "bmax", which specify how the bounding box for printing is to be determined. If the value is "bmovie", the #b frame is used, as just described. If it is "bframe", each frame is printed inside its own bounding box, while if it is "bmax", the largest bounding box of any printable frame in the movie is used for all of them.

Printing vectors maintains quality, but it loses transparency and colour effects. If it is necessary to include these in the printed output, you must use printAsBitmap instead of print. This causes Flash to pre-render the pages, incorporating those effects that cannot be handled in vectors. The bitmap is created at the printer resolution, so the quality is still superior to a screen dump.

Print and screen are different in more than their resolution. Monitors are almost always wider than they are tall, while paper is usually used in 'portrait' orientation, so that it is taller than it is wide. Good page layout takes account of the aspect ratio of the paper, and embodies many conventions that do not transfer to the screen. The relationship between consecutive pages of a printed document is different in kind from that between consecutive frames of an animation. Even though vector printing can ensure that graphics and text transfer smoothly from screen to paper, using the same layout for both media is rarely successful. A useful technique therefore is to design any printable items, such as application forms or brochures, separately and hide them in a movie as clip instances whose _visible property is set to false. To allow them to be printed, you simply need to supply a suitably labelled button with a script attached such as:

```
on (release) {
    print ("product_brochure", "bmovie");
}
```

It should be borne in mind, though, that Flash is not a page layout program, so it is not the best tool for creating high quality printed material.

Exercises and Experiments

1. Take a Web site with which you are familiar and use Flash to provide it with navigation controls.
2. If you always adopt the strategy of mapping properties of an object to XML elements with the same name and no attributes and putting the value of the property in the element content, it is relatively straightforward to write functions to convert an arbitrary object into XML and a suitable XML document into an object. Do so. (You may need to look up typeof in the *ActionScript Reference Guide* in order to handle objects whose properties are themselves objects or arrays.)
3. Retrofitting the XML data to the version of the book shop from earlier chapters may be the sort of thing that happens in the real world, but it is probably not the best way of implementing the system. Design the shop from the ground up to use XML as the data exchange format. It may be helpful to derive the book records from the XML object, and not store the fields explicitly at all. Or it may not.
4. Rewrite the script that prepares the XML object to send the order data so that the object is constructed directly using the XML methods that insert data into a tree instead of building the XML string and parsing it. Which approach do you prefer?
5. What should the server-side script that receives the order data from the book shop do? If you have the facilities, implement it, making any changes to the client system that you find necessary.
6. The text cites some examples of applications that demand the use of sockets. Identify the factors that make HTTP inappropriate. What other types of application require sockets? Can any of the examples cited be implemented satisfactorily without them?
7. Find out the URL and port number of a network time server, and write a server and a client script to display the current time in the corner of a Flash movie. (Assume that the local system's clock is not sufficiently accurate or reliable.)
8. Add features to the book shop movie to allow customers to print a brochure for each book.

further reading

Flash

This book does not claim to tell you everything about Flash, or even about Flash scripting and interactivity. The essential sources for definitive reference material are the manuals distributed with Flash 5: *Using Flash*, *ActionScript Reference Guide* and, for Generator, *Using Generator*. All three are included in printed form with the boxed CD version of Flash, or are available for a small charge if you buy Flash by electronic download. They are also included in PDF and form the basis of the online help system. Chapter 6 of the reference guide, the ActionScript dictionary, is particularly useful to scripters.

There are many Web sites devoted to Flash, including several tutorials. However, like most Web sites, many of these have not been updated for a long time, or have disappeared, so I have not included a list of URLs here. Macromedia's Flash support site, http://www.macromedia.com/support/flash, can be relied on, though. It includes technical notes that deal with matters that the manuals do not cover adequately, some tutorials, and accounts of bugs and commonly encountered problems and workrounds for them. There is also a page of links to other Flash sites on the Web.

I have deliberately almost entirely neglected any discussion of graphic design and animation in this book. The following books concentrate on that side of using Flash.

Hillman Curtis, *Flash Web Design: The Art of Motion Graphics*. New Riders: 2000. This book is written by a graphic designer with considerable experience of using Flash, and shows you, by way of a series of projects, how to go beyond trite animations. Many of the ideas are interesting, although some readers may find the author's writing style a bit off-putting. The first edition uses Flash 4; no Flash 5 version has been announced at the time of writing.

David J. Emberton and J. Scott Hamlin, *Flash 4 Magic*. New Riders: 1999. An extremely popular book, which is valuable because it includes examples of complete projects. The exposition consists of detailed instructions on how to reproduce these projects, a style which may or may not teach you anything, depending on how you learn. *Flash 5 Magic* is in preparation as I write this.

WWW Technologies

Nigel Chapman and Jenny Chapman, *Digital Multimedia*. John Wiley and Sons: 2000. We wrote this as a college textbook, but it can be used as a source of information on the various digital media technologies that are combined on the Web (and elsewhere) including images, vector graphics, animation, video and sound. Chapter 13 describes SMIL, which was mentioned briefly in Chapter 8.

Ian S. Graham, *XHTML 1.0 Web Development Sourcebook*. John Wiley and Sons: 2000. This book provides valuable background information that will help you understand how Flash fits in to the Web. Despite the title, the book is less about XHTML than it is about HTTP, JavaScript, and Web site design. (If you are interested specifically in XHTML, the same author's companion volume: *XHTML 1.0 Language and Design Sourcebook*, John Wiley and Sons: 2000, is the one you want.)

Ian S. Graham and Liam Quin, *XML Specification Guide*. John Wiley and Sons: 1999. The bulk of this book is an annotated version of the XML specification, which is supported by some introductory tutorial chapters. Probably the best thing to read if you need to know more about XML.

Scripting Languages

David Barron, *The World of Scripting Languages*. John Wiley and Sons: 2000. A survey of several of the different languages that are used for scripting on the Web and elsewhere, including Perl, JavaScript and VBScript.

Nigel Chapman, *Perl: The Programmer's Companion*. John Wiley and Sons: 1997. A tutorial introduction to Perl written for those with some programming experience, this should help you understand the server-side scripts that work with Flash to make complete applications.

further reading

David Flanagan, *JavaScript: The Definitive Guide.* O'Reilly and Associates: 1997. Perhaps not entirely definitive, but the best account of JavaScript available in print. Much of the first part, about the core language, has some relevance to ActionScript too.

index

- operator	44
! operator	49
!= operator	48
% operator	44
&& operator	49
* operator	44
+ operator	44, 47, 48
++ operator	51
/ operator	44
;	54
< operator	48
<= operator	48
= operator	50
== operator	48
> operator	48
>= operator	48
\"	46
\\	46
|| operator	49
abstract data types	125
abstraction	107, 155
see also functions, objects and smart clips	
accessibility	8
actions	25
basic	30
button	59
frame	13
Actions panel	28–29, 52
entering statements in	28
expert mode	29
normal mode	28
and curly brackets	53
entering targets	36
active area	23
ActiveX	203, 209, 214
aggregate data structures	68
_alpha	65
alpha	17, 27, 150
and events	88, 95
animated GIFs	7, 232
animation	11, 18
anonymous functions	116, 121
anti-aliasing	5
arguments	108, 114
to constructors	119
arithmetic	44–46
array elements	68
Array object	72
arrays	68–73, 102
associative	128
circular	125
creating	68
of arrays	72
of clip parameters	159
passing to functions	114
assignment	50
of arrays	71
assignment operators	51

B

bandwidth profiler   67
base classes   130
basic actions   25, 30, 233
    Go To   32, 38
    Stop   30
    Tell Target   38
bitmapped images   4, 7
    importing   15
    tracing   16
    uses for, in Flash   15
blocks   52
Boolean values   48
brackets   45
break   57
brochures   236
button events   23–24, 31, 101
buttons   19, 26–28, 59, 188
    active area of   23, 26
    animated   26
    as menu items   87
    for Web site navigation   208
    inside movie clips   82, 94
    sounds in   27
    states of   26
    submit   75

C

caching of Generator objects   194
CGI   173–176
    scripts   183–187, 191
    and XML   226
    as Generator data sources   195
Character panel   76
checkboxes   81–84, 188
    and movie clips   82
classes   119
    base   130
    derived   130
client/server model   1, 171, 229
clip actions   31
clip events   23, 24–25, 31, 96, 99, 101, 104
clip parameters   155
    defining   157
    setting values of   157
Clip Parameters panel   157, 159, 161
closures   116
comments   54, 110
Common Gateway Interface
    see CGI
comparisons   48
conditional expressions   55
conditional statements   52
    single-branched   53, 55
constructors   119–122
continue   58
control structures   52–53
curly brackets   53, 109
    enclosing Generator variables   194
_currentframe   65

D

data entry   102
data event   25, 177, 179–181, 191
data types   44
databases   186
    XML   216
Date object   68
debugger   54
declarations   51
Define Clip Parameters   157, 161
derived classes   130
direct manipulation   93–97, 145, 181
Director   16
Document Type Definitions
    see DTDs
dot notation   64, 113, 119
drag and drop
    see movie clips, draggable
dragOut event   24
dragOver event   24
Dreamweaver   204
_droptarget   65, 95

DTD	216
and record structure	217
duplicateMovieClip	149
dynamic text	76, 78
ECMAScript	3, 9, 43, 122, 211
ecommerce	2, 224
editing text	80–81
element nodes	221
elements of arrays	68
embed HTML element	8, 201
attributes for Flash movies	202
enterFrame event	24, 25
EPS	6
escape	190
escape sequences	47
eval	96, 137
event sounds	22, 27, 67, 234
events	23–26
and variables	58
handling with listeners	153–154
see also button events, clip events and frame events	
Flash 4	82
compatibility with scripting language	49, 96, 178 9
Flash Deployment Kit	215
Flash methods	212–214
Flash movies	7
Flash Player	7, 201
FS commands for	210
Flash Player movies	7, 232
as interfaces to smart clips	160
embedding in HTML	201–204
see also SWF	
floating point numbers	44
displaying	78–80
precision of	45
for loops	56
and arrays	71

for…in loops	129
formal parameters	109, 114
forms	75, 183
and query strings	175
as smart clip interfaces	162
HTML	188
paper	236
frame actions	90
frame events	23
frame rate	11
frame sets	208
frames	11
_framesloaded	65, 67, 113, 191
Freehand	6, 15
fscommand	210
and Flash Player	210
and JavaScript	210
function body	109
functional abstraction	108
functions	108–118
anonymous	116, 121
as arguments	115
as methods of movie clips	143
as objects	122
as values	116
defining	109, 113
higher order	115
recursive	117, 220
gateways	232
see also CGI	
Generator	7, 191–199
data sources	192, 193, 195–196
numerical data	197
objects	193
offline mode	192
online mode	192
templates	192
variables	193, 194, 196–197
Generator Objects palette	193, 197
Generator panel	193
GET HTTP request	172

index

getURL 176, 208–209, 212, 233
global variables 113
GoLive 204
gotoAndPlay 32
gotoAndStop 32
graphic symbols 19

_height 65
host environment 210
host objects 43
HTML 1, 77, 135–137, 201–209
    tags for Flash movies 8, 201
HTTP 1, 172–173, 229
    request headers 173
    requests 172, 185
        sending with loadVariables 176
    response headers 173
    responses 173, 174, 192
        status line 173
HTTPS 184
hypermedia 1
hypertext 1
Hypertext Markup Language
    see HTML
Hypertext Transfer Protocol
    see HTTP

identifiers 50
Illustrator 6, 15
image maps 233
Import From File 29
include directive 29
indexing
    of arrays 68
    of arrays of arrays 72
Infinity 45
inheritance 129–137
    and movie clips 144–151
    and objects 134–137
    and prototypes 130–133
    multiple 133–134

input elements 75–100
    conventional use of 75
    creating with Generator 198–199
    smart clips and 158–168
    see also checkboxes, radio buttons,
        sliders and text fields
input text 76
instance names 20, 34
Instance panel 85
instances 83
    active 17
    naming 34
    of symbols 16
interfaces 151
Internet 1
ISO Latin1 character set 46, 175
iteration
    see loops

JavaScript 2, 9, 25, 43, 55, 209–215
JScript 43

Key object 101
Key.getASCII method 101
Key.getCode method 101
Key.isDown method 104
keyDown event 25, 101
keyframes 14
keyPress event 24, 25, 101
keys 100–104
keyUp event 25, 101

labels 13
    for designating image maps 233
    to designate printable frames 236
layers 13, 138
    and tweening 17
    for actions 87
levels 39
    and target names 40
libraries 16, 138–139, 147

index

shared	139
listeners	153–154
LiveConnect	209
LiveMotion	7
LiveScript	43
load event	24, 25
loading movies	39–41
into clips	41
loadMovie	39
sending variables with	190–191
loadVariables	176–190
local variables	113
logical operators	
AND	49
NOT	49
OR	49
loop counters	56
loops	52, 55, 58, 61
accessing properties using	129
infinite	57
recursion as an alternative to	117
see also for loops	
mask layers	91
Math object	45
Math.random method	70
Math.sqrt method	46
menu items	87
methods	36, 119, 132
as properties	120
calling	36
of Math object	46, 79
of String object	47, 80
this and	120
MIME content types	173, 175
morphing	14, 17
mouseDown event	24, 25
mouseMove event	25
mouseUp event	25
movie clips	19, 143–168
and checkboxes	82
and inheritance	144–151
as objects	36, 143
assigning	62
buttons inside	82, 94
draggable	93–100, 147
loading movies into	41
loading variables into	179–182
printing	236
properties of	64, 143
reference point of	65, 99
see also smart clips	
movie structures	32–34
multiple inheritance	133–134
_name	65
NaN	45, 48, 110
new	119
Number function	48
numbers	44
conversion to Boolean values	49
random	69
object HTML element	8, 202–204
object-oriented programming	118, 145, 151
objects	36, 118–137
and inheritance	134–137
Generator	193
on	31
operators	
arithmetic	44
bitwise	49
Boolean	
see logical operators	
comparison	48
string	47
Paragraph panel	76
param HTML element	202, 203
parameters	
entering	28
to basic actions	25

index

to smart clips
    see clip parameters
_parent 21
Perl 53, 55, 76, 116, 183
    CGI module 185
    DB_File module 186
    server written in 231
pie charts 197
playhead 12, 92
plug-ins 1, 4, 7
    detecting 214–215
pop-up menus 85–89, 188
port numbers 230
POST HTTP request 172, 175, 184, 226
precedence 45
preloading 66
press event 24, 25
print 237
printAsBitmap 237
printing 236–238
product placement 94
properties 36, 119
    accessing using index notation 129
    methods as 120
    of movie clips 64, 143
__proto__ property 121, 130, 134, 136
protocols 172
prototype property 121
prototypes 121–122
    chain of 131
    inheritance and 130–133
Publish Settings 205
    Generator Template 192
    QuickTime 234
    RealPlayer 235
publish templates 205–207, 233

query strings 174
queues 123–128
QuickTime 7, 233–234, 236
    SWF tracks in movies 7, 233

quote marks 46

radio buttons 82, 84–85, 188
    Generator 198
random numbers 69
RealPlayer 234
recursive functions 117, 220
references 62, 71, 114
release event 24, 87
releaseOutside event 24
removeMovieClip 164
rendering 5
reserved words 51
return 109, 120
rollOut event 24
rollOver event 24, 81
rollovers 26
_root 21
_rotation 65

Scalable Vector Graphics
    see SVG
scenes 13
scripts
    CGI *see* CGI
    external 29
    importing from a file 29
scrolling lists 90–93, 188
    Generator 198
selecting frames 15
Selection object 80, 102, 135
selections
    see conditional statements
semicolons 54
sequences 52
servers 1, 171, 174
    custom 231–232
    see also HTTP and CGI
server-side computation
    see CGI

index

SGML 216
shared libraries 139
short-circuit evaluation 49
    pitfalls of 55
sliders 97–100, 153–155
smart clips 86, 155–168
    and input elements 158–168
    parameters
        see clip parameters
    user interfaces to 160–168
        bootstrapped 165–168
SMIL 234–236
sockets
    see XML sockets
sound 22
    adding to buttons 27
Sound object 100
sounds
    see also event sounds and stream sounds
SQL 187
stage 15
startDrag 93, 97
statements
    entering in Actions panel 28
    entering using a text editor 29
static text 76
stop 30, 83
stopDrag 93
stream sounds 22, 234
streaming 66
String function 48
string literals 46
String object 47
String.charAt method 47, 57
String.indexOf method 48, 57
String.length property 47
String.substr method 47
String.substring method 47
strings 46–48
    conversion to numbers 48

structured programming 52
subdomains 178, 191
subroutines
    see functions
SVG 6
SWF 4, 6, 7, 16, 191
    embedding in HTML 202
    exporting from other programs 15
SWT
    see Generator templates
symbols 16
    button
        see buttons
    graphic 19
        using with Generator 198
    instances of 16
    movie clip
        see movie clips
syntax checking 54

_target 65
target names 21, 36, 96, 143
    and levels 40
targetPath 164
targets
    specifying dynamically 63
TCP/IP 1, 172, 229
template variables 206
templates
    see Generator templates and publish templates
text
    formatting with HTML tags 77, 80, 135–137
text fields 75, 76–81, 188
    HTML links in 209
    scrolling 92
text nodes 221
Text Options panel 76–78
this 120
    and base constructors 132
    and movie clips 143

timelines	12–13, 107
_totalframes	65
trace function	54
Track as Menu Item	24, 87
transparency	
see alpha	
tweening	14
and layers	17
and symbols	14
type tool	76
undefined	50, 146
Uniform Resource Locators	
see URLs	
unload event	24, 25
_url	65
URL encoded data	175, 176
URLs	1, 172
and CGI	174
as argument to loadMovie	39
javascript:	212
query strings in	174
user interfaces	
direct manipulation	93
Flash	8
to smart clips	160–168
bootstrapped	165–168
see also input elements	
var	51, 113
variables	49–52, 83
and clips	62
and events	58
and text fields	76
as properties of movie clips	143
Generator	193, 194, 196–197
global	113
loading values from a server	176
local	113
sending to a server	182
smart clip parameters and	155
template	206
VBScript	209
vector graphics	4–6
and animation	4
and resolution	236
and the WWW	6
virtual key codes	101
_visible	65, 237
while	52
white space characters in XML	222
_width	65
with	36, 139
World Wide Web	
see WWW	
World Wide Web Consortium	3
Document Object Model	223
WWW	1
and standards	3
vector graphics and	6
see also HTTP, HTML and URLs	
_x	65, 96
xch	161, 166
XHTML	204, 216
XML	2, 215–232
and CGI scripts	226
declarations	217, 221
differences from HTML	216
sending to a server	226–229
structure models	218
traversal of	220
valid documents	216
well-formed documents	216
white space characters in	222
XML objects	218–229
XML sockets	229–232
XML.attributes property	221
XML.childnodes property	221
XML.load method	218
XML.loaded property	219
XML.nodeName property	221
XML.nodeType property	221
XML.nodeValue property	221
XML.onLoad property	219
XML.removeNode method	222

XML.send method	226	XMLSocket.send method	230
XML.sendAndLoad method	226	_xmouse	65
XML.status property	224	_xscale	65
XMLSocket object	229	_y	65, 96
XMLSocket.connect method	230	_ymouse	65
XMLSocket.onConnect method	230	_yscale	65
XMLSocket.onXML method	230		